GOD AND MYSTERY IN WORDS

GOD AND MYSTERY IN WORDS

Experience through Metaphor and Drama

DAVID BROWN

OXFORD
UNIVERSITY PRESS

OXFORD
UNIVERSITY PRESS

Great Clarendon Street, Oxford OX2 6DP

Oxford University Press is a department of the University of Oxford.
It furthers the University's objective of excellence in research, scholarship,
and education by publishing worldwide in

Oxford New York

Auckland Cape Town Dar es Salaam Hong Kong Karachi
Kuala Lumpur Madrid Melbourne Mexico City Nairobi
New Delhi Shanghai Taipei Toronto

With offices in

Argentina Austria Brazil Chile Czech Republic France Greece
Guatemala Hungary Italy Japan Poland Portugal Singapore
South Korea Switzerland Thailand Turkey Ukraine Vietnam

Oxford is a registered trade mark of Oxford University Press
in the UK and in certain other countries

Published in the United States
by Oxford University Press Inc., New York

British Library Cataloguing in Publication Data
Data available

Library of Congress Cataloging in Publication Data
Data available

Typeset by SPI Publisher Services, Pondicherry, India
Printed in Great Britain
on acid-free paper by
Biddles Ltd., King's Lynn, Norfolk

ISBN 978-0-19-923183-6

1 3 5 7 9 10 8 6 4 2

To Ruth

PREFACE

THIS is the final work of three related volumes that deal with the question of religious experience through culture and the arts. *God and Enchantment of Place: Reclaiming Human Experience* appeared in 2004 (and in paperback in 2006). The second, *God and Grace of Body: Sacrament in Ordinary*, appeared after a three-year gap in 2007. This last volume follows quickly on its heels, as it was written closely in conjunction with its predecessor.

A number of colleagues and friends have read specific chapters or sections, and their help has proved invaluable. In particular, a great debt of gratitude is due, among others, to Rosalind Brown, Christopher Joby, David Fuller, Matthew Guest, Anne Harrison, James Jirtle, Ann Loades, and Robert MacSwain. As with the last volume, I am also grateful to three OUP readers for helpful comments and suggestions. Ann Loades kept a helpful eye on the manuscript as a whole. Her unfailing encouragement and enthusiasm for the project ensured that I kept to the task in hand, even when the difficulties looked formidable and daunting. It is doubtful that I would have got thus far without her aid and support.

The focus of this volume makes it appropriate that it is dedicated to Ruth Miller. Not only has Ruth as my godmother sustained that initial liturgical commitment across the whole span of my life, she also shares with me an interest in poetry and drama.

Appropriately, as I prepare to move to a new appointment in the University of St Andrews, this Preface is completed on the day appointed by the Church to commemorate St Aidan, who came from Scotland (Iona) to evangelize the north of England, my present home. My seventeen years at Durham have been deeply enriching and rewarding, with colleagues in both Cathedral and University contributing to the enlargement of my vision, and for that I am deeply grateful.

D.W.B.

Durham
St Aidan's Day, 2007

ACKNOWLEDGEMENTS

Although every effort has been made to trace and contact copyright holders before publication, the publishers will be pleased to rectify errors or omissions at the earliest opportunity, if they are notified of any.

Excerpt from *Native Mesoamerican Spirituality: Ancient Myths, Discourses, Stories, Doctrines, Hymns, Poems from the Aztec, Yucatec, Quiche-Maya and Other Sacred Traditions*, from the Classics of Western Spirituality, edited by Miguel Léon-Portilla, Copyright © 1980 by Paulist Press, Inc., New York / Mahwah, N.J. Used with permission. www.paulistpress.com.

Words from *The Servant King* by Graham Kendrick © Kevin Mayhew Publishing

Words from *Shine, Jesus, shine* by Graham Kendrick © Kevin Mayhew Publishing.

Words from poetry by Kathleen Raine © Golgonooza Press.

Words from poetry by Les Murray © Carcanet Press.

Words from poetry by Friedrich Hölderlin, trans. by M. Hamburger © Routledge & Kegan Paul.

Words from poetry by Paul Celan in tr. J. Felstiner, *Paul Celan: Poet, Survivor, Jew* (New Haven: Yale University Press, 1995), 84 © Yale University Press.

Words from poetry by Dylan Thomas in D. Brown & D. Fuller, *Signs of Grace: Sacraments in Poetry and Prose* (London: Continuum, 2000), 62-3 © David Higham Associates.

CONTENTS

Introduction

THIS is the final of three volumes on religious experience as mediated through culture and the arts. The intention throughout has been to reclaim the wide variety of contexts in which experience of God has been identified in the past before these were artificially narrowed, as the centuries advanced. It is a process that has accelerated in recent times, with such experience now effectively reduced to explicitly 'religious' scenarios such as worship and responses to prayer. So in the first volume, *God and Enchantment of Place*, I explored how the divine has been found not just in pilgrimage and in religious architecture but also in the home and in town planning, in landscape painting and in gardening.[1] Again, in the second, *God and Grace of Body*, it was emphasized how it was not just the suffering figure of Christ on the Cross or great religious composers such as Bach that elicited such experience but also the body as beautiful and sensual, as well as 'secular' music in everything from hard rock to opera.[2]

This volume pursues a similar strategy but this time more specifically interconnected with worship. In part this intention reflects my own conviction that revealed religion builds on natural religion rather than wholly subverts it. Of course correction is sometimes required but the same can also at times be true for revealed religion. Narrow self-interest and fanaticism can occur equally in both. So, just as *God and Enchantment of Place* began by identifying a sense of the sacramental that makes all of the material world potentially a cipher for the divine and *God and Grace of Body* noted various

---

[1] *God and Enchantment of Place: Reclaiming Human Experience* (Oxford: Oxford University Press, 2004), for architecture, 245–371; for home, 170–89, 308–33; for town planning, 173–83; for landscape painting, 84–136; for gardening, 371–87.

[2] *God and Grace of Body: Sacrament in Ordinary* (Oxford: Oxford University Press, 2007), for suffering, 186–217; for Bach, 250–6; for beautiful and sensual bodies, 19–60; for hard rock, 327–33; for opera, 376–88.

anticipations of the eucharist in ordinary human attitudes to food and to the body, so here I move from a similar wider setting to a more specific focus on liturgy. This is done twice over in the two halves of the book. Part I starts with more general theories about language and the role of metaphor in poetry in instigating experience of the divine before examining more closely how God is communicated through hymn and sermon. Similarly, Part II explores the history of drama and modern theories of its relevance before turning to consideration of liturgical settings of the ordinary of the mass and its performance and setting as a whole.[3]

It is important to stress this strategy at the outset, as it explains why some theological writing that might have been expected to be discussed in what follows in fact finds little, if any, place. So far as possible, I want to engage in as open a dialogue as possible with the wider culture of both past and present, and not simply impose predetermined answers. Despite the many valuable insights he offers, it does seem to me that the work of Hans Urs von Balthasar is seriously deficient in this respect.[4] The application of dramatic metaphors to the Christian revelation allows him to escape from the narrow scholasticism of his youth and even to see drama as sacramental in its intention. But the understanding he has of secular drama is still too firmly fixed by Christian revelation, and so it is through this standard that all else outside is judged and assessed.[5] Not that he is alone in this. To my mind much the same happens with Hans Frei's endorsement of biblical narrative.[6] Such claims are far from denying that there is much of value to learn from the works of both theologians. It is just that I do not want to be constantly waylaid into giving responses to them (or more recent

---

[3] The 'ordinary' are the set, unvarying texts. For more details, see the opening of ch. 6.

[4] *Theodramatik* (in five volumes) is the title of the second major division of Balthasar's most important work.

[5] A critique sometimes made even by those otherwise generally sympathetic to his position. In *Theology and the Drama of History* (Cambridge: Cambridge University Press, 2005), Ben Quash detects too much readiness to find Christian mercy in secular drama and at the same time a general 'epic' desire to resolve issues, in marked contrast to the poetry of Gerard Manley Hopkins in *Wreck of the Deutschland*, which is marked by 'unresolvability': 137–44, 198–205.

[6] H. Frei, *The Eclipse of Biblical Narrative* (New Haven: Yale University Press, 1974).

writing in a similar vein) rather than focusing directly on how I see the lie of the land.[7]

Although nowadays it is the Holy Spirit that is usually credited with working outside of the Church, in the past it was once Christ as Logos.[8] When viewed under that aspect, the experience of the divine in ordinary poetry seems to me not fundamentally different from the experience of Christ in the words of the liturgy. Again, watching a performance of a classical Greek play, observing the Hindu celebration of Divali, and participating in the actions of the eucharist are from a certain perspective essentially kindred religious actions. Of course there are important differences, above all the mediation in the last of Christ's humanity to the believer. But that fact must not be allowed to refuse all comparisons, as though God were absent except under those circumstances. The usual objection to drawing such parallels is that this will inevitably lead to a diminution of Christianity, to acceptance of the lowest common denominator. But such an objection suggests a reader fixated on one particular model of the relationship, with eighteenth-century deism the only possible result. That is not my view. While it is true that Christianity cannot help but be influenced by its wider cultural setting, it is quite wrong to suppose that this must always be to Christianity's disadvantage. It is the wider society, for example, that was largely responsible for stimulating new attitudes towards children, towards hell and towards women.[9] But in the process new insights emerge which can in their turn then be thrown back on that same society, to produce a fresh and challenging critique. This is precisely what happened in respect of the treatment of children.

[7] There are now almost as many imitators of Balthasar as there are of Frei. For a good Roman Catholic example, F. A. Murphy, *The Comedy of Revelation: Paradise Lost and Regained in Biblical Narrative* (Edinburgh: T & T Clark, 2000). For a Protestant pursuing (with qualifications) a similar strategy, K. Vanhoozer, *The Drama of Doctrine: A Canonical–Linguistic Approach* (Louisville: Westminster John Knox, 2005).

[8] Most notably in Origen, *De Principiis* 1. 5–8. For an attempt to reconcile this bald assertion with what he says elsewhere, J. A. McGuckin ed., *Westminster Handbook of Origen* (Louisville: Westminster John Knox, 2004), s.v. Holy Spirit, esp. 126.

[9] For children, *Tradition and Imagination: Revelation and Change* (Oxford: Oxford University Press, 1999), 75–85; for women and hell, *Discipleship and Imagination: Christian Tradition and Truth* (Oxford: Oxford University Press, 2000), 11–31, 130–6.

The new focus on children, including on the infancy of Christ, was part of a much wider social change that was happening during the medieval period. Even so, once internalized, it stiffened Christians to take the lead in due course in seeking reform in the conditions of work and learning imposed on children. In modern Christianity the tragedy is that on the whole the Christian churches have been remarkably slow to produce the cutting edge that might have been expected from their founding documents on these latter two issues: in particular, in the one case an attack on the current shameful treatment of prisoners and on the other objection to the continued marginalization of groups other than women, most notably the mentally disabled.[10]

A similar failure to absorb and respond to external critique seems to me equally characteristic of the topics of this book. As I indicate in the opening chapter, two competing streams have characterized the history of western monotheism: the search for definition and explanation on the one hand and on the other the acceptance of mystery. From the medieval period onwards it has usually been the former that has been in the ascendancy. A notable early illustration of this is afforded by the detailed, careful search in the Middle Ages for precise formulae that could determine the validity or otherwise of each of the seven sacraments. European and American culture have now for some time been in rebellion against this sort of scholasticism that eventually came to characterize Protestantism no less than Roman Catholicism. (Luther's successors ensured that Lutheranism too entered the modern period not substantially different from Calvinism in this respect.) The Church's response has on the whole consisted of rather grudging and reluctant moves towards acceptance of more experience-based worship, but still either set in rigid doctrinal frames or else with such frames abandoned altogether. So a more adequate response is still awaited.

Mystery and doctrine I would suggest go together rather than in competition. There is plenty of support for such a perspective from within Scripture itself, ranging from what happened on Mount Sinai to the Resurrection itself: whether one takes the

---

[10] Hell and the treatment of prisoners are connected because of the way in which opposition to the doctrine of hell was first generated by new understandings of punishment. Britain currently has the highest percentage imprisonment rate in the European Union.

New Testament and the failure of the disciples to recognize Jesus, or in the Old how Moses is vouchsafed only a sight of the back of God.[11] In other words, even as something is revealed or explained, a continuing element of mystery remains. The whole totality is rather like Newman's image of something only vaguely grasped, like an iceberg with at most only one-seventh within our vision. In Newman's own words: 'No revelation can be complete and systematic, from the weakness of the human intellect; so far as it is not such, it is mysterious... The religious truth is neither light nor darkness, but both together; it is like the dim view of a country seen in the twilight, which forms half extricated from the darkness, with broken lines and isolated masses. Revelation, in this way of considering it, is not a revealed system, but consists of a number of detached and incomplete truths belonging to a vast system unrevealed.'[12]

Maximalists and minimalists thus alike err when they make too unqualified claims to knowledge either generally or on specific issues. It is thus quite misleading, I would suggest, to maintain that Moltmann's and Barth's views of the Trinity are at opposite extremes simply because one espouses the limits of the social analogy, the other of the psychological.[13] While viewed in this light that is indeed so, there remains the more fundamental underlying similarity, that here God is defined and explained rather than accepted as glimpsed only very hazily. While we can give intellectual assent to the doctrine, we continue to have no deep grasp of what such assent really means, except when each person of the Trinity is considered separately. To quote Newman once more: 'Break a ray of light into its constituent colours, each is beautiful, each may be enjoyed; attempt to unite them, and perhaps you produce only a dirty white. The pure and indivisible Light is seen only by the blessed inhabitants of heaven; here we have but such faint reflections of it as its diffraction supplies; but they are sufficient for faith and devotion. Attempt to combine them into one, and you

---

[11] For seeing only the back of God, Exod. 33.17–23 (but contrast v. 11); for Jesus as unknown, Luke 24.16; John 20.14.

[12] *Essays Critical and Historical*, 2, 4.

[13] Although Barth talks in terms of revealer, revealed, and mode of revelation, it is clear from his detailed exposition that he wishes to pull his analysis as far as possible in an Augustinian direction, to the idea of 'an eternal repetition'.

gain nothing but a mystery, which you can describe as notion but cannot depict as an imagination.'[14] This is not to deny the worth of more detailed examination of such a doctrine, or to renege on my own earlier attempts to do so, but it is to admit that I should have been firmer in my insistence on the limitations of such analogies.[15]

In theory, a response to such external (and internal) critiques of Christianity could have been made from within the Church's own internal resources. But on the whole this has not happened. Indeed, among those attempting to dialogue with the wider society rather than simply preach, reductionism has usually been the favoured response. Matthew Arnold has no shortage of successors.[16] That is another reason why I have chosen to start from outside, because lessons about such a mixture of mystery and illumination can be drawn no less from the use of words outside the Church than from within. Reductionism is as much of a danger to secular poetry and drama as it is to the more religious context. Good poetry is about expanding horizons but in a way that is suggestive rather than absolutely definitive; good drama is about a narrative that might help to interpret one's own but which also can disclose characters and worlds well outside the horizons of one's own ordinary experience and so still imperfectly understood.

Consider further the issue of metaphor. All of us are familiar with enacted symbols as a way of access to God, most obviously perhaps in the bread and wine of communion. But when it comes to their verbal equivalent in metaphor, the tendency is still to see their role as intellectual rather than as experiential. Metaphor and analogy are there to illumine our understanding of God. It is not that they constitute or create a way of experiencing God. In what follows I want to challenge that assumption, and especially the resultant tendency to think of metaphors as redundant, once we have got the point. While of course some eventually do die, with many there remains, I shall suggest, an inexhaustibility that makes it worth our

---

[14] E. Gilson ed., *Grammar of Assent* (New York: Doubleday, 1955), 116–17 (I, 5.3).

[15] *The Divine Trinity* (London: Duckworth, 1985). I did little more than acknowledge that it is of the essence of an analogy that it will break down at some point.

[16] In ch. 2 I take John Drury as an example.

while to return to them again and again, not only for intellectual stimulation but also as a way into experiencing God. This is not to challenge the valuable work that has been done in establishing the ontological significance of metaphor.[17] But that is hardly its sole purpose, as though to give a definition were in itself to guarantee a complete account of any particular metaphor. That is why liturgical theologians are quite right to play on the variety of possibilities inherent in Christianity's classical metaphors: water not just as cleansing, for example, but also as destructive on the one hand and on the other as refreshing, reinvigorating, and renewing.[18] The metaphor should rightly be allowed to put in play more than one meaning at any one time.

Even then the temptation may be, as with the last example, to conclude that now at last all has been said. But my contention is precisely this, that there can be no certainty about such a stopping-point, and so the move is best resisted. The moral of the parable of the labourers who were all paid the same at the end of the day may well be that grace is indifferent to our deserts and so values all alike, but something important would still be lost without the parable: not just the story but also some further images that come with it, such as Jesus' sympathy with day-labourers who have to hang around all day in the uncertain hope of getting employment.[19] Nor is this merely a 'secular' footnote. What the image encourages is the thought that grace might equally be concerned with the workplace as with our final destiny in heaven. Again, the parable of the shepherd going out to search for the one sheep that is lost may powerfully express God's concern for each and every one of us as individuals, but without the parable we would never think of the burden that God takes on himself in the process: the soiled and plaintive sheep having to be carried across the hills to safety.[20]

As a final example, consider a more obviously doctrinal issue, and the likely reason why so many Christians in the modern world fail to treat the Ascension with any importance. It is that biblical

[17] Most notably in J. M Soskice, *Metaphor and Religious Language* (Oxford: Clarendon Press, 1985).

[18] For implications for baptism, *God and Grace of Body*, ch. 3; for the contribution of liturgical theology, ch. 9.

[19] Matt. 20.1–16, esp. 3 and 6.

[20] Luke 15.3–7. Jeremy Begbie drew my attention to this aspect of the parable.

literalism leads them to the conclusion that it merely marks the conclusion of something much more significant, Jesus' resurrection appearances. But even if the Ascension literally happened in the manner Luke describes, it is without question symbolic of something more important, the exaltation of Jesus' humanity to 'the right hand of God', itself also a metaphor.[21] To state the obvious, there is no right hand side of the invisible God against which Christ's throne could be placed, any more than there would literally be room for all the saved to sit there, if the Christ of Revelation's promise were literally to be fulfilled: 'I will grant him to sit with me on my throne, as I myself have conquered and sat down with my Father on his throne' (3.21). Too literal a reading can very easily turn into the comic: each of the author's 144,000 struggling to find a bit of the throne on which to place their bottom! What is being instigated through such metaphors is reflection that continually forces us beyond the literal, into reflecting on Christ's exaltation, and the hope of a similar exaltation for ourselves, into the nearness of God's presence. But where is that nearness? If one answers heaven, this too is a metaphor since God is omnipresent, not spatially located anywhere. One metaphor thus constantly leads into another, and so definitive closure is for ever precluded. Some sense of what is promised is grasped (the survival of our complete humanity) but the mystery remains (how exactly?), in a way that certainly calls into question all wooden interpretations, among them the relevant Article of the Church of England.[22]

Some may well be willing to accept such an analysis of the implications of the poetic and metaphorical, but insist on drawing a further conclusion, that poetry is therefore necessarily iconoclastic, in such refusal of closure. Certainly, such a case can be plausibly argued. One writer, for instance, sees Blake, Hölderlin, and Sacks as poets in the tradition of Amos.[23] The prophet called into question

---

[21] For Luke's two versions, Luke 24.50–3; Acts 1.6–11; 'the "right hand" of the Creed is derived ultimately from Ps. 110.1 but mediately through repeated use of that verse in proclamation of the gospel in Acts and elsewhere.

[22] Article 4: 'Christ did truly rise again from death, and took again his body, with flesh, bones, and all things appertaining to the perfection of Man's nature; wherewith he ascended into Heaven. and there sitteth . . . ' (Appendix to *Book of Common Prayer* (1662)).

[23] A. Shanks, *What is Truth? Towards a Theological Poetics* (London: Routledge, 2001), esp. 41–59 for his treatment of Amos.

all of Israel's religious institutions. Yet despite the fact that none of his prophecies were fulfilled, that critique was still preserved, presumably as a poetic caution against any such containment of Israel's God. But I am unconvinced that this is metaphor's only religious role, or indeed that it is the only possible type of critique. The problem about critiquing others is that it can all too easily generate its own brand of arrogance, its own over-confidence that God is on one's side. Elsewhere I have already had occasion to observe how the author of the Book of Revelation seems to find evil in everyone else but himself. Not only is every aspect of the ancient world condemned but even many of his fellow Christians, including by implication St Paul himself.[24] While many of his metaphors self-destruct in their own absurdity, such an objection can be reinforced by another common role of metaphor: in making connections that might otherwise go unobserved.[25] The theories of T. S. Eliot and others on this matter are pursued in Chapter 2. Here I want simply to note that, so far from being iconoclastic, this role encourages connection but is no less subversive, for it makes links that the fanatic is always likely to refuse. So, for instance, the eucharist becomes not an exclusively Christian act but one that builds on the symbolism of food in human society more generally, as also more specifically on a shared symbolism for body and blood.

Symbols are but enacted metaphors, and so body and blood could be viewed under either heading. But that does not mean that they are just metaphors or just symbols. They are the means whereby Christ's human presence is mediated to the believer once more, and for that to be experienced it is important that the richness of such imagery be allowed its full force. It is God in the guts, a drinking of the blood which Jewish law reserved for God alone, and as such a means of relating one human being to one very particular human Other, as well as to all others who participate in the shared communion.[26] That is why, although the words

---

[24] For a brief critique of the Book of Revelation, *Discipleship and Imagination*, 158–61.

[25] In talking of such metaphors self-destructing, I allude only to their visual impact: e.g. a sword that could not possibly be held in the mouth, tall skyscraper buildings surrounded by a diminutive city wall and so on. This issue is discussed further in ch. 4.

[26] These ideas are pursued further in *God and Grace of Body*, ch. 3 but also here in ch. 2. The latter chapter in particular notes how even more Protestant

contribute much, they are not enough on their own. The sheer physicality of the actions is necessary to convey the intimacy of the encounter that is on offer.

That is why theology needs to learn from secular discussion of drama no less than of poetry. But once again the danger is that the narrative will be taken to have all the answers rather than concealing even as it discloses. The problem with Frei or a Catholic equivalent like Nicholas Boyle is that it is presumed that the frame of the narrative is now firmly set, and so effectively defined in a way that puts it beyond challenge.[27] But that is not what has happened, even long before the birth of biblical criticism, which is so often seen as the defining moment for the collapse of any such approach. As I argued in *Tradition and Imagination* and *Discipleship and Imagination* the way in which the text has been told has been constantly subject to change in response to the needs and aspirations of the community and indeed of the wider society. Certainly, the challenge of biblical criticism was somewhat different in that it tended to atomise the text. But it too offered the possibility of a story, of gradualism in perception among fallible human beings not unlike ourselves. In my view the Christian faith is richer for that new story, not the poorer. Sometimes it is necessary to hear the original context, sometimes its present customary meaning, and sometimes fresh challenges to that meaning that may eventually carry the community in quite new directions.

As with all plays, there is not one single authoritative performance but various ways in which the story can be told or re-enacted. In a similar way, which performance is the best does not admit of a single answer. Notoriously, Aristotle thought that it could be just as effective to read a play in the privacy of one's own home as to go and watch it.[28] But the experience is of course

---

understandings of the eucharist (such as George Herbert's) find it necessary to use the metaphors with full force.

[27] N. Boyle, *Sacred and Secular Scriptures: A Catholic Approach to Literature* (London: Darton, Longman & Todd, 2004). Boyle insists that a Catholic reading is one determined by the doctrinal interests of the Church and not by historical investigation (e.g. 41, 55, 85). But why cannot the two work together, both contributing to how Christians understand God? It is a false alternative, though all too often applied.

[28] Aristotle, *Poetics* 6, esp. 1450b18–19: 'The power of tragedy is dependent on neither performance nor actors' (my trans).

quite different, even if one has a powerful imagination. There is the opportunity to stop and reflect when turning the pages by oneself, whereas in the theatre the continuity of the action inevitably pulls one along at a rather different pace. More importantly, good acting and characterization also have the power to produce insights that are less easily generated on one's own. Reflective reading of Scripture and liturgical performance are thus not at all the same thing. In the latter case it is vital that some kind of overall vision be encouraged, while at the same time the language should be such as to bear frequent repetition in the kind of imagery that is conjured before the mind's eye. It is the first objective that justifies the use of the traditional prophecies at carol services, despite their original meaning. It is the latter that makes me resent the abandonment in modern Anglican Psalters of some powerful metaphors in Coverdale's translation, despite the fact that the more literal and more banal is what is suggested by the original Hebrew.[29] The dilemma has been with us for some time. The issue was already posed in 1881 by the Revised Version of the Bible, the first of the many new translations that were to follow. There, for example, 'deliver us from the evil one' replaced 'deliver us from evil'. Historically, this may have been what Jesus intended, but effectively it narrowed down the imaginative compass of the prayer, and so its effectiveness in worship.[30]

Another interesting aspect of Aristotle's approach is his stress on the importance of unity of plot.[31] Initially, it might be thought that liturgy is ideally adapted to just such an end. But this is not quite as obvious as it may at first sight seem. Indeed, the existence of (to some extent competing) subplots might actually help with this issue of openness to mystery. For a start, the liturgy is structured in terms of response to Christ rather than as a simple presentation of the drama of his life, death, and resurrection. That is why, for example, services usually begin with confession, not in the nativity. Again, although the story as a whole is told twice (once in the Creed and

---

[29] Explored in ch. 3.

[30] Matt. 6.13. The failure of modern versions of the Lord's Prayer to catch on is a significant comment on the dilemma. Even more than a century later 'the penitent thief' continues to be known by that name rather than the revisers' proposal of the penitent 'robber'.

[31] Aristotle, *Poetics* 7–8: 1450b21–1451a35.

again in the consecration prayer), there are frequent diversions into subplots. Old Testament readings certainly do not always admit of an easy christological slant, while the sermon may well focus on one narrow aspect of the story. So far from being a disadvantage, however, such complications in structure could leave open possible gates to new perspectives. That is important for at least two reasons.

First, rightly or wrongly, what contemporary society values is open narratives rather than predictability. In the past, when biblical stories were the only ones familiar to all, people read them not simply as dramas from the past but also as adaptable to tell stories of their own lives and the events in them. In the process the emphasis was often changed, and conclusions drawn that to our minds often look highly implausible. However, it is a skill that is increasingly disappearing even among practising Christians. Instead, there are a huge variety of secular stories now available which require considerably less adaptation for the reader or viewer to fit themselves into the narrative. The result is that these often take precedence even with the clergy. The average Anglican cleric, for instance, is quite likely to have read far more novels than works of theology over the course of a typical year. Nor is the situation all that different for those among the population who seldom read. In this case life's dilemmas are perhaps most likely to be explored through TV soaps. In particular this genre can provide an easy means for coming to terms with change. So, for instance, the first gay kiss on *Eastenders* and the blessing of a lesbian couple on *Emmerdale* are quite likely to have been significant moments for many in coming to terms with friends or family who were gay. In much the same way the issue was finally broached for a more conservative audience through the long-running radio series *The Archers*, when Brian had to debate how to respond to his son's decision to enter into a civil partnership.

Whether the relation between David and Jonathan or the beloved disciple and Christ might be used to develop more open attitudes on that same issue within the Church is a question which I shall leave here on one side.[32] What we can say for certain is that similar transformations in attitudes have occurred in the past and

[32] That these relations were of sexual kind seems to me implausible, but that would not in itself prevent them from being suborned for such a purpose, as has happened e.g. with Gal. 3.28.

will happen again. My earlier volumes were replete with examples. What worries me about their treatment in much contemporary theology is the widespread failure to acknowledge such change as precisely that. Instead, we are told that it is what the Bible really meant all along. The result is a new form of closure, of the Bible or Church set over against the world with nothing new to learn. Yet even the most superficial of observers cannot but observe, it seems to me, that it was not the Bible that had been over two thousand years preserving the equality of women over against a hostile society but rather was itself part of the problem in reinforcing the wrong sort of attitudes. True openness should involve a willingness also to see such oppressiveness in ourselves and in our ancestors in the faith, instead of merely projecting such faults entirely outwards.

Secondly, people are now much less willing to accept imposed solutions. Yet strategies of control still remain a conspicuous feature of the contemporary Church. While it is important that the heart of the Christian faith should be properly presented, this should not be taken as a licence to impose doctrinal orthodoxy everywhere, whether this be of a conservative or of a liberal kind. While there are far more options in set liturgies than there were in the past, this has often brought with it a wordiness that assumes more doctrinal reference is better rather than less. In short, teaching usually takes priority over image.[33] Again, on the opposite side, as Chapter 3 will indicate, hymns are often edited to reflect new orthodoxies without regard to the poetry of the original, as though congregations are unable to make any assessment for themselves. Nor are composers of new hymns necessarily any better. There is a surprising degree of conservatism in imagery that contrasts markedly with poets (who unfortunately continue to be largely unread in our churches).

But much the same can be said of performance. Past precedent is often thought to be sufficient justification instead of real imaginative engagement with what such actions might be taken to mean in our own day. It is hardly surprising, therefore, that unflattering comparisons are sometimes made between the very conventional character of most liturgy and the ingenuity of some contemporary art, to which it must be admitted the general public flock in large

---

[33] This is not to deny a valuing of imagery. Some is exciting and well deserves credit. But too often it seems introduced only because it is canonical rather than necessarily effective or illuminating at that point.

numbers.[34] Whatever we may think ultimately of the content, there is often an open quality that allows the viewer to explore and reflect imaginatively. Admittedly, this is partly because there is no prior tradition of interpretation that has to be mastered first. But it is also because interaction is encouraged, most obviously in performance and environmental art.[35] It is intriguing to watch people's embarrassment when such art is situated in a church, and the attempt made to generate such a response.[36]

The lack of trust in people themselves coming to the right conclusion is well illustrated by the suspicion with which such modern art is often regarded by Christians. It is important to note that even what is presented in a spirit of hostility does not necessarily have to be read thus. Even the convinced atheist Francis Bacon could produce at least one scene where his obsession with the crucifixion turned into a more positive, almost Christian message.[37] Damien Hirst may lack similar depth, but at least he effectively puts the religious issue on the agenda, while, despite the notoriety of her now (in)famous bed, Tracey Emin can be seen at least at times to take seriously such questions.[38] Perhaps a specific example of how such reversals can occur will help. The video artist Douglas Gordon is undoubtedly hostile to religion. One example of this is the composite work he included in a major exhibition of his work in Edinburgh in 2006. Holbein's well-known woodcut *Allegory of the Law and of the Gospel* in which a tree half bare and half flourishing sharply divides depictions of the two covenants was initially encountered reversed in a mirror with the Christian right-hand

---

[34] Attendance at Tate Modern far outstrips any other gallery in London. The same is true if the Baltic (contemporary art) and the Laing (traditional) are compared in a provincial city like Newcastle.

[35] For helpful surveys, R. Goldberg, *Performance: Live Art since the 60s* (London: Thames & Hudson, 2004); J. Kastner ed., *Land and Environmental Art* (London: Phaidon, 1998).

[36] But not just in churches. The 'reverential' attitude can also affect art galleries, as the Serpentine Gallery found with its 2000 exhibition of the works of Felix Gonzalez-Torres. For a discussion of such approaches, N. Bourriaud, *Relational Aesthetics* (Paris: Les presses du réel, 1998; trans. 2002).

[37] His *Triptych for George Dyer* (1973); discussed in my essay, 'The Incarnation in Twentieth-Century Art' in S. T. Davis, D. Kendall, and G. O'Collins eds., *The Incarnation* (Oxford: Oxford University Press, 2002), 332–64, esp. 350–3.

[38] She has recently accepted a commission from Liverpool Anglican Cathedral for Liverpool's year as Cultural Capital of Europe. *My Bed* dates from 1998; illustration in *Tracey Emin: Works 1963–2006* (New York: Rizzoli, 2006), no page number.

side now seen on the left, and then partially repeated in a felled tree lying on a broken mirror on the floor.[39] The intention was to challenge Holbein's certainties, but equally they could help modern Christians see that their own faith need not be bought at the expense of the degradation of Judaism, nor indeed at the diminution of all left-handers.[40]

Hinduism is often despised by the three western monotheisms as polytheism at its worst. But the way in which its myths present often contradictory aspects to the divine means that Hindus are never absolutely certain of how their experience of God will turn out. The beauty of Shiva as Lord of the dance (Nataraja), for instance, is nicely balanced by him as Bhairava (terrible or frightful) and as essentially aniconic in the linga.[41] It is that openness that Christians need to recover and so with it a greater range to the sort of encounters that are expected to mediate God. Priests dressed in lace and silk gloves in churches built like theatres may suggest drama at its most superficial and corrupt. But the playfulness of God that such a baroque style once implied also characterizes no less serious a book than the Book of Job, where Leviathan and Behemoth seem created solely for the divine pleasure in diversity.[42] In Proverbs it is no less a figure than divine Wisdom herself that plays before God. It is such delight in the unexpected that Christianity needs to recover, as it learns from poetry and drama of the Logos that at one and the same time discloses even as it also veils: the mystery at the heart of words. It is that combination that I wish to explore further in the pages that follow.

As with this volume's predecessors, there is no separate bibliography. Readers need, therefore, to be alerted to the fact that full bibliographical details are given on the first reference to a work within each chapter. Biblical quotations are from the RSV, unless otherwise indicated.

[39] Discussed but only illustrated in part in *Douglas Gordon Superhumanatural* (Edinburgh: National Galleries of Scotland, 2006), 41–3, 54–5.
[40] Deeply embedded of course in Christianity with Christ placed 'at the right hand' of God, but also true of culture more generally, as in the derivation of 'sinister' from the Latin for 'left'.
[41] Although the linga originated as a sexual image, the current treatment of this image suggests more an impact through mystery.
[42] The detailed description of both monsters suggests as much: Job 40.14–41.34 For play in Proverbs, 8.30-1. The church of St John Nepomuk in Munich (Asam brothers, 1733) is a fine example of such a baroque style, with balconies and so forth.

I

Experience through Metaphor

ONE way of characterizing what I am trying to achieve in this part of the book is as an exploration of how language can sometimes be said to function sacramentally, in conveying experiences of divine presence. Initially, this might sound like a rather strange and implausible notion. After all, it may be observed, it is so obviously less physical or material than the usual sort of thing considered as a candidate for such mediation: if not the natural creation itself, then characteristically a close equivalent in human artefacts that deliberately seek to mimic the creation's attributes, as, for example, landscape painting or architecture. By contrast, speech and writing seem so obviously purely human forms of communication. Indeed, even with the Bible itself there has been widespread retreat from the view that God actually communicates directly through the particular words used. Rather, it is more a matter of divine revelation welling up from the person's subconscious. That is to say, it is the recipient's wider experience that conveys a sense of God's presence and purposes rather than precisely those very words. If that is accepted, the point, it might seem, could be made even more forcibly in respect of words in secular contexts: they describe an experience rather than evoke it. Why these apparently conclusive observations are nonetheless anything but, it is the intention of the following chapters to demonstrate.

Words, I shall contend, are not just a medium for conveying something else but sometimes themselves an essential constituent in the experience. Put concisely, God is himself sometimes to be found in and through the words. In order to explore how this might be so, I proceed by four stages. First, I shall explore the competing pressures both within the history of Christianity and outside of it to move in two quite different directions, towards definition and containment in words on the one hand and on the other towards mystery and what might almost be described as inexhaustibility. Thereafter, I shall pick up on that notion of inexhaustibility, particularly as this is reflected in metaphor, and examine how poets have found in metaphor an obvious point of contact with religion, despite the tendency of so many theologians and believers to seek reduction to the literal.

These more general reflections will then be focused in the final two chapters on more concrete examples. The third chapter examines how far Christianity's own history has been deficient in its acceptance and exploration of metaphor within its practice of congregational singing. The psalms are rich in metaphor. Initially, hymns were also quite adventurous. But there is an issue of how far too heavy a reliance on existing biblical imagery has imposed unnecessary restraints on what can be experienced through such words. Indeed, sometimes it seems that it is really the music that is more effective in encouraging and deepening a relationship with God. Finally, in Chapter 4 two apparently disparate aspects of worship are brought together, the continuing reality of preaching and the now lost tradition of illuminated manuscripts. What I want to suggest here is that preaching functions at its best imaginatively through the re-creation of biblical scenes and the bringing alive of its metaphors, and so in a manner not dissimilar from the illuminated manuscript. The contrast between word and image that has prevailed for so much of Christian history (especially within the Protestant tradition) is in my view absurdly overplayed. The excuse for suspicion of the image has been the danger of idolatry, but words no less than visual images can fall subject to such a trap. Wherever the provisional is made absolute, the danger lurks. The modern fundamentalist who claims an absolute character for the precise words as written down is thus no better than the medieval peasant who mistook the statue of Mary or Christ in the local church for the reality itself. What is wrong with both alike is their failure to recognize the openness that is alike inherent in both art forms.

Metaphor and symbol are thus two not unrelated ways of achieving the same goal, of helping the hearer or viewer to move from one form of perception to another, while at the same time recognizing the inevitable limitations of the analogy. Whether symbols are presented directly in specific actions, or indirectly in the painted canvas or the sculpted wood or bronze, the encouragement is there to think through the material into a different type of reality. To see in a Renaissance painting the Christ child pricking his finger on a thorn or a skull at the foot of the cross and leave the matter at that would be totally to misunderstand what is being said through such paintings.[1] The same issue, however, is at stake, not just in obvious symbolism such as this, but no less so where choices are made as to how Christ's body on the cross is presented. Any fool knows that the pain in such a situation must have been acute, but whether it is presented as such is no less a symbolic decision than where Christ's body is allowed to remain beautiful. It is not the facts about Good Friday that are in question but how the artist can best enable us to engage with them. Is divine identification with humanity in its suffering the most important thing that needs to be said, or the fact that God in Christ defeated suffering and death once and for all and so can ensure our own victory over such ills in due course? So a painting that merely portrayed the fact of Christ's suffering and failed to indicate its relevance to us as viewers would in religious terms have to be judged a complete failure. The requirement for engagement through some appropriate form of symbolism is thus just as pertinent in this case as in Romanesque or Renaissance pictures of Christ on the Cross where his body seems not only undamaged but actually beautiful.[2] So, although Raphael and Grünewald diverge hugely on what we see, both have symbolic aims that are not just a function of Renaissance canons of beauty or a northern Gothic concern with realism. In the one case beauty is a symbol of triumph over suffering and death; in the other the accompanying figures are there to help us appropriate the suffering as a means of bringing penitence and new life.[3]

---

[1] The child pricking its finger is there to remind us of Christ's future role in wearing a crown of thorns. The skull alludes not just to Golgotha as 'the place of the skull' but also to the contrast between the first and second Adam. Adam's rebellion led to death (Gen. 3.19); Christ's will lead to new life.

[2] These issues are discussed in chapters 1 and 4 of this volume's predecessor, *God and Grace of Body: Sacrament in Ordinary* (Oxford: Oxford University Press, 2007).

[3] In Grünewald's case seen most obviously in the way in which the figure of Mary Magdalene is made smaller than the other figures and so the size of a typical contemporary donor. Her new relationship with Christ, we are being told, could also be ours.

My point is that to read any serious Christian art literally is almost certainly to misrepresent it. The aim is to engage us as viewers in a particular way of reading reality, and that requires the painting to function as mediator into something other than what superficially appears before our eyes on the canvas: that it happened this way rather than that. Much the same holds in respect, then, of metaphor as the nearest equivalent in the literary medium of the visual or enacted symbol. Of course, statements can be made about Christ that are literally true (e.g. Jesus was crucified under Pontius Pilate); others that sound purely literal but, as we all know, require considerable elucidation and qualification from dogmatics and philosophy (e.g. Christ was God). But it is not such as these that are likely to open us up to an experience of God being mediated through Christ. Rather, this occurs where powerful metaphors are offered of how Christ might impact upon our lives: as, for example, in images of him as Redeemer or Sacrifice. It is a particular way of his story being told that makes the difference: one that refuses, like the painting or sculpture, to halt at the bare facts and instead encourages us to perceive that life as imbued with the sort of significance that the metaphors indicate operates more mundanely elsewhere.

If such examples suggest a somewhat narrow application only to where the gospel story and related material are in play, that is certainly not my point. Rather, what I want to suggest is that wherever metaphor and symbol occur they help to draw apparently different aspects of reality closer together and so help generate a more inclusive conception of the world that we inhabit, and so hint, however tentatively, at a single enfolding reality that lies in God as their common creator. Let me put it another way. Fundamental to religious belief is the conviction that, however much the divine has put of itself into the creation, it remains of a fundamentally different order. So, in trying to conceptualize God, words must necessarily resort to images and metaphors that in the nature of the case draw unexpected connections between different aspects of reality, and indeed derive much of their power precisely from the fact that they are unexpected. Symbols function no differently. Whether spoken, acted, or painted, drawing bread close to body and wine to blood must continue to shock, even as it establishes a more integrated account of reality. The further that process of integration goes, the more it can be taken to suggest everything inhering in a single common underlying reality, the God that is the source of all that is.

That thought is scarcely new. As we shall see, it is an intuition common to a number of poets. In the chapters that follow such is the direction in which my reflections will proceed, precisely because it suggests that, even where we are apparently at our most cerebral in creating new metaphors, the material world once more asserts itself and our imaginative capacities take over. How we act and how we speak move together through symbol and metaphor towards the integration of all reality, and so towards the discovery of the God who lies at the root of all, as the explanatory Logos who is also pure Act, yet in a way that retains mystery and a sense of still more that might be disclosed one day.

I

Logos and Mystery

A tension that exists in almost all forms of religion is that between explanation and mystery, between the conviction that something has been communicated by the divine (revelation) and the feeling that none the less God is infinitely beyond all our imaginings. That tension can be seen reflected in the two words that head this chapter. It is from the Greek for word, *logos*, that we get terms such as logic and logical, and so emphasis on the pursuit of rational explanation. The word mystery is also derived from Greek, but with a quite different thrust. It was used originally of initiatory cults in ancient religions where something was disclosed but still in a way that induced awe and demanded secrecy. Eventually *musterion* came also to be the word used for the Christian sacraments, and nowhere can that tension between knowledge and mystery in the modern sense be seen more clearly. While some theologians continued to speak of mysteries that defied complete human comprehension, others sought for precise definition and explanation. It is that tension that I want to explore further here as a natural way in to the whole issue of metaphor which will be the focus of the second chapter. Metaphors do after all both affirm something to be the case and yet refuse complete identification and closure.

In exploring the Judaeo-Christian tradition in its attitude to words I want to use the history of Logos and Kabbalah as indicative of those two types of approach and the tension between them. Partly because of worries about the connection between *logos* and logical and rational, Christians sometimes resist setting John's use of Logos in the opening chapter of his Gospel against the wider setting of Greek thought. That seems to me a mistake. A search for explanation need not necessarily prove reductive. Indeed, that wider background can be used to suggest the search for a shared divine grounding for all language that promised intelligibility but not necessarily completion. It is only a more pedestrian emphasis that assumed complete intelligibility as the aim, seen most obviously perhaps in the search for divinely sanctioned principles behind the origin of language. But even if this is doubted in the case of Logos, balancing such notions were the kind of ideas to be found in the Kabbalah where words (and even letters) are assumed to have such hidden depths that no completion looks possible. Although in its final form Kabbalah was to find its natural home in medieval Judaism, there is no shortage of earlier precedents, and it was also to influence Christianity, even at the Renaissance when the desire for rationality might have been thought to have been at its most intense.

Christianity's tragedy was that it was eventually to move decisively towards containment, typified by the desire to provide fixed formulae for determining the validity of sacraments. What such aspirations ignored was the wider impact of the rites as a whole, and the way in which words, so far from functioning merely as a test for divine action, could actually in themselves help mediate the divine. So, while this chapter ends with that negative history, it begins by exploring the creative possibilities inherent in both Logos and Kabbalah, even if each had its own inherent danger: too much rationalism in the former, mystery that collapsed into mere nonsense in the latter.

Logos and the Search for Explanation

One obvious way available to the Christian of connecting God and words would be to refer to the description of Christ as Logos or Word. In making that equation the opening chapter of John's Gospel opened up a potentially rich vein of human reflection. This could be halted in its tracks by insisting that at most what is involved is a rich metaphor. Only an analogy, it will be said, is being drawn between Christ and words. It is not that words can be treated as having any real power in their own right. Whether a straightforward Jewish or more Hellenistic background to the passage is assumed, that might well seem to be the case. If purely Jewish antecedents are presupposed and the roots thus seen to lie primarily in the opening chapter of Genesis, the claim amounts to something like this: Jesus is like the Father's words at creation; so he himself and his life are a clear expression of the divine intention for a new humanity in and through him. God uttered a word and the old creation began; he utters a new Word, and so begins the new or restored creation. On that scenario, the second Word is hardly in any sense literally a word. A not dissimilar conclusion might be reached if assumptions operating within the wider Hellenistic culture are presupposed (including the use of *Logos* terminology in both the Platonism and Stoicism of the time). So far from drawing interpretation closer to an emphasis on the importance of words, any dependence on a literal understanding might now seem made even more distant. In those particular philosophies and indeed in culture more generally *logos* was used not to mean just 'word' but, more accurately, 'intelligibility', 'rationality', and 'explanation'. To understand why the term played such a major role in Platonism, it is essential to appreciate that the everyday Greek for 'to give an account' or 'explanation' of something is to 'give its *logos*'.[1] Again, for Stoicism *logos* became the principal term for the divine, precisely because it is the immanence of the divine in our world that gives that world its intelligibility through order and predictability. Against that wider frame of meaning, the claim in John would amount to the assertion that Christ is our principal clue to the world's intelligibility, and so to making sense of our place in it. But, once again, however profound the claim, it can hardly be seen to hinge crucially on word or words as such.

Yet, despite these qualifications, there is, I believe, after all a connection, and one legitimated by the very meaning of *logos*. The Greek term only came to bear these wider meanings in virtue of the fact that there can be no rationality, no intelligibility, without words. It is only thanks to words as diverse as 'table' and 'chair', or 'love' and 'hate' that we can divide up our world and so characterize and make sense of it. So even Christ as lived expression of the divine can still only be communicated to us who have never seen him through the use of words. Not only that, to claim him as the pre-eminent Word is to claim him as the source of the world's explanation, the clue to its meaning; and so all words must find their ultimate rationale in him as the supreme Word. The world will only be given intelligibility or rationality insofar as Christ as Logos is used to further its definition and characterization. So even if John was basing himself only on the inaugural chapter of Genesis, that thought already begins the pull towards the wider Hellenistic

---

[1] The usual Greek expression for 'to give an explanation' of something is *didonai logon*.

resonances, which is precisely what many of the Church Fathers found, as they sought to expound this Gospel.[2] The earlier objection thus in a sense turns back on itself, for it is now clear that for the Creator to be known Christ has to be more than merely nominally a word. He is the expression of an intelligible creator, only insofar as words succeed in conveying that meaning or understanding.

That is why it seems to me a pity that the wider Hellenistic background is not taken more seriously by biblical scholars. Too quickly the possibility is dismissed on the presumption that detailed parallels need to be detected before influence can be acknowledged.[3] Much more probable in my view is the effect of general assumptions at the time about words and their power. Calvin provides an excellent summary of the basic meaning of that opening chapter of John: 'just as men's speech is called the expression of their thoughts, so it is not inappropriate to say that God expresses himself to us by his speech or Word'.[4] However, the way in which he goes on to dismiss the relevance of wider philosophical or cultural assumptions only exposes explicitly what I suspect is assumed implicitly in the minds of many a biblical scholar. As he observes, 'the other meanings of the word are not so appropriate. The Greek certainly means "definition" or "reason" or "calculation"; but I do not wish to enter into philosophical discussion beyond the limits of my faith.' What is thereby ignored is any real engagement with, first, a quite different attitude to words in both Judaism and paganism from what prevails today and, secondly, the way in which that attitude helped generate the search for an overarching Logos that would give a clue to reality as a whole.

[2] For a helpful outline of the way in which Origen combines biblical, Platonic, and Stoic elements in his own creative interpretation, see the helpful summary by J. O'Leary in J. A. McGuckin ed., *The Westminster Handbook to Origen* (Louisville: Westminster John Knox, 2004), 142–4.

[3] C. H. Dodd and Raymond Brown may be usefully contrasted on this point. To establish influence the former postulates detailed parallels with Philo; the latter concludes a purely Hebraic background from the lack of specifics. C. H. Dodd, *The Interpretation of the Fourth Gospel* (Cambridge: Cambridge University Press, 1970 edn.), 263–85, esp. 276–9; R. E. Brown, *The Gospel according to John* (New York: Anchor, 1966), pp. lvi–lix, 519–24, esp. 524.

[4] John Calvin, *Commentary on John*, ed. A. McGrath and J. I. Packer (Wheaton: Crossway, 1994), 13.

In order to indicate what I have in mind, let me take the reader initially to a quite different context, still in the first century AD but to a place apparently far removed from Christianity, the most important shrine of Greek religion, the temple and oracle at Delphi.[5] It was the ancient world's most influential religious centre, its influence in large part created by its famous oracle.[6] People came from near and far to ask for its advice. The trance-like responses given by the female prophets were duly recorded and held in awe by educated and uneducated alike. The best-known priest of the shrine in the first century was the historian and philosopher Plutarch. Not surprisingly for a priest, quite a number of his writings are on religion. One addresses the question of the mysterious third inscription at Delphi. Even today the other two are still quite widely known: the adages 'know yourself' and 'nothing in excess'. But there was a third, simply a letter, the fifth of the Greek alphabet, epsilon or E. Plutarch canvasses a number of possible explanations.[7] Since the letter in Greek is pronounced in exactly the same way as the second person singular of the verb 'to be' (rather like our A), his preferred explanation is that the inscription actually encapsulates an indispensable clue to the nature of divine identity. 'You are' or 'Thou art' marks the essence of God: he alone always exists, and nothing can undermine that existence.[8]

That said, and there is now an obvious connection back to the biblical world. The great revelation at the burning bush to Moses in Exodus 3 takes a similar turn. The Hebrew name for God, Yahweh, is taken to mean 'I am that I am'. In the medieval philosophy of St Thomas Aquinas this was re-expressed as the claim that God is essentially 'He who is'.[9] God alone has his existence in and of

---

[5] For a collection of key texts reflecting ancient attitudes, including on the meaning of 'know yourself': R. Lipsey, *Have You Been to Delphi?* (Albany: State University of New York Press, 2000).

[6] For an impressive attempt by a novelist to recreate its atmosphere and influence, M. Doody, *Aristotle and Poetic Justice* (London: Arrow, 2003).

[7] Seven in all, including the 'if' and 'would that' of enquiry at the shrine, and less likely options such as 'five'. *The E at Delphi* is part of Plutarch's *Moralia* and as such available in the Loeb Classical Library (vol. v).

[8] *The E at Delphi*, 17–21: 391E–394C.

[9] The original sense of Exod. 3.14 may have been more in terms of divine independence of action: 'I will be what I will be'; or 'I create what I create.' However, already with the Septuagint the later view is already well established: 'I am Being.' For the actual range of possibilities: B. S. Childs, *The Book of Exodus* (Louisville: Westminster, 1974), 60–4, 84–7.

himself, with everything else deriving its being from God's. God's name has thus become equivalent to the claim that he is the Source and Creator of all that is. This is also precisely how Plutarch ends his discussion. 'Know yourself', he insists, is not in any sense, as it might be in the modern world, an injunction to gain personal existential knowledge about oneself. Rather, it is essentially a summons to perceive and acknowledge exactly that kind of dependence on a source other than oneself.[10] In other words, 'know yourself' means 'know your proper place in the scheme of things': your dependence on he who alone truly is.

Two quite different examples, then, from the ancient world of attempts to gain access to a deeper reality through the meaning of words, yet coming, intriguingly, to surprisingly similar conclusions. Nor was such fascination with words by any means an isolated phenomenon at that time. Words were commonly taken to function as much more than mere naked signs, just pointing to something other than themselves. Instead, they were seen to provide in themselves a means of access to the nature of reality. This is as much true of the Bible as of the wider ancient world. It is impossible, for example, to read in any other way the narratives of the patriarchs in Genesis where great significance is made to attach to the names they were given.[11] More contrived seem the names given by some of the prophets to their children.[12] Even here, though, caution needs to be exercised against moving too quickly to modern assumptions about arbitrariness. Prophecies based on the punning of similar-sounding words, for example the Hebrew for 'basket of fruit' and 'destruction', may have been seen by contemporaries as more than just fortuitous: it was God who had made the language carry such a heavy import.[13] Certainly, once released even

---

[10] Plutarch's last comment is that 'it is a reminder to a mortal of his own nature and weakness' (my trans.).

[11] So Abraham's name is changed from Abram ('exalted father') to Abraham ('father of a multitude'): Gen. 17.5. Isaac ('he laughs') is so called because of the laughter of his parents at the possibility of so late a birth: Gen. 17.17–19. Jacob is 'the supplanter' or 'he who grabs the heel': Gen. 25.26.

[12] e.g. Isa. 8.1–4.

[13] The example in the text comes from Amos 8.1–3. The verbal similarities might be seen as entirely natural in the context of the fruit's association with autumn or 'the fall', and so with another kind of fall: R. S. Cripps, *A Critical and Exegetical Commentary on the Book of Amos* (London: SPCK, 1960), 240.

God's words were seen as having a power that could act virtually independently of him.[14]

More examples of this kind of attitude will follow shortly. But for the moment I want to stress how such assumptions about words give a quite different resonance to Logos from what otherwise it might have been taken to mean. I have already mentioned its much wider range of meanings than our nearest English equivalent, to include not just word, but also expression, idea, and even definition. That could all too easily suggest a purely philosophical concept, but not if this is set against how words were viewed more generally in the ancient world. They had an element of divine mystery about them, an ability to disclose deeper aspects to the world and thus perhaps also the source of the world itself. It is this dimension that needs to be taken on board when considering how the two major philosophies of the ancient world, Platonism and Stoicism, apply the term. Modern commentators often write as though the choice of the term was dictated by purely philosophical considerations. It was about the search for definition or explanation and only accidentally does this acquire a divine answer. Rather, what I would suggest occurs is an extrapolation from the sense of divine mystery inherent in particular words to the search for an overarching Logos that would explain and give intelligibility to all of reality, though without reducing either to wholly explicable realities. Mystery and wonder are maintained even as explanations are given.[15]

Even then, though, details of the two systems diverged markedly. The Platonic solution expected a resolution in something beyond the world, the Stoic in something immanent or present within it. Against that backdrop John can be seen to be picking up on both possibilities in his first chapter. The Logos of which he speaks is both transcendent (with the Father from the beginning) and also immanent (he became part of our world). It is of course a very large claim. The clue to the world's intelligibility, to making sense of the reality of which we are part, we are being told, lies in Jesus Christ. He is the world's true Logos, its proper explanation, the source of its intelligibility. So, if we read the lines of his Gospel aright, in

---

[14] As in Isa. 55.10–11.
[15] Obviously true of the divine, but I think also of ordinary material reality. Words and their interrelations still retain an element of mystery about them.

effect John promises us a worked-out pattern of explanation against which to interpret our lives.

If that is anything like the right interpretation, then it is hardly surprising if John's Gospel then goes on to play with words to a degree not found in any of the other three. Throughout he is encouraging us to read what he says at more than one level, on both the narrowly historical (the incarnation matters) and with the symbolic given an equally important place. The pre-eminent Word is thus disclosed through words but with words used in all their rich potential. Consider, for example, the first miracle of Jesus that immediately follows in the next chapter. It simply will not do to think only of the stupendous nature of such an event, of water being turned into wine. It is also equally about the new life Christ promises, a life as different as wine is from water. It is through John deliberately playing with words that the clue to such a multiple reading is provided. In introducing the miracle, we are told that it took place 'on the third day'. Highly unlikely to be remembered more than half a century later as an historical detail, what it alerts readers to is the possibility of a resurrection interpretation, confirmed in the way in which the wine comes out of six jars normally used for water in everyday rites of purification. The imperfect six is transformed and completed by the new order. Again, the miracle ends in absurd over-provision, in 180 gallons of the stuff. The point was hardly to encourage a lifetime of hangovers, but to suggest overflowing grace in this new resurrection life. This Logos is the world's point, and so can not only transform readers' lives but also their understanding of the world as a whole. One can only, therefore, express absolute astonishment at the fact that the official Anglican lectionary actually omits the introductory phrase, presumably on the misguided belief that it is an irrelevant historical detail.[16]

In effect, the symbolic power of words is being used by John to bring alive an incident that was already well over half a century old by the time of his writing. The device enables him to draw a past event into his readers' present reality. They are encouraged to envisage the transformation of their lives in the here and now through the power of words to disclose something other than

---

[16] By 'lectionary' I mean here the actual book of texts, not simply the recommended list of readings.

their purely denotational meaning, that to which on the surface they point. In recognizing such a rich mystery to language, John demonstrates that to accept an explanatory sense to Logos is not necessarily to adopt a reductive approach to all language. Indeed, in some ways, as we shall see, his attitude appears not all that distant from Kabbalah. But first I want to illustrate how in the ancient world a preoccupation with words could sometimes be reductive. This is especially evident in the search for the origins of language.

Here a much neglected dialogue of Plato's, *Cratylus*, is of particular interest. One interlocutor (Hermogenes) advocates the view that letters and syllables are entirely arbitrary with no intrinsic connection between them and what the speaker intends to convey. The contrary view is represented by Cratylus. According to him, the constituent syllables of words and even individual letters can afford clues to underlying meaning. Although Plato's teacher, Socrates, is portrayed not infrequently mocking any such attempts, his overall position, I suggest, is one of sympathy: that under appropriate circumstances words could tell us something about the world and so prove not entirely conventional or arbitrary.[17] This might be true, for instance, of the gods' names, or of the original use of terms. Indeed, one of his illustrations can be carried over into English, and so be seen to be not wholly without merit.[18] The English 'r' could be taken to suggest motion since it is found in so many words such as 'tremor,' 'tremble,' 'strike' and so forth, while 'l' slips so easily off the tongue that it might suggest smoothness, as in words such as 'level' or 'sleek'. In fact, the contention is more plausible for Greek than it is for some other languages where (as in English) letters are used to represent a much larger range of sounds, or where the connection is known in any case to be entirely arbitrary.[19]

[17] For an example of Socratic mockery, note his argument, first in support of Heraclitus that all words for the good contain movement, and then the reverse that they denote rest: *Cratylus* 411–14.

[18] *Cratylus* 433b–435b.

[19] English has forty or so phonemes or sounds but only twenty-six letters to represent them. An extreme example of mismatch is Cherokee. In the nineteenth century in his attempt to give written form to his people's language for the first time, Chief Sequoyah chose purely arbitrary correspondences between its characteristic sounds and those of the Latin alphabet.

The details, however, are less interesting than Plato's willingness to examine such possibilities in the first place. Such explorations appear to run counter to his general assumption that this world can only ever be at most a very imperfect reflection of another, better world. It looks as though, in this instance at least, he thought that precisely because words help to provide intelligibility to our world they might also succeed in taking us nearer to understanding the divine underpinning of that world. That God's own name might have some kind of intimate connection with his essential reality is perhaps a natural intuition. At all events Plato did propose that the name 'Zeus' should be connected with the verb 'to be alive' (*zeo*) and its accusative form (*Dia*) with the mediation of that life to us.[20] As such it parallels the attempts of Exodus 3, and is just as implausible. What these hesitant attempts of Plato do illustrate, however, is the pushing towards complete explanation, as though the words in themselves could tell us all we need to know, whether about the nature of God or reality as a whole.

Plato's conviction about the meaning of Zeus was in all probability founded on a much more widespread assumption: that the gift of language itself came from God, and so all language (and not just the name for God) must in some sense reflect its divine origins. If Greek legends involving a role for Cadmus and/or Thoth were one way of speaking of such divine involvement, the way in which Herodotus assigns a key role to the Phoenicians seemed to provide later Jewish and Christian writers with some kind of confirmation that their own God had been involved.[21] After all, Phoenicia was a near neighbour of Palestine. The result was arguments back and forth in the attempt to identify the precise nature of that involvement. Even as late as 1853 the relevant entry in the *Encyclopaedia Britannica* was still declaring that the letters of the alphabet were either due 'to the first man Adam . . . or we must admit that it was not a human, but a divine invention'.[22] The reason why most preferred the second option can be gathered from some words in

---

[20] *Cratylus* 396a–b.

[21] Intriguingly, the legend that Cadmus introduced writing to Greece from Phoenicia may have some historical basis. In 1964 some Mesopotamian cylinder seals were discovered in a Mycenaean site on the Cadmea.

[22] Quoted in J. Drucker, *The Alphabetic Labyrinth* (London: Thames & Hudson, 1999), 26.

John Webster's 1654 work *Academiarum Examen*: 'the causes and
effects of nature are characters or hieroglyphics of his power so
legible that those who will not read them, and by them him, are
without excuse'.[23] In other words, Adam's naming was held to
reflect the meaning already given to things by God. So find the
origin of the words, and that meaning would be known.

That this assumption was based on something rather more than
mere religious fancy is suggested by the way in which even more
secular minds also sought such deeper connections.[24] The decision of
some Christians to use Scripture to argue on the other side (against)
also supports this interpretation. Here the worry was that, if such
decipherment ever became possible, human beings might thereby
gain a handle or even control over God's free action.[25] More than the
theory of evolution, what decisively undermined such ideas was the
discovery of the Rosetta Stone in 1799, and the consequent decipherment of hieroglyphics. As the term implies, hieroglyphs were for long
assumed to be a 'sacred code'. The symbols were taken to mark non-
arbitrary and significant connections between what the symbols portrayed and the words or syllables uttered through them. But once the
Rosetta Stone and subsequent decipherments exploded such a view
even for an apparently pictorial language, the case for ordinary letters
and syllables was also correspondingly undermined.

One irony in all these developments is that modern scholarship
still places the origins of all western notation where Herodotus once
placed it, in the Middle East, if now at a much earlier time.[26] More
relevant to note here, though, is the collapse of such a totalizing
view for words: that they all have a divine origin and so can enable
humanity to access all of reality, including the divine. More modest
ambitions for words are, therefore, necessary. In the next chapter
I shall present those more modest ambitions through an examination of the role of metaphor. First, however, I want to illustrate the

---

[23] Quoted in J. Drucker, *The Alphabetic Labyrinth* (London: Thames & Hudson,
1999), 195.

[24] Hugo and Mallarmé are examples from the nineteenth century, Evans,
Skinner, and Dunand in the twentieth: so Drucker, ibid. 244–5, 295–9.

[25] William Warburton's work of the 1740s (and still being reprinted in the
nineteenth century) is an obvious example: Drucker, ibid. 218–19.

[26] Following the researches of Godfrey Driver, the consensus seems to be that
the Phoenicians were probably responsible for the origins of the alphabet *c*.1700 to
c.1500 BC.

Scylla and Charybdis, the two extremes that need to be avoided: too much mystery or too much explanation. Medieval Judaism may be used to illustrate the former, medieval Christianity the latter. If I had to choose, what I would want to suggest is that, despite the absurdity of so many of its proposals in both its Jewish and nearest Christian equivalents and offshoots, it is the Kabbalah's sense of the mystery in words that theology most needs to hear today. Medieval Christianity's concern with precision in defining when words did or did not carry with them sacramental efficacy, sadly, revealed a strategy all too concerned with human control of the divine.

Language as Mystery: Kabbalah

In order to understand the Kabbalah and its Christian offshoots, it is important first to note how such attitudes spring both out of the Hebrew scriptures and also from earlier traditional but non-mystical ways of reading the text. This must be conceded as soon as due note is taken of how much value, as we saw earlier, the Old Testament itself attributes to words and to names in particular. Punning and attaching a precise significance to personal names alike suggest just such a focus. So too does the extraordinary reverence with which the Tetragrammaton (YHWH) was held. It was not just a matter of what it was taken to mean. Its four letters were customarily written without the help of pointing, that is, of the usual indicators of the vowel sounds needed in pronunciation. Philo tells us that only priests were entitled to utter the name and even then only in the Temple.[27] Otherwise, devout Jews were expected to use Adonai or Lord instead.[28] Later Jewish practice in exegesis exhibited the same kind of attitude. Even non-mystically inclined Jews continued to insist that nothing in Scripture could be arbitrary, if it was truly God's word. Each word and the order in which they appeared must somehow be significant. Sometimes the results were quite startling.[29] Rather than pursue earlier examples

[27] Philo, *Life of Moses* 2. 11.

[28] This is the origin of the mistaken Christian transliteration, Jehovah, in which the vowels for Adonai are combined with the consonants for Yahweh.

[29] Philo is a case in point. For some examples, see his treatment of the patriarchs' names in *De mutatione nominum* 8. 60ff.

here, it would seem best to proceed directly to what are surely to the modern mind the strangest applications of all of such principles, in the mystical tradition known as the Kabbalah.

Nowadays most non-Jews are totally unaware of such a tradition. Yet thanks to their dress its current-day inheritors are among the most conspicuous on our streets, particularly so if one visits New York or Jerusalem. For the Hasidic community, once largely confined to eastern Europe, is now, since the Holocaust, scattered throughout the world, and easily recognizable by their beards and long ear-locks or *peot,* and the *streimel* or squat fur-trimmed hat worn on the sabbath.[30] Among the most prominent are the Lubavitch community, which has been vociferous in its opposition to any surrender of territory back to the Palestinians. It would be unfortunate, however, if Hasidic thought was narrowly identified in this way. It is a rich and diverse tradition that well illustrates how even as transcendent a religion as Judaism can experience pressures to modify its thought in what might be described as a more sacramental or immanent direction.

Hasidic thought in fact takes its origins from the revivalist movement initiated in eighteenth-century Poland by Israel Baal Shem Tov, sometimes known by his abbreviated name of the Besht. Although it is hard to distinguish what were his own ideas and those of predecessors or successors, there is clearly great stress on divine immanence and the joy and enthusiasm this can bring. To this day dance remains a regular feature of Hasidic life, as does a generous supply of alcohol for gatherings on the sabbath and other festive occasions. Hasidism would see itself as in unbroken continuity with the key kabbalistic text, the thirteenth-century *Zohar* that traces its own origins to the second century. Inevitably, reality turns out to be somewhat more complicated.

The tradition in fact seems to have passed through a number of byways, including the influential messianic pretender Shabbatai Zevi (d. 1676). Ultimately more important, though, were two Spanish scholars of the previous century, Moses Cordovero (d. 1570) and Isaac Luria (d. 1572). The former was the more thoroughly immanentist of the two in his ideas, with God seen as present in all things and all

---

[30] *Peot* are based on Lev. 19.27: 'You shall not round off the hair on your temples' (RSV), interpreted as a sign of the continuous stream of mercy that comes from God.

things in God.[31] Luria was more circumspect, drawing a distinction between God in himself (*En Sof*) who withdraws to make space for the world (*Tzimtzum*), and the series of divine emanations (*Sefirot*) that come from him. Yet the net result of these emanations, not least that of Primordial Man (*Adam Kadmon*), was in effect to re-establish a sense of divine immanence after all, even if it was now seen as episodic or partial.[32] It is perhaps, therefore, not surprising that modern Hasidic thought sees no fundamental conflict between Cordovero and Luria. Where, however, it has moved beyond Luria is in seeking to recover 'the holy sparks' that were believed to result from such divine emanations. These were to be found not only in the more obvious areas of religious and moral experience but also equally in every aspect of human life, including food and drink. All life is thus seen as engaged upon the recovery of the holy, and thus of the presence of the divine in our midst.

This detour into Hasidic thought may seem to have taken us far from any notion of the sacramentality of words. In fact it has not, for kabbalistic mysticism found and still finds its *raison d'être* pre-eminently in the *Zohar* and related texts that use detailed attention to divine meanings hidden in the biblical text to justify its imma-nent understanding of God. An example may be given from the very first verse of the Hebrew Bible.[33] In English this runs 'In the beginning God created…'. For Kabbalah, however, the actual word order is also assumed to possess great significance: 'With the beginning—created Elohim.' From that ordering the conclusion is drawn that already there in that first verse is present an allusion to the creation of emanations out of the unfathomable being of Yahweh as En Sof ('that which is without limit'). Elohim is the object of 'creation' for a higher level of divinity.[34] There is no need

---

[31] Some have detected his influence on Spinoza.

[32] Such a central role for what is in effect 'cosmic man' is not found in earlier versions of the Kabbalah. Such a paralleling of macrocosm and microcosm illustrates how intimate, despite *Tzimtzum*, the connection between God and humanity is in Luria's conceptual scheme.

[33] 'The Creation of Elohim' in *Zohar* (London: SPCK, 1983), 49–50.

[34] Although both terms are used for God in the Hebrew Bible and modern translations sometimes do not differentiate between the two, there are some passages that claim Yahweh as God's more intimate name, e.g. Exod. 3. 13–15; 6. 2–3.

to pursue here how that basic assumption develops into ten such emanations.[35] The *Zohar*, unlike the earlier *Bahir*, in any case prefers to speak of the Lights, Garments or Crowns of the King.[36] More important to note is the way in which their emergence is seen as in some sense required and natural. Love balanced by Judgement, for instance, is taken to entail Mercy, with endorsement located in a relevant biblical story.[37] The details of such balancing of the divine attributes are less important than the way in which they are seen to draw the divine progressively closer to the creation. Lowest emanation of all is the Shekhinah, or Divine Presence. The celebration of its marriage to Israel may well have been the origin of the sabbath ritual that has Israel mystically marrying the Sabbath, and is now an important part in much contemporary Jewish ritual whether otherwise influenced by Kabbalah or not.[38]

To this unfolding divine, language is not incidental. It is seen as an essential part of the same process. 'The secret world of the godhead is a world of language, a world of divine names that unfold in accordance with a law of their own. . . . The process of Creation, which proceeds from stage to stage and is reflected in extra divine worlds and of course in nature as well, is not necessarily different from the process that finds its expression in divine words and in the documents of Revelation, in which the divine language is thought to have been reflected.'[39] The social and psychological pressures that led to such notions may well have been a general pessimism about the world at the time.[40] Real effort was seen as required to restore the connection with the divine. If the actual means advocated were at times extraordinarily abstruse or even magical, the positive side was the linking of all of human life, through meditation on the divine words, into the life of God himself. Jacob

---

[35] For a plan of their derivation, *Zohar*, 35.

[36] For *Bahir*, J. Dan ed., *The Early Kabbalah* (New York: Paulist Press, 1986), 57–69. For the work's seminal role, G. Scholem, *Origins of the Kabbalah* (Princeton: Princeton University Press, 1987), esp. 49–198.

[37] In this case the story of the sacrifice of Isaac. Water and fire are seen as reconciled in the harmony of Jacob: *Zohar*, 72–4.

[38] G. Scholem, *On the Kabbalah and its Symbolism* (London: Routledge & Kegan Paul, 1965), 139. For the way in which this is celebrated in contemporary Jewish ritual, see my *God and Grace of Body* (Oxford: Oxford University Press, 2007), 83–4.

[39] Scholem, *Kabbalah and its Symbolism*, 36.

[40] Dan, *Early Kabbalah*, 22–3.

Boehme applying his cobbler's stitches as he meditated in this way is an obvious Christian application of the same idea.[41]

Indeed, in assessing such ideas it is important not to ignore the extent of their influence on Christianity as well, particularly at the Renaissance. Members of the Florentine Academy, for instance, showed a marked interest. Both Pico della Mirandola (d. 1494) and Marsilio Ficino (d. 1499) merged elements of such ideas with their underlying interest in Platonism, helped also by an enthusiasm for the earlier Hermetic tradition that was presumed to be Platonic in its origins.[42] While today the great claim to fame of Johannes Reuchlin (d. 1522) rests on his success in establishing the study of the Hebrew language on a scientific footing,[43] in actual practice much more energy was devoted on his part to trying to make sense of kabbalistic theory. Again, although thanks to his support for Copernicus and his burning at the stake in 1600 the Dominican Giordano Bruno is now more commonly portrayed as a martyr for secular reason, in effect running far more deeply in his thought is the pantheistic influence of the Kabbalah. Certainly, as that burning indicates, some of its ideas were regarded with real suspicion. At the same time it is important not to discount the degree to which the approach in general gained a sympathetic hearing. So, for example, Agrippa's great work of 1531 on the subject, *De occulta philosophia*, was dedicated to Hermann of Wied, the reforming Archbishop of Cologne, who protected him. In England the doctor Robert Fludd's *History of the Macrocosm and Microcosm* (1617–21) not only sought to continue the ideas of Paracelsus (d. 1541) on such matters but also paved the way for more popular Rosicrucian and Freemason versions in the eighteenth century and beyond.

What is defensible in such musings is not the often absurd proposals that went with such detailed engagement with words, but the meditation and reflection that they helped to initiate. So, for example, as Jews pondered over what they saw as the gradual outpouring of God revealed in that opening verse of Genesis, the

[41] *Kabbalah and its Symbolism*, 132. For Boehme's own treatment of the unfolding of God, R. Waterfield ed., *Jacob Boehme: Essential Readings* (Wellingborough: Crucible, 1989), 213–39.

[42] Discussed in this book's companion volume, *God and Enchantment of Place: Reclaiming Human Experience* (Oxford: Oxford University Press, 2004), 72–3.

[43] In his *De rudimentis Hebraicis* of 1506.

words themselves could help generate an experience of God doing just that. God is by definition present everywhere. But unless we are open and searching for that presence, the dividing wall is likely to remain intact. Because Kabbalah involved a search for divine presence and immanence within all the words of Scripture, it entailed a predisposition to experience of such immanence, and so its possibility. If the legend of the golem did suggest manipulation of divine power, this does not seem to have been how the Hasidic tradition in general experienced such focus on words.[44] As their ecstatic worship suggests, it was an engagement with mystery and marvel that was seen as too deep ever to be fully captured by human beings.

Nonetheless, in their enthusiasm to stress such mystery, implausible theories about the meaning of words and the nature of the divine did become common, and so Kabbalah does well illustrate how too much emphasis on mystery could all too easily degenerate into obfuscation. As such it ran in marked contrast to the quite different trend within the medieval Church where, to put it at this starkest, one might speak almost of a divine absence except where certain key definitive words were uttered. What makes this all the more strange is the fact that it was roughly about the same time as the kabbalistic tradition was coming to fruition within Judaism that this new preoccupation with the precise words used in the major sacraments began to affect Christianity.

Language as Formulaic: Sacraments

Since the sacraments also concern human experience, a similar focus to the kabbalistic tradition on an underlying mystery operating everywhere might have been expected. Instead, there is a new focus on a very few words, and the attempt to render them as unmysterious as possible. The explanation lies in the new technical apparatus available to western Christendom in scholastic philosophy and in canon law, coupled with an increasing growth in clerical

---

[44] The magical notion of creating a golem (a new human being) was based on the idea that the permutations of the letters in YHWH had resulted in our world, and so sufficient reflection on the various permutations could provide a way of creating a new such being: Scholem, *Kabbalah and its Symbolism*, 158–204, esp. 168.

power and the desire to maintain this at full strength.[45] Order and control are thus what appear to matter, not mystery and presence. This is certainly not to deny that the latter were sometimes stressed. Indeed, such terms might be what would first come to mind, to describe the medieval mass. My contention is that the detailed discussions that took place and eventually identified very specific words as the precise point at which the major sacramental acts were deemed to have occurred were entered into, not in order to heighten that sense of mystery but rather in order to circumvent it. No hazy boundaries were to stand in the way of clerical control. Performed in any other way than what the hierarchy decreed, and sacramental power was held to be lost.

This might be put more positively in terms of reassuring the faithful that the sacraments were in fact validly performed. An obvious response to such a defence would be to question how much pressure for such definition really came 'from below'. The period during which such decisions were reached was one in which both scholastic philosophy and canon law were held in the highest esteem by the upper echelons of the clergy. Indeed, the most powerful pontiff of the period, Innocent III (d. 1216), did perhaps more than any other pope to enhance the status of canon law, even if earlier suppositions about him having been trained in the discipline himself are now deemed less secure than was once thought.[46] The causes therefore lie in the key intellectual questions of the age rather than in any desire to make the salvation of the great mass of the ordinary people more secure. Why the net result was a deadening rather than an enhancement of sacramentality can best be seen by examining the debate's impact on each of three key sacramental acts.

Take first the eucharist. As a result of the twelfth- and thirteenth-century search for more precise answers the focus moved very much towards the words of institution. Partly in reaction came

---

[45] Seen most obviously perhaps in the Investiture controversy over the source of episcopal temporal and spiritual power. For a discussion of the key period (1099–1122), C. Morris, *The Papal Monarchy: The Western Church 1050 to 1250* (Oxford: Clarendon, 1989), 154–73.

[46] For arguments against him receiving such a training at Bologna: K. Pennington, 'Innocent III and Canon Law' in J. M. Powell ed., *Innocent III* (Washington: Catholic University of America Press, 1994 edn.), 105–10. For the key role of law, including decretals, during his pontificate: J. Sayers, *Innocent III: Leader of Europe 1198–1216* (London: Longman, 1994), 94–124.

the common English expression 'hocus-pocus', used to caricature any piece of pseudo-magic that claims to bring about real change in the world.[47] It is a corruption of the Latin words of institution, *hoc est enim corpus meum* ('for this is my body'). The explicit assertion that this is all that needs to be said stands in marked contrast to the stress among modern liturgists on the importance of the whole anaphora or consecration prayer, if not of the liturgy as whole. Indeed, some early liturgies appear to suggest that no importance was attached to the recitation of specific words as such.[48] Eastern Christendom also provides an interesting contrast, as Orthodoxy has always sat looser to such formulaic approaches. In so far as it has a doctrine, it talks about the indispensability of an epiclesis (an invocation of the Holy Spirit). However, there is no accompanying claim that this is all that is required, as though all else might be omitted and there still be a eucharistic presence.

The way I have put matters thus far may suggest that the blame really lies primarily with lawyers. It would be unfortunate if contemporary prejudices (admittedly sometimes justified!) were exploited in order to carry conviction. In fact, philosophers, as much as canon lawyers, were quick both to exploit and to perpetuate the situation. So, if it is to the time of the ascendancy of ecclesiastical lawyers and to the Fourth Lateran Council of 1215 that we owe the official endorsement of the doctrine of transubstantiation, it is in the philosophical terminology of the later Council of Florence of 1439 that the implications of this way of thinking are carried to full effect. In brief, the Council declares: 'The matter of the eucharist is wheatbread and grape-wine... The form of this sacrament is the words of the Saviour with which he effected this sacrament, for the priest effects this sacrament by speaking in the person of Christ. It is by the power of these very words that the substance of bread is transformed into the body of Christ and the substance of the wine into his blood... The effect which this sacrament produces in the soul of a person who receives it worthily is to unite that person with

---

[47] Here I follow the common explanation, which easily matches how the Latin is pronounced. However, alternative accounts are sometimes given, such as origin in a pseudo-Latin magical formula invented by Latin students, 'hax pax max Deus adimax': *The Shorter Oxford English Dictionary* (London: Oxford University Press, 1983), s.v.

[48] Perhaps the most natural way of reading free, charismatic suggestions of the anonymous, perhaps late first-century work, *Didache*, chapters 9–10.

Christ.'⁴⁹ The matter/form/effect terminology is beautifully precise, and makes good sense in relation to the necessary adjustments required to apply Aristotelian terminology to such new contexts. Even so, something is surely lacking: namely, the sense that something as stupendous as the presence of the God–man cannot possibly be narrowly controlled and defined in this way.

A critic unsympathetic to such a critique might well insist that, whatever the effect of such definitions, they cannot possibly be blamed for lessening the profound sense of mystery which still permeated the medieval mass as a whole. In recent years perhaps Miri Rubin has done more than anyone else in conveying that experiential sense of mystery.⁵⁰ Yet it was a mystery that was still far distant from the true point of communion. As her book well illustrates, it was a mysterious presence over against the worshippers rather than Christ indwelling in them, so as to forge a real unity with the Saviour as the true head of the human race. Certainly Christ was exposed on the altar, but that is where he usually remained.⁵¹ Obviously immanent (in the sense of a presence in our world), the eucharistic host remained nonetheless essentially transcendent, a God momentarily in our midst rather than engaging actively with the communicant in a real personal encounter.

In the case of penance the issue turns out somewhat differently. In the twelfth century theologians had divided over whether contrition (including the intention to confess) was the key element that effected divine forgiveness or priestly absolution as such, and thus the phrase: *Ego te absolvo* ('I absolve you'). Both Peter Abelard and Peter Lombard took the former view. On this understanding the function of the priest's words becomes primarily declarative, indicative of a transformation that had already occurred. Hugh of St Victor, however, argued that divine forgiveness was dependent on the priest's words of absolution. In this he was followed by Aquinas in the succeeding century. Thomas identified the matter of the sacrament with the threefold action of contrition, confession, and satisfaction (the last referring to the token act of regret performed

⁴⁹ From Decretum pro Armeniis (my trans.): Denzinger-Schönmetzer ed., *Enchiridion Symbolorum* (Freiburg: Herder, 1973), 334–5.

⁵⁰ M. Rubin, *Corpus Christi: The Eucharist in Late Medieval Culture* (Cambridge: Cambridge University Press, 1991).

⁵¹ Because of the infrequency of communion. In order to hint at a common feeding, the celebrating priest was envisaged as receiving on behalf of all.

by the penitent after absolution). The form he postulated was the
priest's actual words of absolution, with the sacrament ineffective
without them. Thus, once again as with the eucharist, a narrow set
of words came to be seen as the key element. Although in the later
Middle Ages this position was sometimes challenged or resisted, it
was to become the official view of the Roman Catholic Church at
the Council of Trent.[52]

Sadly, the corruptions that resulted are all too well known. The
desire for priestly absolution often tended to overwhelm any sense
that contrition was also required. The result was that the sacramental act came to be sought for the wrong reasons. As such it was
seen more as a formal way of righting oneself with God rather than
a creative and transforming encounter. Some of the misunderstandings that resulted are recounted by Catholics themselves, among
them a hilarious story from the Irish writer Frank O'Connor about
a seven-year-old boy attempting to make his first confession.[53]

Distortions in popular misunderstandings of sacramental confession and of the eucharist prior to the Second Vatican Council run
closely in parallel. While the penitent in the box focused too
narrowly on the absolving words of the priest, equally the devout
pre-Vatican II Catholic often located his or her primary duty in
simply 'hearing mass'. Sometimes by this was meant not non-com-
municating attendance at one particular service as a whole but rather
hearing as frequently as possible those key words, and those alone.
An extreme example is the well-known story of Matt Talbot. Born
in Dublin in 1856, by the age of twelve he had become an alcoholic
and was sleeping rough. He cured himself by meditating before
tabernacles and racing through the streets to attend as many
elevations of the host as possible, with their accompanying words.[54]

As a final example of such problems, consider ordination. Again,
it was the Aristotelian language of form and matter that led to the
desire for careful distinction between the various orders of ordination. If the 'form' of priesthood came to be associated with the

[52] The debate that led up to Trent is helpfully explored in John Clark, 'Confession
and Re-formation: Walter Hilton's Sacramental Theology' in D. Brown and
A. Loades eds., *The Sacramental Word* (London: SPCK, 1996), 142–53.

[53] 'First Confession' can be found in F. O'Connor, *My Oedipus Complex and
Other Stories* (Oxford: Heinemann, 1998). It is also available in full on the web.

[54] The Venerable Matt Talbot died in 1931.

words, *Accipite Spiritum Sanctum* ('Receive the Holy Spirit'), the desire to identify a specific act for each order of ministry (known as the *porrectio instrumentorum*) generated in its turn some troublesome issues for subsequent discussion. Eventually, the future deacon's 'matter' came to be seen as the delivery of a Gospel book, while paten and chalice were assigned as the specific 'matter' of the new priest. In the nineteenth century the latter criterion was used as one of the grounds for challenging the validity of Anglican orders (they lacked the necessary 'matter'). Pope Pius XII, however, in his *Sacramentum Ordinis* of 1948, came to the realization that such over-subtle qualifications could actually generate as many problems in their turn for his own communion.[55] So the requirement for this particular kind of *porrectio instrumentorum* was abolished, with the laying on of hands now deemed sufficient.

The acceptance of less precision in actions can in retrospect be seen as prophetic of a parallel move in respect of words. Much contemporary Roman Catholic theology, like much Protestant thinking, now stresses the language of the eucharistic prayer as a whole, and indeed sometimes the liturgy in its entirety as this reflects the presence of Christ in his Church.[56] Unfortunately, such trends have not always been accompanied by parallel recognition of the potential richness of language, and so by any willingness to allow the openness of metaphor full play. Instead, there has sometimes been an all too pedestrian desire for new forms of control, in meaning unambiguously set out for worshippers' consumption. That is why I am convinced that the Church has still much to learn from Kabbalah. Of course, its theories lack any secure foundation. But its advocates did at least fully appreciate the importance of retaining mystery to words, an inexhaustible potential for disclosing the divine. Here poets have often been more perceptive than theologians or liturgists. How the Logos might continue to be seen permeating logoi rather than being quite separate and distinct is the issue to which I now turn.

[55] It became apparent that, if this were to be the criterion, there was no absolute continuity of practice in Rome also.

[56] A consequence of the move from a focus on things to personal encounter, seen, for instance, in the theology of Edward Schillebeeckx, *The Eucharist* (London: Sheed & Ward, 1977 edn.), e.g. 136–7. For other examples, D. N. Power, *The Eucharistic Mystery: Revitalising the Tradition* (Dublin: Gill & Macmillan, 1992), 269–90, 343–6.

2

Metaphor and Disclosure

On first reflection it might seem that the general tenor of modern discussion of language pulls against any residual sense of mystery and presence in language.[1] Modern linguistic theory appears to treat language as essentially arbitrary. Saussure, for example, demonstrated the difficulty of claiming that language precisely fits any reality, by highlighting the impossibility of precisely mapping one language against another. None divides up the external world in precisely the same way as any other.[2] More radically, a typical postmodernist philosopher like Derrida has even called into question whether we can get beyond language at all or at any rate, to give a more moderate expression of his thesis, ever do so definitively since any attempt at definition will be found to deconstruct itself in the process of explanation.[3]

Rather than doubting whether language puts us in touch with an external reality (which few of us doubt), a more modest implication to draw from such contentions might be that no detailed precision in such mapping is any more possible. If that is the correct conclusion to be drawn, then, so far from this undermining a sacramental approach, it might actually strengthen its viability, and for the following reason. Sacraments as enacted symbols are often accused of too much imprecision; metaphors, likewise, in the way they point allusively beyond

[1] This chapter builds upon some ideas I originally developed along with Ann Loades in our Introduction to Brown and Loades ed., *Christ: The Sacramental Word* (London: SPCK, 1996), 1–25.

[2] Well illustrated by the problems of translating even as elementary a sentence as 'The cat sat on the mat' from English into French. Decisions about the gender of the cat, the tense of the verb, and type of mat have all to be made before such translation is possible. For further reflections on the example, J. Lyons, 'Structuralism and Linguistics' in D. Robey ed., *Structuralism: An Introduction* (Oxford: Oxford University Press, 1973), 9–10.

[3] For a brief exposition and critique, see my *Continental Philosophy and Modern Theology* (Oxford: Blackwell, 1987), 33–6.

themselves. But, if this feature of metaphor is characteristic of language as a whole, then, so far from being problematic, the common methodology in metaphor and sacrament would merely constitute any substantial or serious attempt to map reality.

Yet it may be said that there remains one overwhelming and obvious objection to treating any such use of language as inherently sacramental, and that is that the entire activity remains an entirely human process, the movement being exclusively from us to that external reality, and not from Logos to logoi. The point is certainly a strong one. Yet some poets are adamant that their metaphors come from elsewhere. So it would seem worth exploring how far it might be legitimate to speak of some metaphors at least as God-given. Biblical metaphors might be so construed. That may seem the clearest category to take. But it is also worth pondering whether the capacity of metaphor to relate apparently disparate realities within the world might not after all reflect some underlying unities behind the divine order in creation.

Some attention has already been given in the previous chapter to the use of Logos at the beginning of John's Gospel. What was not noted there is the recurring temptation among commentators on the passage, despite its focus on word, to substitute alternative 'equivalents' such as 'expression'. 'Word' as a translation on its own, it is felt, undermines the personal character of he who is the Word: Christ himself. Instead of the mere words of the Hebrew scriptures, God has now pre-eminently expressed himself directly through an embodied, personal presence. That way of putting matters of course makes immediate connection with notions of sacramentality, providing, as it does, a powerful link between creation and incarnation. What God has already expressed or given of himself in the pattern of the created order reaches its culmination in the life of Christ, who fully expresses that design for humanity in the divine image of which he is the perfect reflection.

But there is also a cost in such a demoting of John's favoured image. In effect the metaphor has changed. The 'expression' is now that of a divine artist rather than of a craftsman in words. It is really the life that matters rather than any particular words. Yet the Greek term from which is derived our own English word 'poet' originally meant simply 'maker' or 'creator'. That reminds us that the making of phrases and sentences is just as much an artistic, an expressive act. Words can of course be used purely instrumentally; they can even be used as a form of play merely to refer internally to one another, as deconstructionism argues we should understand all language.[4] But their power is surely at their greatest when they act neither purely referentially nor as some form of internal play. Instead, the metaphors and images inherent in them are integral in helping us grasp the totality of whatever reality it is with which we wish to engage. In considering how exactly this happens, my discussion will proceed by three stages. First, I want to explore the rich, often hidden potential of metaphor to establish hitherto unperceived connections, then more specifically at how divine presence is mediated through them, before concluding with some thoughts on the deleterious consequences of modern reductionism.

Interconnectivity and Inexhaustibility

One twentieth-century poet who displayed a fine sensibility to the power of language is Kathleen Raine. For her language is certainly not just an aid to understanding, it also contains the potential to broaden and deepen our experience. As she puts it, 'our treasury of words' speaks 'Of heart's truth, mind's inheritance,/ From one to another told and retold.'[5] Nor is this true merely of connections within the material world; these can also highlight the source from which they ultimately derive. So in her poem 'Word made Flesh' it is the image of word which is retained as she speaks of all creation participating in, and reflecting, that original Word:

> . . .
> Word that articulates the bird that speeds upon the air
> . . .
> Grammar of five-fold rose and six-fold lily
> . . .
> Hieroglyph in whose exact precision is defined
> Feather and insect wing, refraction of multiple eyes.[6]

---

[4] For an example of such a stress on play applied to theological language, M. C. Taylor, *Erring: A Postmodern A/theology* (Chicago: University of Chicago Press, 1984).

[5] From 'Words: For Wendell Berry' in K. Raine, *Living with Mystery: Poems 1987–91* (Ipswich: Golgonooza Press, 1992), 39.

[6] From 'Word made Flesh' in K. Raine, *The Pythoness* (1948); reprinted in *Selected Poems* (Ipswich: Golgonooza Press, 1988), 24.

Language thus need not always be seen as a purely human instrument that can never stretch beyond our world except in the sense of
providing pointers to the possibility of such experience in other
contexts. Sometimes, it can in and of itself function as such
a medium, most obviously in appropriate metaphors helping to
bridge that gap. This is precisely what Raine is attempting to
achieve in her poem: the metaphors help generate the image of
an interconnected world and thus of a God from whom that
intelligibility ultimately derives. But, take note, the poem is not
intended simply to offer an intellectual vision; it also helps us
towards that experience, in and through its metaphors.

It was an issue about which T. S. Eliot thought long and hard. In
one of his finest essays he sets out to defend the seventeenth-
century metaphysical poets against the charge that their imagery is
forced and artificial.[7] In part his defence is historical, that the Civil
War brought about 'a dissociation of sensibility' that separated
thought and feeling, and so it is only to modern ears that their
comparisons seem forced. Ours is a less religiously integrated world.
So 'poets in our civilisation, as it exists at present, must be difficult . . . The poet must become more and more comprehensive,
more allusive, more indirect, in order to force, to dislocate if
necessary, language into his meaning.' That presumably provides
some kind of justification for the difficulty of Eliot's own writing.
But he is also equally insistent that, where thought and sensibility
remained allied, the good poet would still in any case unify experience through associating the apparently unlike, since all reality has
ultimately the same source. 'When a poet's mind is perfectly
equipped for its work, it is constantly amalgamating disparate
experience. The ordinary man's experience is chaotic, irregular,
fragmentary. The latter falls in love, reads Spinoza, and these two
experiences have nothing to do with each other, or with the noise
of the typewriter or the smell of cooking; in the mind of the poet
these experiences are always forming new wholes.'

For Eliot Donne is his ideal model. Perhaps therefore an example
may be drawn from that poet. It is very easy to take Donne's image
of rape in his sonnet 'Batter my heart, three person'd God' as
adding just yet one more paradox to Christianity. But that would

---

[7] 'The Metaphysical Poets' in F. Kermode ed., *Selected Prose of T. S. Eliot*
(London: Faber & Faber, 1975), 59–67, esp. 65, 64.

be totally to misrepresent where the power of this particular image lies, at least for his fellow Christians. It is precisely because Christians are so frighteningly aware of their inability to achieve goodness and holiness on their own that the image of a violent rape generating true freedom is such an effective one:

> Except you'enthrall mee, never shall be free,
> Nor ever chast, except you ravish mee.[8]

God must first gain total control over the believer's life before real change is possible. Even then, it will be a reluctant change because alternatives only gradually lose their attractiveness. So one goes, kicking against the pricks.[9] Even so, the poem need not just function as an aid to understanding past experience. It could also initiate such experience in someone sympathetic to religious belief. The poem's metaphors would enable them to appreciate for the first time what degree of receptivity is necessary if God is effectively to act upon their lives and the requisite openness perhaps then be forthcoming.

Donne's erotic imagery suggests a somewhat different example from the Song of Songs. Chapter 4 contains the famous image of the beloved as 'a garden enclosed', duly developed within the Christian tradition to speak of Mary's virginity. That the emphasis fell primarily there rather than on the refreshing and seductive delights of the garden was a pity, not because the imagery cannot be used to enhance our understanding of virginity but because the metaphor could have been made so much richer had equal attention been given to the garden's other aspects. The fruitfulness of Mary's virginity could have been the main theme. Then, instead of its present limited potential, the image could have opened up the notion of virginity in new directions, for example in thinking how denial might increase rather than diminish the power to act.[10]

The tendency to narrow down the potential of imagery is what I am complaining of here, the supposition that once a particular

---

[8] 'Divine Poems XIV' in J. Donne, *Poetical Works* (London: Oxford University Press, 1937), 299.

[9] As in Luke's description of Paul's conversion, Acts 9.5; 26.14. The imagery is weakened in modern translations (e.g. RSV). 'Goads' tends to be used in the later verse, while in the former it is eliminated, as probably imported from the later context.

[10] For an exploration of virginity in such terms, see my chapter on 'Mary and Virgin Promise' in *Discipleship and Imagination* (Oxford: Oxford University Press, 2000), 226–87.

decoding has been found, more literal language can then replace the metaphor without significant loss. The deleterious consequences can be seen in how scholars have handled the description of the beloved earlier in that same chapter of the Song of Songs. Modern commentators are often dismissive of the imagery as exaggerated or exotic, and difficult to comprehend, if at all, outside of a Middle Eastern context. 'Behold, you are beautiful, my love . . . Your eyes are doves behind your veil. Your hair is like a flock of goats, moving down the slopes of Gilead. Your teeth are like a flock of shorn ewes that have come up from the washing . . . Your lips are like a scarlet thread . . . Your cheeks are like halves of a pomegranate behind your veil. Your neck is like the tower of David, built for an arsenal, whereon hung a thousand bucklers, all of them shields of warriors. Your two breasts are like two fawns, twins of a gazelle that feed among the lilies' (4.1–5). Contrary to the general consensus, to my mind, the imagery is quite marvellous, not least because it helps to illuminate both sides of the equation, the author's appreciation of the natural world no less than the girl's beauty. In other words, the passage can open up the perceptive reader to a new way of experiencing nature as much as female beauty.

If relatively easy to comprehend is the way in which the coyness of the girl is highlighted by the natural diffidence of doves, more problematic may seem the comparison of her hair to a flock of goats. However, it forces us to look at such a herd anew, with their massed ranks from a distance suggesting great flowing tresses of hair. The comparison of her teeth to new shorn ewes reminds us of how seldom white was seen as a colour in the ancient world. It was an age when dyeing was relatively infrequent, and of course teeth more difficult to maintain in condition when impurities in bread were all too common.[11] Again, the comparison of her neck to an armoured tower ceases to surprise when one thinks of the elaborate neckbands still worn in parts of Africa to this day. Finally, her breasts have nothing to do with the twin cheeks of a gazelle's bottom, as some German commentators suggest, but with the bodies of the two gazelles hanging low over the grass, as they feed.[12] Sadly, even

---

[11] With grit affecting the teeth.
[12] Cf. W. Rudolph, *Das Buch Ruth, Das Hohe Lied, Das Klagelieder* (Gütersloh: Gütersloher Verlaghaus, 1962), 147.

with all these points appreciated much of the power of the comparison is lost, if the imagination is reined in too soon. It is precisely through meditating on these scenes and discovering their beauty that the beauty of the girl is brought to life. What initially seems so unlike the girl is part of the same divine creativity that has produced these animal wonders.

Not much may appear to be at stake here, but it does seem to me illustrative of a more general problem: the tendency to tie down biblical and religious metaphors too soon, and so deprive them of much of their potential power. Identify the point, it is assumed, and no more need be said. But part of the point may well be that there is no single point, but a range of possibilities now allowed to be brought into play. Some examples from John's Gospel may help. Take the concluding verse of the first chapter, and Jesus' words to Nathaniel: 'Truly, truly, I say to you, you will see heaven opened, and the angels of God ascending and descending upon the Son of man' (1.51). It is all too easy for the reader to assume a reference back to Jacob's vision at Bethel, and leave matters at that. But John's Greek is deliberately ambiguous. The possibility that Christ is himself the ladder is clearly allowed, with all the richness of suggestion that that possibility allows. Instead of angels having to make the link, a human being can now guarantee us a passage between earth and heaven. It is therefore all the more regrettable that, so far from acknowledging John's creative use of language, explanation is sometimes sought in an ambiguity in the original Hebrew.[13]

Again, in chapter 3 Christ declares that 'as Moses lifted up the serpent in the wilderness, so must the Son of man be lifted up, that whoever believes in him may have eternal life' (3.14–15). Once more, it seems to me doubtful that all that is being claimed is that, just as the brazen figure of a serpent raised on wood once saved the Israelites from death, so Christ will do likewise and by a similar means (the cross).[14] More probable is the supposition that we are being invited to reflect on Christ as serpent, the one who can slough his skin and thus gain immortality but in a way that also

[13] Ladder and Jacob are both masculine nouns in the Hebrew of Gen. 28: the explanation in C. K. Barrett, *The Gospel According to St John* (London: SPCK, 2nd edn., 1978), 187.

[14] Barrett is quite blunt: 'For him (John) the point of the comparison is not the serpent but the lifting up' (214).

can bring health to others.[15] Certainly in Ephesus (often postulated as the place where the Gospel was written) but probably even in Palestine the general symbolism and practices of ancient Greek medicine are likely to have been well known, within which snakes were commonly appropriated for just such a role.[16]

As a final example for the moment, consider John 6 with Christ's declaration that 'unless you eat the flesh of the Son of man and drink his blood, you have no life in you' (v. 54). Depending on overall theological position, biblical commentators can sometimes be quick in decoding this verse in the light of what is said in the rest of the chapter as necessarily entailing a non-literal interpretation: it is a way of referring to Christ's significance, not to his body as such. But his significance is mediated through his humanity and embodiment is essential to being human; so the contrast is quite artificial. My comments are not intended to endorse a purely literal reading, but to suggest that the literal must be allowed long enough play for the complete range of possibilities in the metaphor to be explored. So I do not wish to deny that Bultmann and his followers capture an important element in the meaning, only that they err in refusing time for the full range of possibilities to come into play. To rush quickly to a denial of literal identity is just as foolish as to think that this is the sole meaning. In short, the metaphor is there to give us access to something more, not less.

Intriguingly, it is an insight much more readily conceded by poets than by theologians. Even those of a firmly Protestant persuasion do not hesitate to use eucharistic imagery starkly and without qualification. So, for instance, George Herbert writes:

> Come ye hither all, whom wine
> Doth define,
> Naming you not to your good:
> Weep what ye have drunk amiss,
> And drink this,
> Which before ye drink is blood.[17]

---

[15] In the Book of Wisdom (16.6) the serpent had already been identified as a 'symbol of salvation', while later Barnabas, Justin Martyr, and Tertullian all explicitly talk of the serpent as a 'type' or pattern for Christ (e.g. Barnabas 12.5; Justin Martyr, *First Apology*, 60; Tertullian, *Adversus Marcionem* III. 18).

[16] For the general background in ancient medical practice, see my *God and Grace of Body* (Oxford: Oxford University Press, 2007), 394–405.

[17] 'The Invitation' in J. Tobin ed., *George Herbert: The Complete Poems* (London: Penguin, 1991), 169–70.

Or again, note the winepress imagery that concludes 'The Bunch of Grapes'. If the previous line in this case alerts us to the presence of a metaphor, it is not enough to allay the violence and shock of what follows:

> Who of the law's sour juice sweet wine did make,
> Even God himself, being pressèd for my sake.[18]

Let us try another way of clarifying the issue. By the sacramental is commonly understood the physical or material mediating that which is beyond itself, the spiritual; in the familiar definition, 'the outward and visible sign of an inward and spiritual grace'.[19] From that basic assumption it is easy to jump to the conclusion that only the physical or material can function sacramentally, and so in the case of the incarnation it must be Christ's 'flesh' that accomplishes such mediation, pointing to the divinity that lies behind the fleshly appearance. But the author of the Fourth Gospel by identifying word and flesh demonstrates that word can equally be conceived in sacramental terms. Words are more than sounds; they are signs or symbols pointing beyond themselves, mediating the reality into which they draw us. By calling Christ the Word John effectively declares the language or poetry of the incarnation equally sacramental. Just as the world speaks of the expressed order and pattern of intelligibility from which it draws its origin ('In the beginning was the Word', John 1.1 AV), so now 'the Word made flesh' is 'full of grace and truth' (John 1.14). But words do so, like visual or enacted symbols, in encouraging a looking beyond themselves, an appreciation of their suggestiveness, not their completeness.

Fascinating light is thrown on the sacramental character of words by the American poet, Emily Dickinson, in her poem 'A Word made Flesh'. There she characterizes all words as seeking to enable us to participate in something beyond themselves. However, a word 'has not the power to die' unless it succeeds in this perfectly; then:

> It may expire if He—
> 'Made Flesh and dwelt among us'—
> Could condescension be

[18] Tobin, *Herbert*, 120.
[19] As in the definition of a sacrament in the Catechism of the *Book of Common Prayer* (1662).

> Like this consent of language,
> This loved Philology.[20]

But can even the incarnate Word succeed perfectly? Will not even divine language stumble and stutter? Clearly at one level most Christians would wish to deny this. Christ as God's Word must be the only adequate measure of truth:

> Therefore these filthy rags of speech, this coil
> Of statement, comment, query and response,
> Tatters all too contaminate for use
> Have no renewing: He, the Truth, is, too,
> The Word.[21]

Such are the sentiments of one of Robert Browning's dramatic characters, and in this case probably also the poet's own. But, another poet, W. H. Auden, is perhaps nearer the truth, when he insists that, although the Word brings reconciliation of opposites and restraint to Imagination's 'promiscuous fornication with her own images', it is a practical definition and intelligibility, not complete understanding: 'But here and now the Word which is implicit in the Beginning and in the End is become immediately explicit, and that which hitherto we could only passively fear as the incomprehensible I AM, henceforth we may actively love with comprehension that HE IS.'[22] God is 'the perfect poet', not in making all known to us in the Word made flesh, but all that we need know and love.[23]

Word and flesh are not then opposites: both alike are capable of functioning sacramentally; both alike participate in but do not exhaust that to which they refer. So in considering what John

---

[20] For full text, T. H. Johnson ed., *The Complete Poems of Emily Dickinson* (London: Faber & Faber, 1975), 675–6. I have altered her original punctuation to make the text more easily intelligible. For another fine poem reflecting on the power of words: 534–5.
[21] R. Browning, *The Ring and the Book*, x. 373–7; ed. R. D. Altick (Harmondsworth: Penguin, 1971), 487.
[22] From W. H. Auden, 'Meditation of Simeon' in *For The Time Being* (London: Faber & Faber, 1953), 105–11, esp. 109, 108.
[23] The phrase is Browning's in *Paracelsus*, II. 648; in I. Jack and M. Smith eds., *The Poetical Works of Robert Browning* (Oxford: Clarendon, 1983), i. 265. For an excellent study of Browning's reflections on the incarnate Word, W. Whitla, *The Central Truth: The Incarnation in Robert Browning's Poetry* (Toronto: University of Toronto Press, 1963).

meant by his claim, it is worth pondering whether as well as identifying the person of Christ with the Word he did not also intend the words he assigns to Christ also to participate in that relation, in disclosing the divine. If so, it might suggest that those who wish to challenge Bultmann's anti-sacramental reading of the Fourth Gospel focus on the wrong place, when most attention is given to Bultmann's claims that key sections of the sixth chapter are due to a later editor.[24] Nor can the argument be decided simply by the question of whether explicit reference is made to the two dominical sacraments. Rather, what matters is how John uses language. He practises a deep engagement with words in order to make Christ present to the reader, particularly with the sort of language that can pull us beyond surface meaning. A good example of this is the subtle interplay of water, wine, and blood in the story of the first miracle at Cana, or again the way in which the language of ascension can appear in the most surprising of contexts.[25] John's talk of the Word 'tabernacling among us' (John 1. 14) is thus no isolated exception. As the Temple or Tent of Meeting once brought the divine presence into the people's midst, so now Jesus and the words of this Gospel can do so.

Sometimes such an effect can be achieved by a single powerful metaphor; sometimes it takes several to complement each other. Sometimes too apparent conflicts may be introduced. The temptation is then to seek an easy resolution, whereas the capacity for something to be disclosed may come precisely from maintaining that tension in its full power. Again John's Gospel may be used to provide some examples. The Lord who has declared himself the source of living water is later found on a cross, uttering the cry: 'I thirst.'[26] The same Gospel that has made the taking of flesh so central can nonetheless declare: 'The flesh profiteth nothing' (John 6.63 AV). The temptation (which needs to be resisted) is to suppose that such conflicts can be resolved by reduction ('flesh' not to be

---

[24] In his *Gospel of John* (Oxford: Blackwell, 1971) Bultmann declares of John that 'the truth is that the sacraments are superfluous for him' (472). Although I think the debate improved when given a different focus, for strong arguments in favour of John 6.51–8 being original see C. K. Barrett, *Essays on John* (London: SPCK, 1982), 37–49.

[25] The Ascension is discussed in the Introduction; Cana in *God and Grace of Body*, 163–4, 166–7.

[26] Contrast John 4.14 and 19.28.

valued in its own right, 'living water' only a metaphor). But Christ's ability to satisfy our spiritual thirst is actually first dependent on his entering into that physical thirst, in his becoming one of us and all that that might entail. So the two references actually complement and reinforce one another. Likewise, it is no accident that the value of flesh is strongly asserted and strongly denied within the same chapter. It is only by allowing both assertions to interact constantly with one another that crude literalism about the sacrament on the one hand and mere memorialism on the other will be avoided.

God 'making' himself flesh (the 'poetry' of the incarnate Word) inevitably meant a plurality of images and metaphors, as language struggled to capture the mystery of what had happened. The words, like the flesh itself, function sacramentally in both pointing to a divine reality beyond themselves, while at the same time mediating, however inadequately, something of that reality. But that will only be fully appreciated if the interconnectivity of metaphor and its irreducibility are allowed full play. It is by returning to a poem or biblical text again and again that something closer to full enlightenment may dawn, not by repeated harping on about a single point that has allegedly been made. But, as I have already stressed several times, it is not just a matter of intellectual understanding, it is also sometimes a case of God thereby being brought close. Metaphor can itself provide us with an experience of divine presence.

Metaphor and Divine Presence

Christians have at times been as suspicious of metaphor as they have been of the visual image. It is felt that at most it offers a second-best, something at one remove from reality itself. That suspicion is also often accompanied by the conviction that those who speak in metaphors are inevitably seeking to take a step back from realist commitments. While certainly this is sometimes the case, there is no necessary implication that this is so. Indeed, one of the contributors to *The Myth of God Incarnate* marked her conversion to the other side of the debate by indicating that it was precisely reflection on the import of metaphor that had brought her to this change of mind.[27]

[27] Frances Young, 'From Analysis to Overlay: A Sacramental Approach to Christology' in Brown and Loades, *Christ: The Sacramental Word*, 40–56.

Paul's commitment to a doctrine of incarnation, she argues, can only be fully appreciated in the context of recognition that his language is really one of 'sacramental interpenetration', that is, an imaginative interplay of texts and images. By being used simultaneously to speak of God and Jesus, the metaphors Paul uses effectively identify them as occupying the single space that is Christ, both God and human being. The imaginative or metaphorical identification thus carries with it ontological implications no less stringent than the literal.[28] Metaphors can thus yield genuinely new knowledge that is by no means reducible to some weaker version of what might have been said, had a more literal or analytic approach been adopted. More pertinent here, metaphor can also open up the type of experience that revealed Christ to be acting in God's place and so divine.

With that said, the reader can perhaps now appreciate why I claimed in Chapter 1 that there was some truth after all in the mystical approach to words that dominated the Jewish Kabbalah tradition. What modern literalism has lost is the sense that words in themselves might communicate an experience rather than necessarily only be effective, if directed entirely beyond and outside themselves. That is, it is not always necessary to step outside of words, as it were, in order for their full impact to be felt. Rather, by drawing in already existing elements of our understanding, the words can reconstitute our experience to give fresh insight into other aspects of reality. Failure to appreciate this fact is one of the contributing factors, I believe, to the rather wooden approach to the sacraments that so characterized the medieval period. All the focus had moved to set formulae and away from the impact of liturgical language as a whole.

This is not to deny the importance of establishing minimum conditions for a sacrament, determining what must be done in order for there to be a reasonable expectation of Christ's presence and action. In the case of the eucharist, it would be odd, to say the very least, if no reference were made to the words uttered by Christ at the Last Supper. So, even if these were absent from some of our earliest liturgies, the Church was nonetheless right to insist on their use.[29] But

[28] For a detailed argument to this effect, J. M. Soskice, *Metaphor and Religious Language* (Oxford: Clarendon Press, 1985).

[29] Absence is the most natural interpretation of the second-century *Didache* where chs. 9–10 seem to offer a eucharistic prayer but with no words of institution.

to go on from that admission and suppose everything else incidental to Christ's sacramental presence would be equally to err in the opposite direction. Two quite different questions need to be addressed: when, objectively, Christ may be said to be present; and when, subjectively, that presence is most likely to become a personal reality for the communicant. In the former case it is necessary to ask which formulae best reflect the intentions of the Church and under what circumstances they may appropriately be said to be realized. Here the notion of the sacraments functioning *ex opere operato* has its legitimate place. The activity of God cannot be made to depend either on the holiness or otherwise of the priest or on the recipient's degree of attentiveness but only on 'the rite properly executed'. This is not to say that God is bound by such rules. The divine can circumvent human arrogance and folly, and still bring salvation. But it is to call such guidance helpful and appropriate.

Quite different and of more relevance here, is the subjective question. So long as body and blood are thought of as things, it is very easy to suppose that the words of institution might be enough. However, as soon as Christ's presence is conceived in more personalist terms, as with all personal relations it then becomes a cluster of images that mediate the 'other' rather than any one particular item or word. So, for instance, if an individual walks into an empty room, it is seldom one thing that tells him or her that it belongs to a close relation or friend, but numerous small indicators—the way the cushions are strewn, the newspapers in the magazine rack, the half-drunk cup of tea with the biscuit on the saucer, and so forth. The images reinforce one another in generating a sense of the 'other's' presence.[30] Nor does this change should the 'other' appear. The 'other' is seen as other in gesture, intonation, and twinkle of the eye, all of which activate memories of the 'other' as having precisely these characteristics.[31]

Similarly with the eucharist. Words, even the words of institution, can do little of themselves to evoke a sense of presence. What matters is how they resonate, their ability to build image upon image in a way that brings to life that sense of presence. In some

---

[30] Even negative judgements can sometimes take this form, as in Jean-Paul Sartre's comments about the unexpected absence of his friend Pierre from a café: *Being and Nothingness* (London: Methuen, 1958), 9–11.

[31] Another philosopher relevant here is Emmanuel Levinas in his comments on 'The Face': *Totality and Infinity* (The Hague: Nijhoff, 1979), §§ III–IV.

respects this is a lesson modern liturgy has learnt. For instance, instead of a narrow focus on Christ's death, the anaphora or consecration prayer now seeks to encapsulate the entire history of human salvation. The Christ of the infancy narratives, of the ministry and of the resurrection is thus brought to remembrance no less than the Jesus of the passion. Yet at the same time there remains a fear of the allusive, as though what may not be immediately understood must therefore be misunderstood. Consider, for instance, the retreat of both the Church of England and the Roman Catholic Church from the image of Christ not only tabernacling within us but coming to a home in need, as in the traditional words before receiving communion: 'Lord, I am not worthy that thou shouldst come under my roof, but speak the word only and my soul shall be healed.'[32] Now replaced by the prosaic: 'Lord, I am not worthy to receive you', the image of receiving food is merely repeated. Thereby is lost all the wonderful resonances of the analogy, however remote, of Christ now deigning to tabernacle in our flesh as once he did at the incarnation, specifically in the home of the pagan centurion who had asked for his help. Similarly, the lively image especially created by the English scholar, David Frost, of us like shipwrecked sailors 'grasping' at a hope was in the *Alternative Service Book* reduced to the flat 'a hope set before us'.[33]

Just as the application of the term 'Word' to the incarnate Christ did not leave things as they were but changed how the term was understood, so sacramental words cannot be said to achieve their purpose simply as mediating words, quite distinct from what they are intending to convey. It matters deeply that they should resonate and interact with as wide a range of ways of perceiving Christ as possible, at the same time in a manner which grounds each allusion as part of the identity of what it is to be the incarnate Lord who is also Lord of the Church. The fact that such a qualification necessitates a degree of conservatism in the choice of imagery should not mislead into supposing that the imagery does not therefore matter, or that it cannot be used in new or even startling ways.

---

[32] Matt. 8.8.

[33] In the so-called 'Prodigal Son Prayer' that may conclude the eucharist and which has survived into *Common Worship* (2000). General Synod voted to 'correct' the prayer, apparently anxious both about whether one could 'grasp at' a hope, and also perturbed by talk of human beings taking initiatives before God.

Both in the history of the Bible and in subsequent church history unexpected and innovative use of traditional language is to be observed, as is the enriching interplay of allusions across textual references in Scripture itself.[34] Yet in marked contrast to sixteenth- and seventeenth-century translators of the Bible, our modern pre-occupation equates accuracy with the elimination of ambiguity, with narrowing (no doubt, sometimes rightly) the possible range of meanings.[35] It suggests a less meditative, less engaged way of reading the text. Because of their hostility to visual imagery, Juda-ism and Islam are usually deemed to be anti-sacramental religions. Although this is largely true, their treatment of their sacred texts suggests another perspective. For Hasidic Judaism in particular, as we saw earlier, each word, and indeed sometimes each letter, is taken to have the power to convey the sense of the presence of God.[36] The ritual chanting that takes place in the mosque can also be similarly interpreted. The music of the words cannot be further qualified by translation without remainder into native languages because those Arabic words are the inexhaustible vehicle through which God speaks to the believer. That sense of Scripture as sacrament, as the vehicle of God's presence, occasionally finds twentieth-century parallels within Christianity, as in the extraor-dinary effect upon Simone Weil of frequent recital of the Lord's Prayer in Greek as she went about her work in the fields.[37] But, on the whole, current western practice assumes one meaning in the text, and our quest complete, once this meaning is found.

Western theology has paid a high price in its constant temptation towards such reductionism. If the imagery of baptism can be reduced to remission of sins, the whole rite becomes problematic in a world which has ceased to believe that babies are deeply infected by original sin. If penance is no more than the receiving of absolution, the penitent's recurring sins will remain as problematic

[34] For illustrations, G. B. Caird, *The Language and Imagery of the Bible* (London: Duckworth, 1980); S. Prickett, *Words and Word* (Cambridge: Cambridge University Press, 1986).

[35] Cf. Prickett, *Words and Word*, ch. 1.

[36] For a modern Jewish poem that continues that tradition, meditating on each word of the first verse of Genesis: Anne Winters, 'The First Verse'; in D. Curzon ed., *Modern Poems on the Bible* (Philadelphia: Jewish Publication Society, 1994), 33–6.

[37] S. Weil, *Waiting on God* (London: Routledge & Kegan Paul, 1951), 23–4.

as ever. If the eucharist is only about Christ's death or the mere fact of his presence, then it too becomes difficult where belief in substitutionary atonement no longer seems plausible, or such presence fails to suggest any sense of a transforming relationship. These are issues to which I shall return in the concluding chapter where liturgy will be a more central concern.

But the problems are by no means narrowly liturgical. Doctrines are similarly undermined when focus is narrowed: if, for example, resurrection is defined by the empty tomb, or ascension as an event forty days later. For it is precisely as focused images bearing more than one meaning that such doctrines maintain their power: with resurrection summing up new life generally, or ascension humanity's permanent place in the divine scheme of things. In such contexts the defined words inevitably burst out beyond any attempt to contain them. It is precisely because of the open-ended character of the images that they are able not only to exercise their power, but also to move us towards thinking in a manner transcendent to the words, of God himself. All imagery forces beyond containment. Although in more ordinary contexts this usually only makes listeners or readers turn their attention laterally or sideways to think of another earthly parallel, the process has at least begun of thinking analogically, and analogy is of course of the essence of religion. The words induce us to move beyond their literal meaning towards thinking in a quite different way and so, potentially, of a quite different order of reality.

If all this is true, it is perhaps scarcely surprising that poets have often claimed a close relationship, even identity between poetry and religion. It is a theme taken up by a number of poets, among them the contemporary Australian poet Les Murray. For him:

> Full religion is the large poem in loving repetition;
> . . .
>
> and God is the poetry caught in any religion,
> caught, not imprisoned. Caught as in a mirror
> that he attracted, being in the world as poetry
> is in the poem, a law against closure.[38]

That resistance to closure, the refusal to accept that any word or deed has fully expressed all that need be said, the persistence of

---

[38] From 'Poetry and Religion' in Les Murray, *Collected Poems* (Manchester: Carcanet, 1991), 272–3.

transcendence as a point of contact between the two, is a theme
which he reiterates elsewhere:

> Art is what can't be summarised:
> it has joined creation from our side,
> entered Nature, become a fact
> and acquired presence,
> . . .
> Art's best is a standing miracle
> . . .
> an anomaly, finite but inexhaustible,
> . . .
> a passage, a whole pattern
> that has shifted the immeasurable
> first step into Heaven.[39]

The notion of both poetry and religion conveying an 'inexhaustible presence' is of course not a new one. Christianity has a long
tradition of viewing God as author of two books—Scripture and
nature; and in seeing both as artistic creations it endorsed what had
already become a pagan commonplace. Augustine even applies the
analogy to God's providential ordering of history; for him it is
'a beautiful poem' in which 'the beauty of the world's history is
constituted through the clash of contraries as a kind of eloquence in
events, instead of in words'.[40] Again, in the Middle Ages we find
Boccaccio so stressing the extent to which God uses poetic devices
in Scripture, that poetry and Bible can be virtually identified as the
same thing: 'theology and poesy may be considered to be almost
one and the same thing'.[41]

It is perhaps, however, Coleridge with whom this claim is most
strongly associated. In *Confessions of an Inquiring Spirit* he launches a
tirade against the deadening hand of biblical literalism, which he
sees as effectively destroying the power of biblical imagery: it 'plants
the vineyard of the Word with thorns for me'.[42] Earlier in his
Lectures on Literature he had sought to define what it is that makes

---

[39] From 'Satis Passio' in *Collected Poems*, 220–1.

[40] My trans.; *City of God* 11. 18.

[41] Boccaccio, 'Life of Dante' in P. H. Wicksteed ed., *The Early Lives of Dante*
(London: Chatto & Windus, 1907), 67, 72. 'Theology' is here used as equivalent to
'divine Scripture'.

[42] S. T. Coleridge, *Confessions of an Inquiring Spirit* (Philadelphia: Fortress,
1988), 28 (Letter 2).

'religion ... the poetry of all mankind'. Like poetry, religion 'bids us while we are sitting in the dark round our little fire still look at the mountain tops'.[43] Either by generalizing or by distancing us from our immediate concerns, Coleridge suggests, both pull us onto an altogether different plain, but for that to be possible a certain type of use of language—imagery—is indispensable.

Inevitably such imagery comes from the natural, created world, and so the question of the relation between divine and human poetry or 'making' is raised. For Plato art stood at two removes from reality; it imitated nature, itself an imitation of the ideal world of the Forms. But, intriguingly, also to Plato should be attributed the view that the inspiration of the poet should be compared to a form of madness. Although his suggestion has sometimes been used as a strategy for demoting the artist's status, Renaissance Neoplatonism was adamant that it should be treated as a compliment. Coupled with the authority of Plato, there was the possibility of an analogy with the mystic inspiration of the Old Testament prophet.[44] Milton, for instance, talks of poetic inspiration coming 'by devout prayer to that eternal Spirit who can enrich with all utterance and knowledge, and sends out his Seraphim with the hallow'd fire of his Altar to touch and purify the lips of whom he pleases'.[45] The allusion to Isaiah 6.6–7 is repeated in his poem 'On the Morning of Christ's Nativity' where he speaks of the Muse 'From out his secret Altar toucht with hallow'd fire'. In *Paradise Lost* (3. 1–55) he opts instead for a comparison with classical poets and seers, blind like himself—Homer and Teiresias.

Such analogies which bypass nature made poetry less derivative, and even allowed for the possibility that the poet's creation could surpass the natural order. This is the position advocated by another poet, Sir Philip Sidney: 'Nature never set forth the earth in so rich tapestry as divers poets have done ... Her world is brazen, the poets only deliver a golden.' Although such a claim could easily have

[43] R. A. Foakes ed., *Lectures 1808–19 on Literature* (London: Routledge & Kegan Paul, 1987), i. 325, 326 (Lecture 8).

[44] For the origins of the parallel between poet and prophet, J. L. Kugel ed., *Poetry and Prophecy: The Beginnings of a Literary Tradition* (Ithaca: Cornell University Press, 1990). The parallel was also adopted by Robert Lowth in his influential *Lectures on the Sacred Poetry of the Hebrews* of 1787.

[45] J. Milton, 'The Reason of Church Government' in *The Works of John Milton* (New York: Columbia University Press, 1931), iii. 1. 241.

been used to denigrate the divine, that is clearly no part of Sidney's intention:

> Neither let it be deemed too saucy a comparison to balance the highest point of man's wit with the efficacy of Nature; but rather give right honour to the heavenly Maker of that maker, who, having made man to his own likeness, set him beyond and over all his works of that second nature: which in nothing he showeth so much as in poetry, when with the force of a divine breath he bringeth things forth surpassing her doings.[46]

The argument is less likely to appeal today in a world in which we have become more sensitive to the dangers of human arrogance in relation to the rest of creation. Perhaps a better way of justifying Sidney's point is to draw a parallel with landscape art. By the way in which such artists present nature they can enable us to see the order, mystery, or transcendence that is not immediately perceptible to our own eyes. Poets might perform a not dissimilar function.

Nor is it a contention of which we should fight shy today. Nature has its focused symbols which find their appropriate place in the Christian religion, such as water, bread, and wine, but that focus surely gains added intensity and power by the use to which these symbols have been put, not only in the Bible as a literary creation but also in the Christian tradition of liturgy and poetry. In John Keble we find the sacramental character of this relation made quite explicit: 'Poetry lends religion her wealth of symbols and similes; religion restores them again to poetry, clothed with so splendid a radiance that they appear to be no longer symbols, but to partake (I might almost say) of the nature of sacraments.'[47]

Such an exaltation of the role of the artist (even if literary) may seem to have taken us far from Platonism. But the position of Platonism is much more complex on this matter than is usually acknowledged. It is all too easy to take the dying Socrates' longing for release from the body as normative, and certainly in the Neoplatonism of Plotinus a strongly ascetical side was developed. But against that must be set the positive estimate of the world given by Plato in dialogues such as *Timaeus* or the *Symposium*. Again, Plotinus not only conceives of the world as emanating from God

---

[46] P. Sidney, *An Apology for Poetry* (Manchester: Manchester University Press, 1965), 101.

[47] J. Keble, *Lectures on Poetry* (Oxford: Clarendon, 1912), ii. 480.

but also has a long tract against the Gnostics, defending the inherent goodness of the world.[48] Plato's theory of Forms can in fact be read in two different ways: as suggesting that anything really worthwhile exists elsewhere, because the world is always pointing to something other than itself; or else as claiming that precisely because this world imitates or participates in that other world necessarily it has an inherent, transcendent value. Clearly, the more closely one follows the latter account, the nearer one comes to a sacramental position. But increasingly we live in a world where both perspectives are under threat. So I want to end this chapter by looking more closely at modern reductionism and its consequences.

Modern Reductionism and its Consequences

In discussing the way in which metaphors communicate presence, much has already been said by way of implication against reductionism. But it is worth focusing a little more closely on the issue, since it is so characteristic of our own age, both in its pessimism about any linking of different worlds and, more surprisingly perhaps, in its unwillingness to give space to different points of view. That is why I want to end by illustrating how even metaphors in the hands of non-believers can work creatively for the believer. But I begin with the nineteenth-century poet who is often taken as marking the real beginning of such trends.

Matthew Arnold is often taken as the key nineteenth-century literary figure who denied that religious imagery pointed beyond itself, while in the twentieth century philosophers like Derrida even went so far as to deny that any texts, religious or otherwise, have a life outside of themselves. Whereas Derrida's position is often dismissed as incoherent, that of Matthew Arnold continues to evoke a sympathetic response, particularly from those who like him have either lost their faith or else are teetering on the edge. In a famous essay he wrote:

Our religion has materialised itself in the fact, in the supposed fact; it has attached its emotion to the fact, and now the fact is failing it. But for poetry the idea is everything; the rest is a world of illusion, of divine

[48] *Enneads* 2. 9.

illusion. Poetry attaches its emotion to the idea; the idea is the fact. The strongest part of our religion today is its unconscious poetry.[49]

In part anticipated by Shelley's talk of 'the poetry in the doctrines of Jesus Christ', Arnold writes as the son of a famous cleric, Thomas Arnold, onetime headmaster of Rugby School.[50] He is determined to save something of Christianity from all the undermining of belief that had taken place during his own lifetime through the impact of biblical criticism and scientific discovery (though he is quite clear about the inadequacy of science by itself to save). Nonetheless, one may question his solution. A more recent representative of that position may be used to illustrate its limitations.

John Drury has published material on the New Testament, on the visual arts, and on literature. A recurring theme has been the way in which undue concern with the narrowly factual reduces any potential impact both aesthetically and spiritually. So, for example, although he does not wish to deny the achievements of historical biblical scholarship, these in his view have been bought at the cost of a real engagement of the imagination with the text. With that part of his analysis I cannot but agree. More problematic is the way in which he goes on from this to develop a 'nothing but' or reductionist approach. He wants to 'tie the poet and the sacred Scriptures so fast together as to invite glossing the clause about Christ in the Nicene Creed, "he rose again according to the Scriptures" as "he rose again according to poetry".'[51]

In that particular essay there then follows a comparative analysis of two poems on the resurrection (one by Hopkins and one by Herbert), with the Herbert poem judged superior because of its this-worldly reference. The estimate has become moral and meta-physical, rather than allowing the poems in their own right to pull us out of ourselves into fresh perceptions of how things might be. The language traps us where we are, rather than taking us where we might be. Significantly, we can be well-nigh certain that, unlike Drury, the two poets would have endorsed each other's poems. For

[49] M. Arnold, 'The Study of Poetry' in *Essays in Criticism: Second Series* (London: Macmillan, 1888), 663.

[50] For Shelley's comment in his 'A Defence of Poetry', R. Ingpen and W. E. Peck eds., *The Complete Works of Percy Bysshe Shelley* (London: Ernest Benn, 1965), vii. 126.

[51] J. Drury, 'According to Poetry' in S. Barton and G. Stanton eds., *Resurrection* (London: SPCK, 1994), 202.

both, the transcendent dimension was an essential element in imagery's power, whether the metaphors are used to point to an unfamiliar or totally other world. Drury's preferred Herbert poem 'The Flower' succeeds because it draws us into thinking of flowers repeatedly dying and coming to birth in a way which might be possible with our own repeated 'deaths' in a single life.[52] But no less effective is Herbert's more challenging 'Death' where we have to think hard how 'our Saviour's death did put some blood/ Into thy face.' In fact, the corpse blushes into life as if in the presence of its lover. My point is that we need to engage with a poet's metaphors on their terms rather than ours. Only that way can poetry provide the possibility of access to new understandings and experience. It is for similar reasons that I am also suspicious of Drury's approach to Christian art.[53] Certainly he provides common ground between believer and non-believer but at the cost of neither actually discovering anything really new. Yet believers no less than non-believers could find their imaginations renewed and stretched, were something more like the original intentions of the artists allowed full play.

It is just such a transcendence that is resisted by modern deconstructionism, not least by Derrida himself who has proclaimed that 'there is nothing outside the text': *il n'y a pas de hors texte.*[54] It is a position which is strongly challenged by George Steiner in his *Real Presences*, where, in an argument similar to that defended here, he maintains that literature gains its power precisely through the sense of presence within it of something beyond itself, or, putting matters the other way around, through its ability to disclose a transcendence beyond itself.[55] The argument was taken up a few years later by Valentine Cunningham in his book *In the Reading Gaol*, a title which is a play upon both Oscar Wilde's famous poem and the jail or prison into which modern accounts of reading have thrown

[52] For 'The Flower', George Herbert, *The Complete English Poems* (London: Penguin, 1991), 156–7; for 'Death', 175–6.

[53] J. Drury, *Painting the Word* (New Haven: Yale University Press, 1999). For my critique, 'The Glory of God Revealed in Art and Music: Learning form Pagans' in M. Chapman ed., *Celebrating Creation* (London: Darton, Longman & Todd, 2004), 43–56, esp.51–3.

[54] French version, 1967; trans. G. C. Spivak, *Of Grammatology* (Baltimore: Johns Hopkins University Press, 1976), 158.

[55] G. Steiner, *Real Presences* (London: Faber & Faber, 1989), esp. 137–232.

us. Cunningham insists upon the inescapably theological character of the success of literature, should it indeed succeed:

The question of presence, of what is made really present or not, in writing and reading, is, as Eliot knew and George Steiner keeps insisting, of course theological and biblical . . . The issue is, in the end, sacramental; the table at which the literary parasite sits looks oddly akin to a eucharistic one.[56]

Initially the parallel may seem far-fetched, but the point is that, like the eucharist, words have the power to open us up to new worlds. The modern tendency is to treat words as though they were there simply to convey information, whereas the power of meditative practices lies precisely in their ability to force us beyond standing apart from the words into inhabiting what they are trying to convey. Just as Ignatian spirituality encouraged the reader of the narrative of Christ's life to walk beside him and so experience directly his impact upon oneself, so there is a corresponding need to reject immediate identification of literal equivalents for biblical metaphors and instead allow them time for our imaginations to work their full impact on our lives.

As an example consider what might be meant in calling God a rock. In the story of Israel's desert wanderings Moses strikes a rock, and water gushes forth to relieve the thirst of the Israelites wandering in the desert (Num. 20.2-13). Paul in 1 Corinthians (10.4) takes up the image and transforms it into a metaphor for Christ. Paul identifies the rock with Christ, and suggests that it or he followed them through the desert, continually refreshing them, and so will do the same for us today. Although the metaphor of God as rock is found in numerous places in the Old Testament, not a few commentators have remarked that Paul here stretches such imagery to breaking point. The whole point about rocks, one might have thought, was their stability and immovability, whereas Paul allows the rock to change location as often as do the people themselves. No doubt that is one reason why commentators, rather than trying to defend Paul, often seek to assign blame elsewhere. We are told that he is building on an existing, strange Jewish legend that had already elaborately reworked the Old Testament passage.[57]

[56] V. Cunningham, *In the Reading Gaol* (Oxford: Blackwell, 1994), 393.

[57] The view of both Conzelmann and Fiorenza. Some, though, do concede the possibility that the midrash is Paul's own: e.g. N. Watson, *The First Epistle to the Corinthians* (London: Epworth, 1992), 98.

To my mind, however, further reflection should have suggested a quite different conclusion: that Paul is actually building creatively on the potentialities inherent in just such a metaphor. Certainly, permanence and stability is the first thing that occurs when mention is made of rocks in a climate such as Britain's. But that is not necessarily what comes immediately to mind in the Middle East. Imagine great tracts of desert, and an intense sun beating down. What a relief it must have been to see a rock on the horizon, with the certain guarantee of shade from the oppressive sun and also perhaps the possibility of refreshing one's thirst! A rocky outcrop was so often where desert springs were located. Isaiah, for example, speaks of the righteous king being rather like 'the shadow of a great rock in a thirsty land' (NIV: 32.2). Similar allusions occur in the story of David and in several of the psalms. So the problem is not so much St Paul as ourselves: our lack of imagination in thinking ourselves into a different culture, and so the possibility of alternative meanings. Protection and refreshment turn out to be the point, rather than stability and resistance to change.

An isolated example, it may be said, but it is in reality a common problem. As readers we all too quickly jump to a single meaning, whereas Scripture derives much of its power from the fact that its images are multivalent; that is, they allow our imaginations the possibility of moving in more than one direction. It should therefore come as no surprise that, apart from the meanings already identified, rock can also be used of divine judgement in both Old Testament and New (Deut. 32.30; Rom. 9.32). Nor is it hard to see why. Rocks can be threatening and destructive, as, for example, when overhanging a cliff or hit by a plough. Our imaginations have to learn to explore and to discriminate, and that is something we do not always do.

To change the illustration to one discussed in this volume's predecessor, think of water.[58] The Church became obsessed with its cleansing role. So through most of the Church's history this was to remain the doctrinal core to baptism. It was the place where our sins were washed away, and, if you were a child, then a special sin was invented, what the Church called original sin, sin inherited from Adam. But is that the only metaphorical meaning for water? Surely not. Water can also be a destructive force, as in the story of the Flood and, more pertinently here, a source of refreshment and

---

[58] In *God and Grace of Body*, 156–65.

renewal. If we take the teaching of John the Baptist or Paul as our model, then of course repentance must lie at the core of the sacrament, but, intriguingly, not if we reflect on Christ's own baptism or what St John the Evangelist has to say on the subject. Instead of being backward-looking, the focus is now on the future, on new beginnings as with the inauguration of Jesus' ministry. The result is a nice irony in the modern world. Clergy who baptize still look largely to the past as they perform the act, to the washing away of sin. However, when the unchurched bring their children for baptism what they are usually after is a blessing, and that could well be a more accurate perception of what Christ had in mind at his own baptism: grace and help with the future pattern of his ministry; grace and help with the future direction of the child. It also accords better with how the unchurched might explain the symbolism involved. They are unlikely to declare their new born child unclean and in need of a bath. More probably, the event will be seen as more like the spiritual equivalent of the refreshing shower they take after exercise or first thing in the morning. It marks a new beginning.

The point I am trying to make with these examples is actually quite a simple one. Our language is richer than our prejudices, and so will on many an occasion afford new insights, if only we are prepared to listen and reflect. Just as the imagery of rock or water can open up new possibilities, so sometimes even where the context seems hostile, the end result may prove quite otherwise. Take, for instance, a famous poem from the eighteenth century, Hölderlin's 'Brot und Wein' (Bread and Wine). Initial impressions are all of a Romantic classicism, according to which our own world is as 'night' compared with the 'day' that was once classical Greece. So for most of the poem it looks as though 'the god who is to come' is Dionysus or Bacchus and that it is he who will bring recovery: 'a wine-cup more full, a life more intense and more daring'. But then comes the surprise of the ending:

Meanwhile, though, to us shadows comes the Son of the Highest,
Comes the Syrian and down into our gloom bears his torch.
Blissful, the wise men see it; in souls that were captive there gleams a
Smile, and their eyes shall yet thaw in response to the light.[59]

[59] Trans. M. Hamburger, *Friedrich Hölderlin: Poems and Fragments* (London: Routledge & Kegan Paul, 1966), 242–3.

The identification of Christ and Bacchus is startling, but all the more effective as a result. Our night is not total blackness; the bread and wine continue to speak of a divine presence, and so give hope.[60] Put more prosaically, classicism and Christianity are in the end not set against each other as day against night: both are enlarged. Through patient reading we are given a vision of Christianity as it might be, the water of our lives, to revert to an earlier example, turned into an absurd overprovision of wine.

As one might expect from the twentieth century, examples far more thorough-going in their negation than Hölderlin do occur. Yet, even here, the final result is not necessarily wholly antipathetical, if one is prepared to persevere. Whether or not this was also the intention of the poet is not the main issue. Authorial intention may in the end not be resoluble. The point rather is that for religious believers even the apparent negation of their perspective can draw them into its renewal, as new potentials and new aspects are explored. An intriguing case to consider because it seems concerned to subvert Hölderlin with a much more negative view of the present is Paul Celan's 'Die Winzer' (The Vintagers). It was written by him shortly after reading Heidegger's essay on Hölderlin's 'Brot und Wein'. Celan admired both men. In Heidegger's case the admiration was ironical in view of the philosopher's ambivalent attitude towards the Nazis. Having lost both parents in the Holocaust, Celan found it difficult to commit himself to the German language; yet it was Heidegger who in his view gave back to German its *limpidité* (lucidity).[61] The poem opens with an allusion to the Holocaust:

> They harvest the wine of their eyes,
> they crush out all of the weeping, this also:
> thus willed by the night.[62]

At one level the positive biblical images of the wine are subverted and turned into night. Yet at another level the very fact that Celan

---

[60] For a similar interpretation, D. Constantine, *Hölderlin* (Oxford: Clarendon Press, 1988), 199–206.

[61] D. J. Schmidt, 'Between Meridians and Other Lines: Between Heidegger and Celan' in H. M. Block ed., *The Poetry of Paul Celan* (New York: Peter Lang, 1991), 30–7.

[62] Trans. J. Felstiner, *Paul Celan: Poet, Survivor, Jew* (New Haven: Yale University Press, 1995), 84.

expresses himself in German at all speaks of hope. The use of the language (German) and of the imagery (biblical) hint at the possibility that God might after all have the last word, that the harvest of tears could become a vintage wine crop, as it were, if only the past is acknowledged for what it was.

Dylan Thomas offers a British parallel. A superficial reading of his short poem 'This bread I break was once the oat' might suggest that the poem is intended as a direct attack on Christianity.[63] So far from being life-giving symbols the eucharistic elements might just as well be reversed, with wine into vine and bread once more into corn, since what they most evoke is humanity's destructive potential. The 'oat' that 'was merry' and 'the grape's joy' are made to yield to a 'flesh' that 'breaks' and 'blood' as 'desolation in the vein'.

> Man in the day or wine at night
> Laid the crops low, broke the grape's joy.

Given that Thomas was not a Christian, this might seem to be the required reading. But symbols are more powerful than their authors, and so the poem ends with a nice ambiguity.

> My wine you drink, my bread you snap.

No doubt Thomas intended the earth to be the speaker, but for the Christian the first half of the line most naturally suggests Christ himself. So the desecration of the earth stretches to misuse of the eucharist itself, and so deepens perception of what can occur in the sacrament rather than the reverse: Christ's continuing availability, whatever we do to him in the rite, or more widely in his creation.

In the history of Christian theology some theologians have been suspicious of words, arguing that, if used at all, they should always point beyond themselves.[64] Certainly, reference beyond the text ought to be part of their purpose. But, if our argument here is correct, equally important is another strand of the Christian tradition that sees the words as themselves 'comestible', to be 'chewed and digested'.[65] As Anselm enjoins, 'taste the goodness of your Redeemer . . . chew his words as a honey-comb . . . chew by

---

[63] For the full text of the poem and a commentary, D. Brown and D. Fuller, *Signs of Grace: Sacraments in Poetry and Prose* (London: Continuum, 2000), 62–3.

[64] e.g. Augustine, *De doctrina Christiana* 1. 13; 3. 9.

[65] Cunningham, *Reading Gaol*, 203.

thinking, suck by understanding, swallow by loving and rejoicing. Rejoice in chewing, be glad in sucking, delight in swallowing.'[66] Only by such lingering delight over words will their full richness be discovered.

Whether within the biblical text or beyond, words can and do thus function sacramentally, despite all their apparent clash and dissonance. For it is precisely through meditation upon such imagery that our participation in the Word made flesh is most effectively deepened. Chewing the eucharistic elements and chewing words should thus not be seen as opposed activities. Words, no less than the Word himself, can be fully sacramental. If Dorothy Sayers is right, Dante combined the incarnate Christ with the books of the Bible in a single eucharistic procession: Word, words, and sacrament all as one. Whether a correct account or not, it was a wise intuition.[67] Not only is metaphor thereby granted its full power, it is seen to be part of a larger mystery, the Logos that permeates all of creation and so provides the foundation for things unlike to be illuminatingly compared, as well as things like.

Although to my mind biblical metaphors are not as yet given enough attention, there is also a danger in how I have been arguing here: that their very inexhaustibility will be used as a justification for never going beyond them, especially when that point is supplemented by appeal to their canonical character. The Church has faced such an issue before, when it wrestled with the question of whether the psalms were always sufficient in themselves for Christian worship. Not all the lessons of that earlier debate, as we shall see in the next chapter, have as yet been fully appropriated.

---

[66] From the opening of 'A Meditation on Human Redemption' in J. Hopkins and H. W. Richardson eds., *Anselm of Canterbury* (London: SCM Press, 1974), i. 137.
[67] D. L. Sayers ed., *Dante: The Divine Comedy: Purgatory* (Harmondsworth: Penguin, 1955), 298–306 (on Canto 29). For a different view, P. Armour, *Dante's Griffin and the History of the World* (Oxford: Clarendon, 1989), 1–14.

3
Hymns and Psalms

To place consideration of congregational singing before preaching (which follows in the next chapter) might seem perverse. Partly such a decision reflects the declining status of the sermon in churches generally. But it is also possible to put matters more positively. Although hymn singing is often treated as a sort of Cinderella subject and so seldom gains the attention it deserves from theologians, the words of hymns are frequently what are most deeply imprinted on worshippers' memories.[1] They are thus quite often the last thing to go when advancing senility strikes. As a result, though seldom explicitly considered, they are none the less quite commonly not only what conditions people's expectations of experience of God, but also where for many such experience is primarily to be found.

To the degree to which the explanation for this lies in the sharp contrast now often drawn between religion and the rest of life, it is a matter of deep regret. If Sunday worship is required to be always the spiritual highlight of the believer's week, it will soon disappoint. Certainly, as Augustine once claimed, praise should be the central element in worship and so also in the hymn, but that does not mean that praise is the only way of encountering God.[2] As I have sought to emphasize across these three volumes, God can in fact be experienced in a great range of human activities. The sacred–secular contrast is a modern one, and wrongly endorsed.

Before, however, considering the role of language in such experience, some more general remarks first on the setting of hymns in the context of worship would seem apposite. For a start, it is important to stress that such experience in worship should

---

[1] Even a Methodist theologian like Geoffrey Wainwright gives only relatively few pages of his systematic theology to the topic: *Doxology* (London: Epworth, 1980), 198–217.

[2] In his *Commentary on Psalms*, 72 where hymns are progressively identified as praise, praise to God, and praise to God sung.

emerge out of life as a whole, and not be directly sought in so narrow a context. Consider the following parallel. It would be quite wrong to cultivate a particular friendship simply because of the pleasure it brings (that would be to fail to value friends in their own right). Nonetheless it is quite likely that pleasure will be a consequence, in the delight the other's presence provides. So similarly worship should be given to God because he is valued in and of himself irrespective of any experiences it may bring, but concomitantly certain further experiences are still quite likely to follow. Indeed, precisely because praise is pre-eminently an expression of gratitude for the way the world is, the disposition of one's life and so forth, it would be odd if praise did not blossom into song as an expression of the exuberant nature of such thankfulness. That is no doubt one reason why the stories of grace with which the Bible abounds are often themselves surrounded in the liturgy with song.[3] At the same time were the songs sung with the aim of such exuberance in mind, the central focus would have moved wrongly from the divine 'object' to the human subject. Under such circumstances the practice would be quite rightly condemned by those who insist that worship should continue, even where such feelings do not seem likely to be generated: for example, in a cold, sparsely attended church in which the music is performed quite indifferently. As in duties to friends and family, an obligation to worship is owed to God even where the circumstances make it likely that it will be more chore than joy.

That conceded, though, it would be quite wrong to go on from this to conclude that all else is therefore indifferent. In *God and Enchantment of Place* I observed how landscape painting can help give better shape to our perceptions of the presence of the divine in the natural world.[4] By picking out and emphasizing certain features rather than others, what is partially hidden becomes more perspicacious; similarly, then, in the organization of worship. Words and music combine to bring into sharper focus or relief that for which some may already know themselves deeply indebted to God but need reminding. Yet others may still be learning of the fact. That is why much criticism of the emotional character of

[3] For a similar view, G. W. Lathrop, *Holy Things: A Liturgical Theology* (Minneapolis: Fortress, 1993), 18–19.
[4] (Oxford: Oxford University Press, 2004), 84–152.

nineteenth-century evangelical hymnody seems to me misplaced. Entirely laudable motives lay behind the desire to keep alive the original conversion experience that brought the individual to faith in the first place. Thereby the individual was renewed in the sense of gratitude that motivates worship. It was only when everything became subordinate to the emotional 'feel' of the experience that things began to go badly wrong: for example, when it was asserted that this was necessarily better or more 'real' than the calmer dispositions that were reflected in hymns such as Addison's 'The spacious firmament on high'.[5]

Addison was actually engaged in essentially the same task of evoking and intensifying an original experience, in this case clarifying a particular way of reading the natural world. Despite the huge differences in external presentation, therefore, it is not there that any debate should be focused in my view but rather on whether the two experiences complement one another or suggest incompatible accounts of the nature of divinity. I shall return to the matter later, but for the moment let me observe that huge differences in experiential 'feel' cannot of themselves be taken to indicate comparable differences in their object. In a similar way two individuals may share the same friend, but experience the friend in quite different ways, one very much through bodily contact, the other without obvious signs of affection, for instance. What this may indicate is contrasts in style rather than any significant differences in the true nature of the friend as such.

None of this, I hasten to add, should be taken to imply that experience is always to the fore. Singing in worship can fulfil a great variety of other purposes (apart, that is, from praise or worship itself), among them the fostering of communal identity and the exposition of credal commitments. It is simply that the possibility for experience of the divine is my concern here. Nor should it be thought that singing achieves that possibility in only one kind of way. As with landscape painting, such ways may include reminding the individual of where such experience has occurred in their life in the past, renewing or creating that experience at this particular time, or directing the individual to how it might be achieved in the future.

---

[5] Although soon taken up as a hymn, it was first published as an Ode in an appendix to an essay on 'Faith and Devotion' in the *Spectator* (23 August 1712).

In exploring how the music of worship thus recalls, renews, or initiates experience and the contribution that metaphor and symbol make I shall begin by offering some reflections on the historical background to our present situation. Thereafter, I shall focus on the issues raised by imagery that goes beyond explicit biblical precedent (including what criteria might be applied in our own day), the question of match between music and words, and, finally, the range of experience to which such writing might appeal.

Hymns in their Historical Context

Although hymns made an early appearance in the Christian tradition, it is only relatively gradually that these came to exercise such a major role in the worship of Protestant Christianity. Their active encouragement in the Roman Catholic mass is even more recent, largely since the Second Vatican Council. Admittedly, the need was recognized much earlier. Already in the middle of the nineteenth century the Anglican convert F. W. Faber was lamenting 'the few in the Garden of the Soul' and contrasting the spell that the *Olney Hymns* continued to exercise on him,[6] and the strong support given by the German Hymn Book to 'the now decaying cause of Protestantism'.[7] But despite his own efforts, progress was still slow.[8]

With the rise of more informal worship styles throughout the western Church, some might contend that it is the worship song or 'chorus' to which more attention should now be given.[9] Certainly, it would be wrong to dismiss such forms of singing as naive, and not merely because of their widespread dissemination. Early precedents for a high degree of repetition such as is characteristic of this type of singing can be found in the wording of Psalm 136 and in repeated use of the Jesus Prayer.[10] Even classical music has its parallels in the

---

[6] This was a joint work of John Newton and William Cowper at Olney.

[7] F. W. Faber, *Hymns* (London: Richardson, 1862), xv, xvi (from the 1849 Preface).

[8] *The Westminster Hymnal* of 1912 was a notable landmark, but still weak in comparison to the present situation.

[9] 'Worship song' is now the more common terminology, not least because not all exhibit the repetitive nature of the 'chorus'.

[10] Psalm 136 has the repeated refrain, 'for his mercy endures for ever'. The Jesus Prayer ('Lord Jesus Christ, Son of God, have mercy on me') dates from the sixth century and has migrated westward from the Byzantine Hesychast or quietist movement.

ostinato or repeated rhythmic, melodic, or harmonic patterns in pieces such as Ravel's *Bolero* and Pachelbel's *Canon*.[11] Nor should we think of only one basic type. Some, for example, inhibit movement while others positively encourage it.[12] Repetition at times fosters exuberant praise, while at others it can encourage a meditative, almost mystic contemplation. Where content is minimal, how much further worshippers are likely to be carried in their understanding of God will clearly very much depend either on the individual's anterior resources or else on what is provided elsewhere in the service. The former is obviously too wide an issue to explore here. Accompanying hymns, however, could provide exactly the right kind of supplement.[13] That is one reason for devoting more attention to them here. Another is the fact that, however popular the worship song now is within church circles, in the population at large it is still the hymn that holds its own, as the popularity of the TV series *Songs of Praise*, the choice of music at weddings and funerals, and so on, continue to demonstrate. None of this is to deny that the issue may be quite different for the present generation of children when they become adults.[14] Also relevant to note is the existence of a sort of half-way house in 'songs' that are more complex than choruses but usually simpler than hymns.[15]

Most Anglicans would now find it difficult to imagine an alternative world, but in fact it is only as recently as the nineteenth century that hymn singing properly entered the life of the Church of England. Of course, there had been hymns long before this. The Gnostics and the Arians were known for their hymns, and so one

---

[11] Examples quoted in Anne Harrison's helpful discussion, *Sing it Again: The Place of Short Songs in Worship* (Cambridge: Grove Books, 2003), 9.

[12] Harrison contrasts the stillness recommended by the Taizé Community with the movement encouraged by the Wild Goose Group of the Iona Community: 13–21, esp. 21. More dramatic contrasts occur when clapping and dancing are encouraged.

[13] Harrison offers an intriguing example of integration: Graham Kendrick's refrain, 'My Rock, my Rock, my Jesus, my Rock' set in between the verses of Augustus Toplady's hymn 'Rock of ages': 7.

[14] The contrast between what was sung in schools in the 1960s and now is highlighted (with examples) in R. Brown, *How Hymns Shape our Lives* (Cambridge: Grove Books, 2001), 17.

[15] Well illustrated by the two-volume 2002 CD with All Souls Orchestra under Noel Tredinnick: *The Best of Prom Praise: Hymns and Songs* (1—'I Will Sing the Wondrous Story'; 2—'Praise, my Soul, the King of Heaven').

reason for early Christian compositions was in response as a teaching aid. For instance, John Chrysostom organized hymn singing
through the streets of Constantinople in reaction to Arian processions of a similar character, and this was also a motive behind
Ambrose's writing in Milan.[16] That was in the fourth century.
The earliest surviving complete Christian hymn comes from almost
two centuries earlier, a hymn to Christ, 'Bridle of colts untamed',
preserved by Clement of Alexandria.[17] It is marvellously rich in its
imagery. 'Bridle of untamed foals, wing of unerring birds, unwa-
vering helm of ships, shepherd of royal lambs, gather your artless
children to sing in a holy way' is how it opens. Again and again in
its short compass the reader is brought up with a start, thanks to
powerful metaphors such as the author's talk of 'tender mouths
suckled at the nipple of the Logos'. Possibly earlier but less explicitly Christian is the collection preserved in Syriac and known as
the *Odes of Solomon*.[18] In one Jesus is envisaged singing in the midst
of the congregation through their own vocal chords, as it were.[19] It
was the more restrained Ambrose, however, who effectively set the
pattern for the west, as can be seen not only from his own compositions but also in the sort of poetry employed by his successors,
among them Prudentius, Sedulius, Fortunatus, and the two Tho-
mases (of Celano and Aquino).[20] In considering their work it is
essential to note that experience of and through hymns was still
mainly clerical, since the use of their compositions was largely
confined to the various daily services set by the Roman Breviary.[21]

[16] Ambrose's hymns, the Arians alleged, acted like magic spells: Ambrose, *sermo contra Auxentium*, 34.

[17] For the text used and the translation in full, M. Kiley ed., *Prayer from Alexander to Constantine* (London: Routledge, 1997), 296–303.

[18] It has been argued that they must have been written before 125 AD: M. Lattke, 'Dating the *Odes of Solomon*', *Antichthon* 27 (1993), 45–58. For the complete text, J. H. Charlesworth ed., *The Odes of Solomon* (Oxford: Clarendon, 1973).

[19] *Odes*, 31. 3–4. Although he makes most use of Psalm 22 (73–102), the author's image is also taken up by R. M. Kidd in his book *With One Voice: Discovering Christ's Song in our Worship* (Grand Rapids: Baker, 2005), 177.

[20] John Mason Neale (d. 1866) did more than any other individual in attempt-ing to secure through translation a permanent place for such writers in the canon of hymnody. Ambrose, Prudentius, Sedulius, and Thomas Aquinas all still have several hymns each in the *New English Hymnal* (1986).

[21] For a commentary on such hymns, J. Connelly, *Hymns of the Roman Liturgy* (London: Longmans, 1957). For an edited Latin edition, A. S. Walpole ed., *Early Latin Hymns* (Cambridge: Cambridge University Press, 1922).

Unless we count the *Gloria in excelsis*, hymns were not used at mass. So, apart from on pilgrimage or later at benediction, hymns would not have formed a normal part of the experience of the laity. This subordinate role indicated their essentially secondary character.

Nor is it true that the Reformation brought marked change. Certainly, Martin Luther adopted a positive and encouraging attitude, producing several compositions of his own, most notably *Ein feste Burg* ('A mighty stronghold is our God'), where both words and melody are his. But this was not the attitude among the Protestant Reformers more generally. Calvin in particular was adamantly opposed. The resources of Scripture, he thought, should be sufficient. So only congregational psalm singing was allowed (itself of course an important innovation), and in this England followed suit.[22] Although hymn writers such as Isaac Watts and Charles Wesley had ensured that hymn singing had become a common pattern in much of Nonconformity by the late eighteenth century, the Church of England was much slower to move. There was a strange irony in this, as both the Wesley brothers had remained priests of the Church of England till their deaths. Yet, turn up at your parish church in 1800 and one would still have found a small band in the gallery, with the parish clerk leading the psalm singing by a method known as lining out—singing one line at a time with the congregation then repeating it. Readers familiar with the novels of Thomas Hardy and George Eliot will be aware of the pandemonium that was sometimes the result.

Both Eliot and Hardy, however, expressed regret at the change: Eliot in *Amos Barton*, one of her short novels making up *Scenes of Clerical Life*, and Hardy in *Under the Greenwood Tree*. It is worth pausing, therefore, to consider whether such regret amounts to anything more than the nostalgia of agnostics who had once been committed Christians. Hardy in particular introduces an element of the tragic: 'The old choir, with humbled hearts, no longer took their seats in the gallery as heretofore ... but were scattered about with their wives in different parts of the church. Having nothing to do with conducting the service for almost the first time in their lives, they all felt awkward, out of place, abashed, and

---

[22] Zwingli went even further, banning all singing and instrumental music in church, and that despite his own undoubted musical gifts: P. Westermeyer, *Te Deum: The Church and Music* (Minneapolis: Fortress, 1998), 149–53.

inconvenienced by their hands. . . . the venerable body of musicians
could not help thinking that the simpler notes they had been wont
to bring forth were more in keeping with the simplicity of their old
church than the crowded chords and interludes it was {the orga-
nist's} pleasure to produce.'[23] In a Preface of 1896 Hardy added the
observation that not only had such groups been virtually self-
financing they also ensured the meeting of sacred and secular.
Not least was this so in their practice of beginning their music
books at one end with sacred entries and with secular at the other,
and these often meeting in the middle.[24] What certainly was lost
was the full participation of ordinary village folk. Even so it is
unlikely that this type of contribution would have survived anyway.
Radio and other forms of mass communication ensured that professionalism came to be seen as the expected norm, even in more
popular forms of music. More worrying, a century and a half
further on, is the way in which the organ has so completely
triumphed that even a poor instrument or a good one played
badly is still commonly thought preferable to any other form of
accompaniment. Hardy was wrong to think simplicity the issue, but
communicability certainly is. The Church surely needs once more
to ask what aids people's experience of God and what does not.

In bringing us to our present situation the north of England was
for once quicker in accepting change than was the south. The first
attempt to produce a hymnbook in the south (by Reginald Heber)
was actually vetoed by the then Archbishop of Canterbury, whereas
in 1820 the Archbishop of York supported a comparable effort in
the north.[25] The collection emanated from Sheffield, where a once
radical local journalist and poet, James Montgomery, played a
leading role.[26] In earlier life Montgomery had attempted to undermine Scripture in a series of irreverent contributions that he wrote
for the paper he edited, *The Sheffield Iris*. Now, however, he sought

---

[23] T. Hardy, *Under the Greenwood Tree* (Oxford: Oxford University Press, 1985),
IV. v. 167.

[24] Ibid. 3–4.

[25] I. Bradley, *Abide with Me: The World of Victorian Hymns* (London: SCM Press,
1997), 16, 19–20.

[26] Seen as a supporter of the French Revolution, Montgomery was imprisoned
several times. A change of view came with Napoleon's invasion of Switzerland that
also led to the poem that first gave him national fame, 'The Wanderer of Switzerland'
(1806), This poem he placed first in his collected *Poetical Works* (4th edn., 1854).

to use his undoubted skills more positively. At least eight of his hymns are still in most modern hymnbooks, among them 'Hail to the Lord's Anointed', 'Angels from the realms of glory', and 'Songs of praise the angels sang'. Two on the theme of prayer deserve to be better known, 'Lord, teach us how to pray aright' and 'Prayer is the soul's sincere desire'. The latter contains some of the finest lines ever written on prayer as 'the Christian's vital breath', 'the Christian's native air':

> Prayer is the burden of a sigh,
> The falling of a tear,
> The upward glancing of an eye,
> When none but God is near.

Montgomery starts with need but advances the singer into the experience of intimacy and joy that prayer can also bring. It is a splendid example of how the good hymn writer meets us where we are, in order to draw us into a new dimension. What, sadly, this hymn also illustrates is how failure lurks just around the corner if words cannot become firmly anchored to a particular tune. It has been sung to more than half a dozen familiar melodies but none has so far won general acceptance.[27]

Despite the innovative work of Montgomery it was only really with the phenomenal success of *Hymns Ancient and Modern* (1861) and its successive editions that the hymn finally achieved an unassailable ascendancy. That collection has sometimes been attacked for cultural imperialism, in the way in which its use was disseminated throughout the empire. But, just as its first editors drew on earlier sources, so also did subsequent editions elsewhere in the English–speaking world succeed in producing their own distinctive medley of foreign borrowings and native product.[28] Although other collections also played their part in securing the triumph of the hymn, their significance lies more in aspects of their contribution

[27] Six are listed in J. R. Watson ed., *An Annotated Anthology of Hymns* (Oxford: Oxford University Press, 2002), 251. Intriguingly, the latest editions of *Hymns Ancient and Modern* (now called *Common Praise*) and of *The English Hymnal* (NEH) now offer two more.

[28] The result was an unusual marketing ploy in response to just such an attack from Archbishop Rowan Williams. Adverts described the latest version (*Common Praise*) as 'less a cultural sin—more a global phenomenon': e.g. *Church Times* (25 November 2005), 20.

rather than in the work as a whole. So, for instance, *The English Hymnal* (1906) was especially important in reviving pre-Reformation traditions of hymnody and also in recognizing the importance of memorable tunes, including folk tunes. Again, Percy Dearmer's *Songs of Praise* (1925) represented an important reminder that hymnody should aspire to poetry as a norm and not just occasionally, even if the editor did sometimes overreach himself in the inclusion of unsuitable lyrics from Shakespeare and the like.[29] In such cases the stature of the poet seems to be treated as more pertinent than the content of the poetry as such.

It is the appropriate nature and quality of the imagery that I now want to address in more detail. Thereafter attention will focus on what distinctive contribution the accompanying music can make and the related issue of how far the form of the experience might be affected by content and with what results.

Going beyond the Psalms: the Legitimacy of New Imagery

In considering the suitability or otherwise of particular words it is important to acknowledge that hymns are a medium of expression with their own distinctive criteria of appropriateness. 'Every word communicating the maximum and most precise thought in a minimum of syllables . . . they must also elicit personal involvement and response on the part of the worshippers.'[30] Because they are intended to appeal to a range of different intellects and no time is offered for prior reflection on their meaning, only language that is relatively easily accessible can work. But this emphatically should not entail the absence of the poetic.[31] While the vital need for some basic immediate comprehension might seem to pull in that direction, on the other side needs to be set the inherited rich tradition of metaphors within any particular religious community on which the writer can easily draw without obfuscating meaning. So 'lamb',

[29] For a list of the poets included and a critique, J. R. Watson, *The English Hymn* (Oxford: Clarendon Press, 1997), 523–30, esp. 524–5. Dearmer had also been a member of the editorial committee for the *English Hymnal*.
[30] Two of the criteria listed by M. Clarkson, *The Singing Heart* (Carol Stream, Ill.: Hope, 1989), 12. Her complete list repays study.
[31] Clarkson speaks of 'words of simplicity, clarity, beauty and strength'.

'rock', 'water', and other such metaphors all start with a much
larger potential for building new forms of expression than would
be true in purely secular poetry where context and reflection can
only gradually build relevant meanings.

In the creative use of such building blocks the psalms of course
set an important precedent which translators into English and other
modern languages were rightly concerned to maintain. Indeed, one
reason for the slow acceptance of hymns in England may well have
been the quality of the work of Tate and Brady (their so-called
'New Version' of 1696) as successors to the more pedestrian Sternhold and Hopkins (1562).[32] Both accepted the restraints of normal
verse metre, which is not the case with the version by Miles
Coverdale that is to be found bound with the 1662 Prayer Book.
Ironically, it was only after the rise of the hymn that Coverdale's
version came fully into its own, as higher standards of choral singing
made possible the more widespread use of Anglican chant.[33] Even
recent revisions have so far failed to displace his achievement.
Although bad as well as good motives have played their part in
such resistance, questions of poetics are worth taking seriously as
they raise more than merely aesthetic issues. It is the writer's
metaphors that help to engage our attention and thus our imaginations. Their inclusion can also pose important theological questions
about the proper application of old material to new situations. It is
often assumed without a moment's forethought that the best version to sing of any biblical text must be that closest to the original's
meaning. But that is to confuse authorial intention with what might
be the quite different context to which the text is now to be applied
in the singing. Even the writers of the psalms themselves adapt and
change meanings, to ensure continuing spiritual relevance. If that
was the right approach on their part, the same principle might also
entitle hymn writers to go beyond the stage to which biblical
metaphors had developed by the time of the closure of the canon.
That hymn writers themselves realized that no small issue was at

[32] Two of their paraphrases are still commonly found in modern hymnbooks:
'Through all the changing scenes of life' (based on Psalm 34) and 'As pants the hart
for cooling streams' (Psalm 42). Sternhold and Hopkins also have one survivor:
'All people that on earth do dwell ('The old hundredth').

[33] The use of Anglican chant apparently first arose in the Chapel Royal. Many
seventeenth-century Prayer Books were bound with metrical versions of the
psalms rather than Coverdale's.

stake is well indicated by Montgomery's choice of the title *The Christian Psalmist* (1825) for his own collection of hymns. More pertinently, as we shall see, a not dissimilar title was also adopted in the case of Isaac Watts.

Consider Psalm 144 as an example. Thanks to modern discoveries such as the Dead Sea Scrolls, our knowledge of the development of Hebrew is now immeasurably improved. As a result it becomes possible to date more accurately some of the psalms.[34] In this case some of the words used in its second half can now definitely be identified as Aramaic rather than Hebrew. So that suggests a time when the use of Hebrew was declining, and Aramaic, the *lingua franca* of the Middle East, was taking over. By contrast, the first half of the psalm is written in pure Hebrew, with numerous verbal parallels to Psalm 18. A likely possibility, therefore, is that an early version of the psalm has been rewritten for fresh use sometime during the post-exilic period, that is to say probably in the fifth century BC or later, and in the process given a quite different meaning from Psalm 18. Although it still opens with words of praise, instead of a royal thanksgiving Psalm 144 quickly turns instead into a royal lament. God is accused of deserting his people and urged to act now: 'Bow thy heavens, O Lord, and come down.' Nonetheless, the psalm ends on a confident note with its vision of the people once more blessed, with flocks flourishing and sons and daughters of whom the king can be proud. So it looks as though what we have is an existing psalm adapted for new circumstances in a more troubled world.[35]

Because Hebrew was less well understood in Coverdale's day than it is now, it would not have been possible for him to reflect on such developments. Although there are some exceptions, his tendency is therefore to assume that it is his duty to adopt more literal meanings, a practice that does not always advance the spiritual potential of the text. Take, for example, how the daughters are described in this same psalm (v. 12). We know now that in keeping with its character as a royal psalm the image is of the daughter's beauty adorning the royal palace in the same way as its sculptured

---

[34] Quite a number of other criteria are available, among them theological content and a reluctance to use 'Yahweh' of God: J. Day, *Psalms* (Sheffield: Sheffield Academic Press, 1990), 34–6, 113–15, 123–4.

[35] For further details, A. Weiser, *The Psalms* (London: SCM Press, 1962), 822–5, esp. 824; L. C. Allen, *Psalms* 101–150 (Waco, Tex.: Word, 1983), 286–92, esp. 291.

cornices do. Coverdale followed earlier Greek and Latin translations. Even so, he translates more literally: 'that our daughters may
be as the polished corner of the temple' (v. 12). That literalism is a
pity, because those earlier versions—the Greek Septuagint and
Latin Vulgate—had already developed a rich, alternative vein of
spirituality based on a less literal reading—as Jerome's Vulgate puts
it, the daughters are to be an adornment like the temple, in other
words, noted for their prayer and piety.[36]

If that is one small example of a spiritual meaning developed by
church tradition that Coverdale rejects (wrongly in my view), at
other times he is more conservative in a way that shows up the
poverty of modern literalism. In Psalm 84 he follows precedent and
offers us the beautiful, familiar lines about those 'who going
through the vale of misery use it for a well' (v. 6); in other words,
they discover God in adversity. Literally, however, all the verse
meant is that people are fortunate when, in the words of the New
English Bible, 'as they pass through a thirsty valley, they find water
from a spring'. Again, in another psalm about Joseph (105.18)
Coverdale describes how 'the iron entered into his soul'. Modern
versions by contrast disclose all too quickly the utterly prosaic
character of the original: in prison Joseph had in fact an iron collar
put round his neck. The same more literal translation principles are
adopted in the version of the Psalter now bound with the modern
Anglican Prayer Book, *Common Worship* (2000).[37] The later Christian tradition had universalized such experience, and so made its
appropriation in quite different contexts much easier, whereas the
literal distances what happens from our own particular concerns.

Nor is it even the case that the literal always guarantees easier
intelligibility. An amusing case in point is the image in Psalm 119,
verse 83: 'I am become like a bottle in the smoke.' Those who
attend choral evensong on the twenty-fifth evening of the month
could scarcely be anything other than puzzled. Yet had Coverdale
followed the Septuagint and Vulgate, such perplexity would not
have arisen. Both speak of 'a bottle in the frost'. Singers and readers
are alike aware that glass is likely to crack in extreme cold, and so
the image is of a person easily broken in adversity. What, however,

---

[36] *Ut similitudo templi.*
[37] This has 'Who going through the valley find there a spring' (84.5) and 'his
neck was ringed with iron' (105.18).

had been discovered in the meantime was that glass bottles were rarely used in ancient Palestine and Egypt, except to collect tears as a sign of mourning: hence Psalm 56, verse 8: 'put my tears in thy bottle'. Instead, Jewish bottles were generally of skin, and so what the obscure verse really means is that like a skin bottle the psalmist feels himself darkened and shrivelled by the smoke of adversity. The translation is accurate, but has lost in the process easy intelligibility.

Of course, many another verse could be quoted where Coverdale or the modern translator removes obscurity and actually helps with the accessibility of the passage. My point is simply that the argument cannot be assumed always to go in the same direction in each case. In particular, in opening up new possibilities for experience of God through the words, what is less literal, less tied to the past, may well be the more successful. Consider one last example. As with Psalm 144, Psalm 108 attempts an application to new circumstances of two earlier psalms which are now combined, parts of psalms 57 and 60. Again like Psalm 144, the combination is likely to date from the post-exilic period, and so probably also from a period when all the various little nations referred to in the second half of the psalm had either been conquered or disappeared altogether, as with Edom, against whom the psalmist's main fury is directed.[38] Moab and Edom were two small nations on the far side of the River Jordan. So, were we to read the request literally: 'Moab my wash-pot' and 'over Edom will I cast my shoe', we would end up endorsing the present Israeli government's expansionist policies against the Palestinians, and indeed urging them on to take over part of Jordan as well. So long as the two nations had existed, they were regarded by the Jews with special hostility.[39] Both nations were probably conquered under David and again under king Omri, but they in turn got their revenge (particularly in Edom's case) through regular incursions from the south and perhaps also participation in the sack of Jerusalem itself in 586. Then, centuries later, came the final pièce de résistance, when

---

[38] Although willing to concede a date later than the fall of Jerusalem, Allen still wishes to place the psalm at a point where Edom remained a real threat: Allen, *Psalms 101–150*, 69. To my mind, however, the combination of the two psalms gives the message of Ps. 108 a more universal quality.

[39] The Book of Ruth with its story of Ruth the Moabite as David's ancestor (4.22; the concluding verse) is usually read as a protest against such attitudes.

someone from Edom, King Herod the Great, eventually became ruler over the entire land of Israel.

In the intervening period, however, in the centuries immediately preceding Herod when this psalm was probably written, the old animosities were for a while dormant, for Moab and Edom had already been made subject to Arab invasions from the east. So almost certainly, whereas Psalm 60 intended the references literally, by the time Psalm 108 came to be written Moab and Edom were now functioning more generally as symbols of what constituted any kind of threat. Indeed, that was exactly how the later Church came to read this psalm. That more spiritual reading can now be expressed more powerfully than was ever the case over the past two millennia or more. In 1868 the Mesha Stele or Moabite Stone was discovered. What its inscription revealed was how close Moabites and Edomites were to the Jews. They even spoke almost exactly the same language, Hebrew with only very small variations. Moab also had a not altogether dissimilar theology regarding their own god Chemosh. So we may think of the final revision of the psalm as asking for victory over that most insidious enemy of all, what is closest to us but corrupting of our vocation and discipleship.

It is against such a background of the changing deployment of psalms both within the canon and beyond that I suggest we place the adaptation of psalms to more explicitly Christian purposes and the eventual creation of hymns as Christian psalms, as it were, in their own right. Here Isaac Watts (d. 1748) is the great innovator.[40] Just as the authors of Psalms 108 and 144 recast the content and themes of earlier psalms to make them more easily rekindle experience of God in their own day, so Watts reorientates his 'translations' as though the psalmists were writing for Watts's own times. This is made self-evidently clear by the full title Watts gives to this aspect of his work: *The Psalms of David, imitated in the language of the New Testament and applied to the Christian state and worship*. He declares that 'the royal author is most honoured when he is made most intelligible; and when his admirable composures are copied in such language as gives light and joy to the saints that live two thousand

---

[40] As with all the other major hymn writers discussed here, there is a CD devoted to their key works available in the Kingsway series *The Hymn Makers* (two in the case of Charles Wesley).

years after him'.[41] If Watts's best-known hymn in this vein 'O God,
our help in ages past' (based on Psalm 90.1-5) does not step outside
Old Testament possibilities, many go very much further.[42] So, for
instance, Psalm 22 becomes Christ's own words.[43]

Again, his version of Psalm 72 opens with the familiar words,
'Jesus shall reign where'er the sun' and then goes on to become a
celebration of the visit of the three kings to the infant Christ. In
similar vein the second half of Psalm 98 now directly alludes to the
incarnation:[44]

> Joy to the world, the Lord is come!
> Let earth receive her king;
> Let every heart prepare him room,
> And heaven and nature sing.

Psalm 137, however, is one of the few cases where he decides to
leave the text as it is. Because of the vengeance against children
advocated in the concluding lines ('Blessed shall he be that taketh
thy children: and throweth them against the stones'), Watts
observes: 'this particular psalm could not be well converted into
Christianity, and accordingly it appears here in its Jewish form.'[45]

Montgomery a century later acts in much the same fashion. 'Hail
to the Lord's Anointed/ Great David's greater Son' is in fact a
Christian version of Psalm 72, while many another psalm is made
just as explicit. So, for instance, his version of Psalm 24 opens:

> Lift up your heads, ye gates of brass
> Ye bars of iron, yield,
> And let the king of glory pass.
> The cross is in the field.[46]

[41] G. Burder ed., *The Works of the Reverend and Learned Isaac Watts* (London,
1810), iv. 115.

[42] Watts's original version, though more difficult to sing, was more personalized: 'Our God, our help . . .'

[43] Initially he began by thinking that all should be given a christological
reference. That proved much less successful than his later decision to adapt them
to the circumstances of his own day.

[44] In 'Jesus shall reign' most modern hymnbooks sadly omit the imagery of the
kings, and so the debt to Ps. 72 is much less obvious. For the full version, D. Davie
ed., *The Psalms in English* (London: Penguin, 1996), 198.

[45] Quoted from Watts's *Reliquiae Juveniles* (1734) in Davie, *The Psalms in
English*, 212. For some examples of Watts's work, 188–212.

[46] Ibid. 265. For other examples from Montgomery, 264–73.

In such practice Watts and Montgomery may have been its clearest and most gifted exponents, but they were by no means unique. Between the sixteenth and the eighteenth centuries the approach was commonplace, and included some of our greatest poets, Milton among them. If his best-known adaptation has more the character of a paraphrase,[47] Milton did not hesitate elsewhere to include allusions not only to Christ but also to his own personal situation.[48] Similar examples might be quoted from Charles Wesley and Christopher Smart.[49] The same technique was also applied to other passages of Scripture, as in the work of Philip Doddridge and William Cowper.[50]

Ironically, almost certainly the reason for the decline in such practice had little to do with theology. It was much more a matter of wider cultural developments. With the Romantic movement valuing individual originality above all else, poets were in effect offering themselves up for contempt if they merely adapted or improved upon the writings of others. Fortunately, some of this rich tradition has survived into modern hymnbooks, but not the principle of development as essential for new contexts, which is a great pity.[51] While it is important to value the Jewish roots from which Christianity has come, it is quite wrong when this is taken to entail respect for literal accuracy even in contexts of worship, where other values ought to be to the fore. One recent discussion of the psalms reminds us of how crucial metaphor is to the imaginative power of the psalms in their original context.[52] Borrowing

[47] 'Let us with a gladsome mind'; based on Psalm 136.

[48] He alludes to his own blindness in his version of Psalm 6: Davie, *The Psalms in English*, 136.

[49] Psalm 51 in Wesley's hands becomes a celebration of Christ's atoning work: Davie, *The Psalms in English*, 214–15. Smart's version of Psalm 74 opens, 'Lord Jesus': 246.

[50] As in Doddridge's 'Hark the glad sound!' and Cowper's 'Hark my soul! it is the Lord,' both of which produce a new vision from a medley of different biblical texts.

[51] Though there are some exceptions, as in the writings of Martin Leckebusch, Timothy Dudley Smith, and John Bell. These might be contrasted with the general tendency of worship songs to use direct quotation.

[52] W. P. Brown, *Seeing the Psalms: A Theology of Metaphor* (Louisville: Westminster John Knox Press, 2002). The importance of the visual is underlined by the inclusion of illustrations of twenty-one pagan images that may have played their part in creating the imagery of the psalms.

from the visual imagery of the surrounding religions, the Hebrew poets sought to transform them from visual icons into verbal metaphors that were compatible with Israelite religion but in a way that continued to appeal strongly to the imagination. 'A raid on the inarticulate' thus became possible, the move 'from sense to transcendence, from the describable to the ineffable'.[53] 'It is on the anvil of experience that the metaphor is forged': the aim was not simply to record but rather to envision an alternative world, one in which God is active, integrating the totality of our present experience into a unity with himself and his purposes.[54]

The problem is that it just will not do to say, as Hooker once did, that the Psalms cannot be bettered.[55] Watts was exactly right about those concluding lines of Psalm 137. That is why they are rightly best omitted from Christian worship, and indeed Psalm 58 altogether. The Fathers attempted to obviate the problem by offering non-literal interpretations, but these fail in the disputed cases precisely because here the metaphorical interpretation runs so obviously counter to the literal rather than developing it.[56] Equally, however, the Church should not be afraid of improvements that do succeed in giving a richer metaphorical resonance without destroying the original Jewish context, as in the examples I quoted earlier. To some extent this is now conceded in service books like *Common Worship*. In Psalm 122, verse 3 the likely meaning is quite prosaic; a reference is being made to the density of the city's housing: 'whose houses stand close together within her walls'.[57] Fortunately, however, such translations have yielded to something more traditional: 'Jerusalem built as a city that is at unity in itself.' Likewise it is unlikely that the author of Psalm 23 intended any

[53] Brown, *Seeing the Psalms*, 9. The first quotation is a borrowing from T. S. Eliot's *Four Quartets* (East Coker, 16).

[54] Brown, *Seeing the Psalms*, 213–15, esp. 213. However, his contention that verbal metaphors are more successful than visual images in avoiding definition of the divine seems to me incorrect. Like paintings, it all depends on how they are used. See further Chapter 8 of this book.

[55] Quoted without reference in Davie, *The Psalms in English*, xxv–xxvi.

[56] For examples from Cassiodorus and Jerome, J. Manley ed., *Grace for Grace: The Psalter and the Holy Fathers* (Crestwood, NY: St Vladimir's Seminary Press, 2003), 204–5, 576–7. Jerome, for instance, wants to treat the infants as 'evil thoughts'. For a more natural development with Psalm 137 in all its horror, see John Oldham's version in Davie, *The Psalms in English*, 163–7.

[57] The *Revised Psalter* translation of 1966.

allusion to death. Nonetheless, 'the valley of the shadow of death' has been retained.[58] The pity is that that principle has not been conceded more extensively. As a distinguished biblical scholar once remarked, rather than turning Jerusalem into a real slum ('houses closely packed together'), what we need to ask is: 'if we are using the Psalter liturgically, what do things like this matter?'[59] More important is the way in which the liturgical version can provide easier access to the experiential. Precisely because the developed metaphor universalizes the situation, individual worshippers will find it easier to apply the imagery to their own context.

Watts by no means confined such creativity to the Psalms. One can detect a similar process at work in his treatment of New Testament texts. So, for example, although his famous hymn 'When I survey the wondrous cross' takes Galatians 6.14 as its starting point, that is all it is really—a starting point, as singers are drawn into a powerful visual re-enactment of the crucifixion. In the manner of so much medieval religion and also Catholic visual piety of his time, we are encouraged to experience the impact of God on our lives through envisaging ourselves bystanders at the crucifixion.[60] And one might add, more than bystanders. His imagery is so powerful that it is almost like standing in front of some great medieval painting. Like the painter he uses the power of his pen to make us see more clearly what we might not otherwise have fully grasped, even had we been at the actual scene.

Sometimes objection is taken to the penultimate verse:

> His dying crimson like a robe
> Spreads o'er his body on the Tree

If the image is found too bloody, the hesitation seems odd in an age like our own that actually appears to revel in work such as Grünewald's Isenheim Altarpiece. If it is right to portray the agony of the crucifixion visually in all its gruesome explicitness, it is hard to see what can be wrong with providing similar gore in words.

---

[58] Here again the *Revised Psalter* translated more accurately, if more prosaically: 'Yea, though I walk through the darkest valley.'

[59] H. F. D. Sparks, *On Translations of the Bible* (London: Athlone Press, 1973), 17–18, esp. 18.

[60] As in Ignatius Loyola's injunction in his *Spiritual Exercises*: 'represent to yourself in imagination': first day of second week, second contemplation, second preliminary.

However, almost certainly it was not to the awfulness of the event
that Watts wished to draw attention. 'Survey' implies viewing
things from a distance where 'the pus and the sweat, the scab and
the coagulation and the stink' would no longer be visible.[61] From
afar the cruel gibbet could become a 'wondrous cross' and 'thorns
compose so rich a crown', in the manner of so much baroque
poetry and painting of the time.[62] To object to either interpretation, however, seems to me equally misconceived. It suggests a
reluctance to allow hymns to address any more than merely
a narrow range of emotions, as though to expose ourselves to
them publicly in song must necessarily produce embarrassment or
still worse deleterious consequences. The range of experience from
which hymns may legitimately draw is an issue to which I shall
return in due course.

Conflicting Contemporary Criteria

In the meantime, arising out of my discussion thus far is the more
general question of how far this process may go. If the hymns of
Montgomery and Watts were intended to advance upon the psalms,
might a similar legitimacy be claimed for yet further developments
in our own day? Indeed, given the huge differences between the
type of society in which we now live and ancient Palestine, is that
not inevitable? In actual practice, however, there has been extraordinarily deep resistance to hymns like 'God of concrete, God of
steel', and not, it must be said, with necessarily the best of
motives.[63] In that particular hymn's case, an aversion to too much
mention of the modern world seems to have played altogether too
large a role. A more commendable motive might have been its
paucity of imagery, with each modern invention only mentioned

[61] D. Davie, *The Eighteenth-Century Hymn* (Cambridge: Cambridge University
Press, 1993), 39–44, esp. 40.
[62] P. N. Brooks, *Hymns as Homilies* (Leominster: Gracewing, 1997), 50–63, esp.
59–60 where a fascinating contrast is drawn with a Studdert Kennedy poem on the
same theme. For baroque parallels (the painter Annibale Carracci and the poet
M. C. Sarbiewski), Davie, *Eighteenth-Century Hymn*, 42, 44.
[63] Originally composed for *100 Hymns for Today* (1969), it was incorporated
into *Hymns Ancient and Modern Revised* (1983) but dropped from that hymnbook's
latest revision *Common Praise* (2000).

rather than actually described.[64] In general, modification of existing lyrics to reflect more adequately what is now believed is a far more common strategy that any attempt to create new imagery. That can only be regretted.

Commentators can sometimes be unthinkingly doctrinaire on this point. Britain's leading expert on hymnody quotes Aristotle in support, to the effect that 'the traditional stories must be kept as they are'.[65] But *contra* Aristotle that is precisely what the Greek tragedians and poets did not do. Imaginative adaptation, we now realize, played a much larger role than Aristotle appears to concede.[66] Similarly in hymns their memorability is often secured precisely through new images or new versions of old stories rather than simply a reworking of the old. So the full version of Watts's hymn 'Jesus shall reign where'er the sun' not only includes the post-biblical tradition of the wise men as kings but also how all now known nations and continents come to do Christ honour.[67] Similarly, we may admire Graham Kendrick's image of 'hands that flung stars into space/ to cruel nails surrendered', but the startling image of Christ's original act of creation is scarcely scriptural.[68] Again, Wesley's fine hymn 'O thou who camest from above/ the pure celestial fire t'impart' is a marvellous meditation on what is an entirely literal and utterly prosaic injunction in its original Old Testament source, about keeping an altar fire permanently lit.[69] And so the list might go on.[70] Indeed, sometimes biblical metaphors are adopted too readily without considering their adequacy.

[64] The only exceptions are 'soaring satellite' and 'lightning's livid line' (the latter scarcely modern).

[65] J. R. Watson, *Hymns and Literature: Form and Interpretation* (Michael Ramsey Lecture, Durham, 2003), 2–3.

[66] For a brief study of the way in which Greek myths were changed and adapted, see my *Tradition and Imagination* (Oxford: Oxford University Press, 1999), 171–207.

[67] 'And Europe her best tribute brings;/ From north to south the princes meet.' For the full version, Watson, *Anthology*, 142.

[68] From his song 'The Servant King'. For full text, G. Kendrick, *Behind the Songs* (Stowmarket: Kevin Mayhew, 2001), 87. For another, thoughtful example: 'God is watching us now/ through a baby's eyes' (109).

[69] Lev. 6.13. For further comment, T. Berger, *Theology in Hymns?* (Nashville: Kingswood, 1995), 102–4.

[70] It is not without relevance to their originality that Daniel B. Stevick chose as the title for his book about Wesley's eucharistic hymns: *The Altar's Fire: Charles Wesley's Hymns on the Lord's Supper* (Peterborough: Epworth, 2004).

Thus, despite its biblical basis, Wesley's 'Hail the Sun of Righteousness...Risen with healing in his Wings' jars as an image,
unless some classical knowledge is presupposed and so the transformation of Apollo's wings as those of the Sun God into Christ's
own.[71]

In our own day, however, what perhaps causes the greater
controversy is the alteration of existing hymns to conform more
closely to what is now seen as acceptable theology. Some American
denominations have gone very far indeed down this route. A good
example of this is what happened with the United Church of
Christ's *New Century Hymnal* of 1995. Even conservative denominations such as the Baptists have been concerned in revisions to
provide inclusive language, but in this case the revision committee
went very much further, seeking to remove all traces of 'sexism'
and what were seen as tired or redundant metaphors.[72] The result
was the decision to omit even the term 'Lord', as well as reshape old
hymns to what was seen as a more contemporary theology.[73] So, for
example, in 'Come, thou fount of every blessing' not only did the
obscure reference to 'my Ebenezer' go but also talk of a 'redeeming
love' that 'interposed his precious blood'.[74] Although there were
resignations, the committee eventually carried the day, and the
hymnal has in fact been widely adopted.[75]

It is an approach that would be strongly supported by the
English-born hymn writer, Brian Wren.[76] He also is worried by

[71] The solution offered in the text is my own. The classical allusion would have
been natural to an eighteenth-century writer. Davie, however, finds its worrying,
and wonders whether Wesley might even have been tempted to continue Malachi
4.2 where it is immediately supplemented (in the AV) by talk of calves growing up
in the stall: *Eighteenth-Century Hymn*, 87–9.

[72] For an account of the creation of modern hymnbooks for the two denominations, see S. A. Marini, *Sacred Song in America* (Chicago: University of Illinois
Press, 2003), 184–212. Conservative Christians are usually happy to adopt inclusive language for human beings, less happy about removing gendered terms from
God.

[73] For the debate about 'Lord': Marini, 197–9.

[74] Marini, *Sacred Song in America*, 199–200. 'Ebenezer' is a reference to 1 Sam.
7.12. In removing the other imagery, the Calvinist roots of the denomination were
also obliterated.

[75] For sales figures, Marini, *Sacred Song in America*, 209–10.

[76] He has spent much of his life in the United States, and is currently Professor
of Worship at Columbia Theological Seminary.

the male authority overtones of 'Lord'.[77] 'Father-like,' he believes, must be balanced by some such phrase as 'mother-like'. 'Kingship' too must go, in favour of a more suitable metaphor such as 'president' that does not smack of unquestioning obedience.[78] Even John Newton's 'Amazing Grace' comes under suspicion because of what he regards as its negative image of the gospel removing blindness, negative at least for those permanently deprived of their sight. By way of contrast he quotes with approval an image of Thomas reading Christ's wounds 'like Braille'.[79]

It is hard not to see all of this as political correctness gone one stage too far. One of the key features of metaphor is surely its inadequacy: that, however rich and illuminating the original comparison may be, it is not literal precisely because inevitably it will break down or fail at some point. It is of the essence of language learnt for application in ordinary human contexts that it will only partially succeed in talking of God. Indeed, that is a theme taken up by hymn writers themselves. John Mason declares of God 'Thou art a sea without a shore,/ A sun without a sphere', while Charles Wesley talks of being 'Plunged in the Godhead's deepest sea,/ And lost in thine immensity'.[80] So it is only to be expected that images will reflect some aspects of meaning of which we may well not approve. Nor will proposed substitutes necessarily fare any better.

New metaphors will simply introduce fresh problems. 'President' may remove the element of tyranny that 'king' sometimes carries with it, but in its turn fails to convey transcendence or otherness.[81] Certainly, American memories of monarchy are much more bound up with oppression than is the case in Britain.[82] Yet, even if one thinks only of the United States, 'president' can

---

[77] B. Wren, *Praying Twice: The Music and Words of Congregational Song* (Louisville: Westminster John Knox Press, 2000), 244–52, esp. 247–9.

[78] For father-like, 317; for king and president, 225–35, esp. 231, 233.

[79] Wren, *Praying Twice*, 179–80.

[80] The Mason quotation is taken from the final verse of his hymn, 'How shall I sing that majesty?'; Wesley's words from his hymn, 'Come, Holy Ghost, all quickening fire'. Ultimately, the imagery is from Augustine: *Confessions* 7. 5, where God is compared to an immense sea permeating every aspect of the world like a sponge.

[81] It is also of course much more difficult to rhyme.

[82] Americans are likely to immediately think of their War of Independence, whereas with monarchy continuing in Britain any oppressive royal actions remain in the dim and distant past.

also exercise a negative role in reminding listeners of just how exclusive rather than inclusive such forms of government can sometimes be.[83] Such conflicting considerations suggest to me that the greater the variety and forms of imagery there are in the hymnbook the better the situation is. In pulling against one another, rival metaphors can then help generate a better balance. In so doing they would function not unlike Scripture itself, where the very diversity and incompatibility of texts enclosed within the same volume, I would argue, helps to keep religious commitment and engagement alive.[84] Part of the problem in America may in any case be a purely practical one. Because American hymnbooks set the words under the music, worshippers never see the poem in the round.[85] The result is that they are much more likely to be fazed by individual words than other nations, though with the increasing use of overhead projectors in Britain and elsewhere this may well change here too.[86]

That is not of course to argue against all change. Because it is taken to suggest the wrong model for children, most modern English hymnbooks omit the verse from Frances Alexander's hymn 'Once in royal David's city' that declares: 'Christian children all must be/ Mild, obedient, good as he.' Similarly, I would argue against 'no crying he makes' in 'Away in a manger' on the grounds that it plays to every parent's fantasy of the child that never disturbs their night hours. What should be presented is a wholly realistic image of a completely normal humanity in the Christ-child. My own support for these two instances might suggest that the principles are really the same in both the English and American case; the only difference is in the degree or extent of change proposed. But there are, I think, important differences. As I tried to indicate above, the right question to pose is not whether something less than the full truth is offered (that will always be the case) but whether

[83] American democracy is essentially a plutocracy, where only the wealthy can get elected, which makes it scarcely surprising that there has never been a president from any of the minority races.
[84] See my argument in *Discipleship and Imagination: Christian Tradition and Truth* (Oxford: Oxford University Press, 2000), 293–342, esp. 295–317.
[85] Brown, *How Hymns Shape our Lives*, 6–7.
[86] In a recent visit to Poland I was astonished to see that the practice had spread to Poland. The white screens look totally out of place in the country's baroque churches.

the resultant imagery helps or hinders access to that reality that is fundamentally other than ourselves. Literal claims are just that, either right or wrong, whereas metaphors are in the nature of the case only ever partially successful.

What I find wrong with the two carols in their original form is precisely what seems to me wrong in the changes now endorsed by the American church. Both draw Christ into our conception of how *we* think things ought to be rather than pulling us in the reverse direction, into seeing our world from a new perspective. Nor is my objection to the excluded psalms any different. It is because they pander to human nature at its most self-centred, with God made to assume the same hates, that they should be rejected. So far from drawing individuals out of themselves, they reinforce their own negative subjectivity. By contrast, imagery that is only partially adequate can still often work on our imaginations, offering engagement, illumination, and challenge.

But there is also another reason why it is important that hymns should not be tampered with too often, and that is because it affects their memorability. George Herbert has often been quoted by hymn writers:

> A verse may find him, who a sermon flies,
> And turn delight into a sacrifice.[87]

Being written in verse of course helps, but that is presumably not quite Herbert's point. Rather, retention in the memory is most effectively secured when significant content is allied with powerful imagery and simple versification. So changing or abandoning the imagery is of no small moment.

In a late essay D. H. Lawrence observed how even 'the rather banal Nonconformist hymns that penetrated through and through my childhood' remained deeply embedded in the consciousness of his later life.[88] If those words suggest no more than the power of early learning by rote, it is clear from the essay as a whole that Lawrence has rather more in mind. While he refuses to concede

---

[87] From the first stanza of 'The Church-Porch' (ll. 5–6): J. Tobin ed., *George Herbert: The Complete Poems* (London: Penguin, 1991), 6.

[88] 'Hymns in a Man's Life' in A. Beal ed., *D. H. Lawrence: Selected Literary Criticism* (London: Heinemann, 1955), 6. The piece was originally written as a newspaper article in 1928, two years before his death.

that they might have conveyed doctrine to the young boy, he readily speaks of a sense of wonder and mystery. There was 'no hardening into the commonplace'.[89] So, although Lawrence as an adult was soon lost to Christianity, a religious sensibility continued to play a significant part in his own creativity.[90] A more recent acknowledgement of the same phenomenon has come from Alan Bennett. As a product of English state education in the 1940s and '50s he admits to retaining a ready memory for the words of hymns from childhood. Although the admission is grudging, clearly for him they have helped in enabling some form of identification with religious belief: 'I have never found it easy to belong. So much repels. Hymns help. They blur.'[91]

Music's Contribution

In such retention in the memory music of course also plays a vital part. Another agnostic like Lawrence can help throw light on the matter. Ralph Vaughan Williams was musical editor for *The English Hymnal*. In his section of the Preface he insists that 'where there is congregational singing it is important that familiar melodies should be employed, or at least those which have stood the test of time'. He therefore objected to new material specially composed for the occasion. At the same time he insisted that 'old favourites' ought not to be a criterion sufficient to itself, since most were likely in any case only to date from 1861.[92] To his mind some of these exhibited a quality of 'music that would not be tolerated in any place of secular entertainment'. So he ranged widely across European and American history in his attempt to find suitable tunes, often employing traditional melodies that hitherto had not had exclusively religious associations, and (despite his earlier admonition) also including some original compositions of his own. While it would be easy to read how Vaughan Williams behaved as largely a matter of musical snobbery, this was far from being so. As he himself expresses the

[89] Ibid. 7.
[90] Not only in 'Christian' novels such as *The Rainbow* (1915) but also in his novel of an alternative religion, *The Plumed Serpent* (1926).
[91] From a talk on Radio 4 (22 December 2001).
[92] The date of the first edition of *Hymns Ancient and Modern*.

matter in a memorable phrase, 'it is indeed a moral rather than a musical issue'. Simplicity was sometimes exactly right, but it was important that words and music should in fact pull in the same direction, conveying the same mood, with the music augmenting the sense of the words rather than simply allowing them to be sung.

As with Lawrence it has become fashionable to talk of Vaughan Williams's 'atheism'.[93] Admittedly, it is a term that the composer did use occasionally of himself. In accepting one such commission he declared that 'there is no reason why an atheist could not write a good Mass'. But more commonly his language is mystical, as when he speaks of the ability of music 'to look through the magic casements and see what lies behind'.[94] The very range and number of his religious compositions does suggest a degree of sympathetic accommodation. Crucially, his *Five Mystical Songs* display an extraordinarily fine ability to place himself in the same frame of mind as a devout poet like Herbert, and so perfectly match words and music. To talk thus of his engagement in the *English Hymnal* as 'down-to-earth, socially minded, humanistic' or as 'a project of cultural, not religious evangelism' thus seems to me quite misguided.[95] Of course he did not subscribe to the specificities of the Church's programme but that did not mean that he could not see himself engaged in opening more general spiritual vistas. If further confirmation is needed, one need only listen once more to his two most famous hymn tunes, *Down Ampney* for Bianco da Siena's 'Come down, O Love divine' and *Sine Nomine* for William Walsham How's 'For all the saints'.[96] One reason why How's poem is deliberately long and drawn-out is to suggest the struggle that was necessary towards the final climax described in the concluding chapters of Revelation.[97] Vaughan Williams captures that mood

[93] e.g. J. Day, *Vaughan Williams* (Oxford: Oxford University Press, 3rd edn., 1998), 30.

[94] Both passages quoted in S. Heffer, *Vaughan Williams* (London: Phoenix, 2000), 54, 11.

[95] Day, *Vaughan Williams*, 30; Heffer, *Vaughan Williams*, 29.

[96] Day's inability to sympathize with the composer on religion is well indicated by the fact that both Walsham How's names have been incorrectly spelled through three editions (cf. 31).

[97] A more practical reason was that the hymn was originally written for a church procession.

exactly in his music's vitality and joy.[98] The repeated Alleluia
adds to that effect (How's original had only one). With Bianco's
images of 'ardour glowing', 'holy flame bestowing', and 'earthly
passions . . . to dust and ashes in its heat consuming' some may argue
that a more robust tune was required for 'Come Down', but that
is to ignore what it is that is coming down—'Love divine'. The
gentle serenity of the music has a rhythm and pattern of phrase
lengths that suggests change but a change that works gradually to
our benefit, a work of love not compulsion.

By contrast, no great search is required to locate the deadening
effect of the arbitrary tune. For example, the common American
practice of singing 'It came upon the midnight clear' to the gently
waltzing or lullaby sound of *Carol* clearly runs counter to the strong
protests in the words against the world's continuing injustices ('two
thousand years of wrong').[99] However, rather than personalizing
matters too far, exactly the same point can be made by arbitrarily
exchanging words and music between any two well-known hymns
where the metres are compatible. A good example to take is 'My
song is love unknown' and 'Ye holy angels bright'.[100] John Darwall's tune (the 148th) is ideal for the latter, as its rising scales and
trumpet-like phrases convey a joyful confidence that matches the
words. However, transferred to 'My song is love unknown', the
effect is to make the crucifixion altogether too easy an achievement, with an almost docetic Christ the result. By contrast, John
Ireland's *Love Unknown*, the tune commonly used for the other
hymn, fits its mood exactly, particularly in the unsettling change
from an E flat to a D flat chord at 'O who am I' and again with
'Then "Crucify!" was all their breath'. The final 'This is my Friend'
then comes as a decisive and welcome relief of tension after such
musical applications in the previous verbal contexts. All that
subtlety goes with Darwall's melody used instead, while if its own

---

[98] Even the title of the composition may suggest Vaughan Williams's more
than nominal engagement, for it is most naturally taken to refer to the great band
of anonymous saints ('without name'): cf. Watson, *Anthology*, 345.

[99] The example is noted in Wren, *Praying Twice*, 345.

[100] Here I am taking up a suggestion made by T. Hone, 'When in our Music
God is Glorified' in J. Astley, T. Hone, and M. Savage eds., *Creative Chords: Studies
in Music, Theology and Christian Formation* (Leominster: Gracewing, 2000), 143–71,
esp. 156–7.

tune is applied to 'Ye holy angels' it introduces a complexity that carries no obvious meaning.

These are but a few examples. Plenty of others could be quoted. For example Hubert Parry's tune for 'Dear Lord and Father of mankind' seems to capture perfectly the mood of the words, not only suggesting a soothing calm but helping to create it. There is a nice irony here since the tune was borrowed from a quite different original use. Even so, it was at the instigation of someone who saw the music's potential, and that use was endorsed by Parry himself.[101] When an entire congregation follows the organ and is reduced to *pianissimo* for the final 'O still small voice of calm', many have spoken of a strong sense of a more than human peace, and that is powerfully conveyed by a composer who was, like Vaughan Williams, himself an agnostic. Again, take a recent popular success, Graham Kendrick's 'Lord, the light of your love is shining'. As the author and composer himself admits, the verses initially made little impact until some considerable time later the chorus occurred to him, 'Shine, Jesus, shine'.[102] There can be no doubt that this is why it became the most popular such song of the 1990s, with words and music alike relevant in accounting for the phenomenon. Musically, the sudden jump of an octave at the chorus helps create confidence and conviction. The basic image, though based on earlier, related precedents, is itself new and startling:

> Shine, Jesus, shine
> Fill this land with the Father's glory,
> Blaze, Spirit, blaze
> Set our hearts on fire.

Of course, extraneous associations may also play their part, but not necessarily, it should be stressed, to the detriment of the possibility of religious experience. 'Guide me, O thou great Jehovah' at rugby matches and 'Abide with me' at the Cup Final may initially seem far removed from any real notion of religion.[103] But,

---

[101] A former pupil and friend, the Director of Music at Repton School, suggested the new use for what Parry had written for his oratorio *Judith*.

[102] Kendrick, *Behind the Songs*, 152.

[103] The Cup Final tradition began in 1927 at the suggestion of the then FA Secretary, Sir Alfred Wall, and with the strong support of George V and Queen Mary: Bradley, *Abide with Me*, 225.

however tangentially the words may first have been appropriated, their very familiarity may help generate quite other reactions than mere crowd camaraderie in other contexts such as weddings or funerals or even a conventional service. If this sounds implausible, it is worth reflecting on the degree to which the popularity of a number of contemporary hymns depends in part on the way in which they have helped provide easier access for those whose main orientation is towards pop music. So, for instance, it is largely thanks to Pat Boone that 'The old rugged cross' became a firm favourite, just as Cat Stevens was crucial to the rise in popularity of 'Morning has broken'.[104] Even Patrick Appleford's 'Living Lord' which was created as part of the parish communion movement had its origins in Cliff Richard's 'Living doll'.[105]

Sometimes this can produce profound ambiguities about what is really meant. While the religious origins of Newton's 'Amazing Grace' are not in question, there seems little doubt that for some in the twentieth century the words became simply a secular celebration of the human capacity for self-recovery.[106] As Judy Collins remarks, 'the melody itself is haunting and healing, even without the transforming words'.[107] Yet it is that very melody that also helped to ensure that the words could continue to challenge and direct towards a more profound meaning, as indeed singers like Collins herself and Aretha Franklin sought to make clear.[108] So in the end that wider use did the song no harm. Instead, it ensured greater longevity for that deeper meaning. In a similar way, melodies from Bach, Handel, Palestrina, Praetorius, and Tallis have helped to draw the lover of classical music into more effective use of the hymn.[109]

[104] A. Barr, *Songs of Praise: The Nation's Favourite Hymns* (London: Lion, 2002), 58, 70.

[105] Ibid., 48.

[106] Stressed in one account of the history of the song: S. Turner, *Amazing Grace* (Oxford: Lion, 2002), 207. Singers have included Rod Stewart (223–5), Yes, Bryan Ferry, and Sinead O'Connor (234–5).

[107] In her introduction to Turner's book, 10–13, esp. 13. The tune (*New Britain*), though composed in 1835, only dates since 1900 in its present form: Turner, *Amazing Grace*, 164 169.

[108] For Franklin, Turner, *Amazing Grace*, 220–2.

[109] A dense but valuable book on the role of music in hymnody is E. Routley, *The Music of Christian Hymnody* (London: Independent Press, 1957).

Range of Experience

Yet leaving open the possibility of that more spiritual experience can also generate a fresh set of tensions in its turn. In the modern Church some are so concerned to create the experience that words and music are reduced to the minimum in the repeated chorus. There is nothing wrong with this in itself. No doubt the resultant experience is often uplifting and helpful. The concern comes when this is the sole diet, for then the persons involved will lack the richness and variety of experience that hymns potentially can provide. On the other hand that potential richness is severely curtailed by many of the hymn's defenders in a false effort to ward off all emotionalism. So, for example, both John Keble and John Ellerton have contributed familiar hymns.[110] Yet both fought shy of any display of emotion, Keble evoking a principle of reserve in matters of religion and Ellerton the necessity of avoiding appeal to the inward and personal in the context of public worship.[111] It is almost as though there was nothing worse than for the singer to be wholly absorbed in the experience of singing some particular hymn. The irony is that such restraint often generates its own form of introspection. Singers now become all too aware of their own personal contribution: whether their own voice is quite in tune, how others round about them are doing, and so on. The result is in effect a Cartesian mind standing apart from the body's performance and assessing it and those around. The issue is surely one of appropriate balance, with both divine praise and reflection on human experience working together to procure rounded individuals giving their lives in trust to God.[112]

Certainly, the totality of the human person needs to be taken more seriously, our emotions no less than our voices, our bodies no less than our minds. It is often forgotten how hymns have in effect movement built into them either through the telling of a story or progression within a theme. So our bodies are actually being encouraged to react and respond, as the story or mood develops.

[110] Keble's best-known hymn is probably 'New every morning is the love' and Ellerton's 'The day thou gavest'.
[111] For further details, Watson, *English Hymn*, 329–31, 399–400.
[112] For a defence of Wesley's success in obtaining such a balance, B. L. Manning, *The Hymns of Wesley and Watts* (London: Epworth, 1942), esp. 28–30.

It is an aspect of song that contemporary evangelicalism now takes more seriously than did its historical antecedents.[113] It is, therefore, a particular pity that in the process no comparable understanding has been given to the work of the Victorians and earlier. Instead, many of the most characteristic Victorian hymns (words and tunes) continue to be marginalized or even abandoned. Yet, while the bodily response may have been implicit rather than dramatic, we know from novels and letters of the time how deeply such hymns could move individuals and affect their composure.

To object that words or tunes are 'sentimental' or 'romantic' or 'overblown' may be true, but one suspects that such comments reflect knee-jerk forms of political correctness rather than any deeply felt critique. Take John Bacchus Dykes. The number of his hymn tunes still appearing in hymnbooks progressively declined as the twentieth century advanced, with even many of these only surviving as alternatives.[114] So, if *Melita* survives absolutely for 'Eternal Father, strong to save' and *Nicaea* for 'Holy, Holy, Holy! Lord God Almighty!', his three once most popular tunes now all appear under threat. Many contemporary hymnbooks list his *Dominus regit me* as only one option for 'The King of love my Shepherd is' (with the Irish melody *St Columba* as alternative), just as *Hollingside* is made to battle it out with Parry's *Aberystwyth* as the right tune for 'Jesu, Lover of my soul'. *Lux Benigna* fares even worse. Once a universal favourite, it is now commonly dropped altogether for Newman's 'Lead, kindly Light' in favour of Harris's *Alberta*.

In the twentieth century *Lux Benigna* has come in for some particularly severe criticism. In his influential work *Oxford Apostles* Geoffrey Faber wrote that 'it needs an effort to dissociate the poem from the dreary, drawling tune fitted to it by the Reverend John Bacchus Dykes'.[115] Again, a number of twentieth-century histories of church music have singled the tune out as representative of Victorian melodies at their worst, over-emotional and excessive in its use of the dominant seventh, 'a chord of fatal fascination to the Victorians'.[116] Newman himself, however, thought that the

---

[113] As in G. Kendrick, *Worship* (Eastbourne: Kingsway, 1984), e.g. 109–10.
[114] The latest supplement to the *English Hymnal, New English Praise* (2006), has, however, reintroduced three of Dykes's tunes.
[115] G. Faber, *The Oxford Apostles* (London: Penguin, 1954), 315.
[116] C. H. Phillips, *The Singing Church* (London: Mowbrays, 1979), 171–2.

popularity of the poem was in large measure due to the quality of the tune.[117] Nor was such admiration for Dykes confined to amateur musicians such as Newman. Sir John Stainer was also strong in his support.[118] Certainly, it must be conceded that with *Alberta* there is a better fit between musical and metrical accent. For example, the hiatus before 'a distant scene' in Dykes's tune disappears. Even so, Dykes enters imaginatively fully into the pessimism of Newman's mood at the time and so through the music helps to transcend it. Indeed, Dykes's music even seems to capture something of the context in which the poem was originally created, Newman storm-tossed on the Bay of Biscay.

The same point about imaginative range might also be made by consideration of a quite different sort of ecclesiastical tradition, the evangelical fervour behind the compositions of Dwight Moody and Ira Sankey. These two American evangelists (Moody was the preacher and Sankey the singer) had a huge impact through their missions to Britain in the early 1870s. They are even credited with finally securing acceptance of the organ into Scottish churches.[119] More relevant here is the fact that thanks to their influence certain types of hymns about conversion now found a place in more conventional hymnbooks.[120] In the case of the *English Hymnal*, for example, such songs were included in a section at the end entitled 'For Mission Services' and with the explicit caveat 'not for ordinary use'.[121] Modern hymnbooks seldom resort to such a division. Nonetheless some such hymns have successfully migrated elsewhere.[122] It is a pity that others have not.[123] However, less important than the relative merits of which have survived and

---

[117] J. T. Fowler, *Life and Letters of John Bacchus Dykes* (London, 1897), 104.

[118] For relevant quotation, Bradley, *Abide with Me*, 203.

[119] For the story of the Barclay Free Church organ, Bradley, *Abide with Me*, 181–2.

[120] Sankey wrote many of his own hymns. It is a pity therefore that, on the CD in the Kingsway Hymn Makers series devoted to his music, all are to compositions by other authors.

[121] Could the explanation lie in Vaughan Williams's snobbishness about the type of music being advocated?

[122] 'I heard the voice of Jesus say'; 'O Jesus, I have promised'; 'Stand up! Stand up for Jesus'; 'Thou didst leave thy throne and thy kingly crown'.

[123] Gone from the New English Hymnal are the following: 'Take my life and let it be/ Consecrated, Lord, to thee'; 'Safe in the arms of Jesus'; 'Tell me the old, old story'; 'There were ninety and nine' (the music in this case Sankey's own).

which not is the issue of how in actual fact such hymns once functioned and might continue to do so. Despite the suggestion of that early edition of the *English Hymnal* that they were really only significant for those about to change stance, subsequent research has tended to suggest that their real function is as a way of keeping the experience of conversion alive: a means of ensuring that an earlier enthusiasm does not grow dim.[124]

Hymns can of course play a number of other roles not directly related to questions of experience. Several of Frances Alexander's surviving hymns, for example, were originally intended as part of a series giving children instruction in the Apostles' Creed.[125] Again, even those that are about experience may on occasion function as reminders of past experience rather than as instigators to more of the same. But none of this justifies the reticence about experience that has characterized so much of the history of hymnody. Whatever the intention, Alexander's 'All things bright and beautiful' could still initiate an experience of God through creation, just as 'There is a green hill far away' might instigate a fresh encounter, through story, with the crucified Lord. Indeed, one of the intriguing things about these two hymns is that whereas the latter has in effect migrated to become an adult hymn and that is perhaps one reason why its original Victorian melody has survived, each generation of children seems to want a new tune for 'All things bright and beautiful' that more nearly touches their own experience.[126] So the first widely known tune by W. H. Monk has long since gone, and been replaced by *Royal Oak* by Martin Shaw (d. 1958). Even that has been displaced, for listeners at least, by John Rutter's anthem version. Not that there is only ever one right way of establishing such contact with God through nature. If Mrs Alexander offers to the child a gentle hand in nature, it is the ordered, reasonable character of the divine creation that is there for contemplation in Joseph Addison's 'The spacious firmament on high'. Stuart Hine's 'How great thou art' offers a complete contrast. Here it is the more awesome and unpredictable that is stressed:

[124] J. Kent, *Holding the Fort: Studies in Victorian Revivalism* (London: Epworth, 1978), 225; Watson, *English Hymn*, 491.

[125] Apart from the two mentioned in the text, note 'Once in royal David's city' and 'He is risen, he is risen!'

[126] Though the Victorian melody paired with it only acquired that association twenty years after the hymn's composition.

'mighty thunder' and 'lofty mountain grandeur' replace Addison's 'reason's ear'.[127]

Instead of lamenting the variety of such theologies, to my mind we should welcome them. They are not necessarily inconsistent. They can help feed different characters or the same character in different moods. Indeed, compilers of hymnbooks implicitly recognize this in the range of denomination and churchmanship upon which they draw, far broader than in any other church context. Because from our own espoused theological perspective particular hymns seem less than entirely adequate, this should not be taken to entail that the attempt should therefore be made to preclude their use. They can still open vistas, however partial. Indeed, their very lack of density in a particular direction may well make the limited imagery they employ more readily accessible. So, for example, three hymns by Unitarians have made it into most modern hymnbooks: 'Nearer, my God, to thee', 'City of God, how broad and far', and, perhaps most surprisingly of all, 'It came upon the midnight clear'. Again, an extreme evangelical like F. R. Havergal with her 'Take my life and let it be' is made to sit alongside Matthew Bridges' deliberately provocative image of Mary as 'mystic rose' in his 'Crown him with many crowns'. Two explicit statements of directly opposed theological positions can even find their way into the same hymnbook. Charles Wesley's Arminianism stood in opposition to Whitefield's strong Calvinist doctrine of predestination. Yet Wesley's famous conversion hymn about free grace available to all, 'And can it be?' is now found jostling for place with 'Rock of Ages'.[128] That hymn was written by a devoted disciple of Whitefield and intended to reflect his theology of everything thrown onto an incomprehensible and arbitrary divine decision.[129] Hymns are also sometimes suborned for quite different purposes from what their author intended. So, for example, nowadays 'The Church's one foundation' is quite commonly sung at ecumenical gatherings, whereas its original intention was precisely to exclude a particular

---

[127] One suspects that few singers now realize that 'reason's ear' was intended as a substitute for the now discredited 'harmony of the spheres'.

[128] Strictly speaking, another less familiar hymn was the one written most immediately after his conversion: Watson, *Anthology*, 165.

[129] For the background to Augustus Montague Toplady's hymn, Brooks, *Hymns as Homilies*, 81–97. He once described Charles's brother, John, as 'a low and puny tadpole in divinity' (87).

type of Christian: the liberal modernizer as represented by Bishop Colenso of Natal.[130]

The sad thing, though, is that in some ways the present range of hymnody is still altogether too narrow. Certainly when measured against the psalms there appears to be continued reluctance to explore the whole range of human emotion and experience. Quite a few writers of the past wrote in pain or suffering. Unfortunately, that often expressed itself in advocacy of simple acceptance of the divine will rather than any serious attempt to struggle through towards such acceptance, surely more characteristic of human experience. Thus one would never dream that Rinkart's 'Now thank we all our God' was in fact written during a severe outbreak of plague, or that Charlotte Elliott's 'Just as I am, without one plea' hid beneath it a more rebellious nature that had compared her illness to a difficult, demanding husband.[131] In particular, one looks almost in vain for more negative emotions, such as bewilderment and sorrow, far less anger against God. Possible exceptions from the traditional repertoire might include 'O Love that will not let me go' and 'O for a closer walk with God'.[132] John Bell of the Iona Community finds the lack especially prominent in the modern chorus tradition, which seems reluctant to move beyond praise and confidence.[133] Yet space is needed to work through the more negative emotions, if a false optimism is to be avoided. As an example Bell offers one of his own hymns, written for a mother who had lost her handicapped child an hour or so after birth:

> So through the mess of anger, grief and tiredness,
> Through tensions which are not yet reconciled
> We give to God the worship of our sorrow
> And our dear child.[134]

[130] The subject of major controversy in the 1860s. For more details about the hymn, Watson, *Anthology*, 338–9.

[131] For Rinkart's hymn, Watson, *Anthology*, 73–4. If *The Invalid's Hymn Book* (1836) made Elliott famous, some of the verse in her *Thoughts in Verse on Sacred Subjects* (1869) tells a rather different tale about her real attitudes. I am indebted to Nancy Cho for drawing this to my attention.

[132] A recent addition to some hymnbooks is 'We lay our broken world in sorrow . . . As if you were not there'.

[133] 'The lost tradition of lament' in S. Darlington and A. Kreider eds., *Composing Music for Worship* (Norwich: Canterbury Press, 2003), 104–16, esp. 107–11.

[134] Ibid. 114; the penultimate verse of 'We cannot care for you the way we wanted'.

Another area where more effort has of late been expended is in producing hymns that offer a political and social vision. They are still, however, in relatively short supply, often hidden under sections such as 'National' or 'Kingdom of God' where they fight for space with sentiments of a quite different kind. It can be useful to measure one tradition against another. In *God and Grace of Body* I explored at some length African American experience of song in the United States.[135] There my argument was that blues, jazz, soul, and even rap can all, to varying degrees, be seen as a response to the failure of the gospel music tradition to continue consideration of the range of experience that had once found its way into the spiritual. The dilemmas and anxieties of ordinary human living were now reflected elsewhere. Nor was this done without reference to religion. All the genres just mentioned have achieved significant spiritual expression. The tragedy was that it was now an exploration that largely existed outside the Church. There is the same danger in more conventional hymnody. It will only appeal to a limited range within the population at large, if its metaphors remain firmly fixed in the past and the issues it focuses on are deliberately uncontroversial. Traditions flourish by being dynamic and creative, not by simply holding firm to the past.

Those who write new hymns today are quite commonly aware of the complexities of this past history, even if they choose to ignore its potential implications for their own present practice. In the case of the issues that will be our concern in the following chapter, however, such knowledge seems largely lost. Few clergy are aware of the history of preaching. Even academics frequently contrast the verbal and visual in a way that lacks all plausible foundation.

[135] *God and Grace of Body: Sacrament in Ordinary* (Oxford: Oxford University Press, 2007), ch. 7.

4
Verbal and Visual Images

INEVITABLY, such a chapter heading will strike most readers at first sight as a strange and improbable amalgam of ideas: two quite different sorts of things treated as though they were one. But, if I am right about words thus far, the traditional Protestant contrast between words and images cannot be allowed to stand. Words are potentially just as seductive as images, and so inherently in just as much danger of misleading the worshipper into idolatry as any visual image. The preacher has the ability to entice the listener into as corrupting and controlling an image of God as any construct offered by artist or sculptor. If that is the negative side of the equation that I want to suggest here, the positive is the capacity of a good preacher's words to act just as sacramentally as any image: to draw the listener into an experience of the God who is always present and ready to address us, whenever opportunity presents itself. So what I want to do is approach the issue by three stages: first, examining the positive sacramental side of preaching; then, offering a comparison with the earlier, largely but by no means exclusively monastic tradition of illuminated books; before, finally, providing some assessment of the relative likelihood of either verbal or visual degenerating into idolatry.

Preaching as Sacrament

From one perspective at least, modern Roman Catholic theology could be viewed as having been in implicit revolt for some time against the medieval obsession with a rather narrow set of words as determinative of sacramental validity.[1] What the various movements from the nineteenth century onwards and into the twentieth (most

[1] As discussed in the final section of Ch. 1. The Ceciliam movement, Solesmes and what happens thereafter are examined in Ch. 6.

notably at this time the Benedictine communities at Maria Laach in Germany and at Collegeville, Minnesota) all implicitly demonstrated through their desire for liturgical reform was recognition of the fact that divine presence is mediated not primarily through formal acts alone but by the general 'feel' of the liturgy as a whole. If in earlier days there was considerable caution and reserve about how this might be best expressed and a strong tendency to look for precedents in the past (as in the nineteenth-century Cecilian movement and at Solesmes), more recent writing has accepted the need for a major reorientation. The focus should no more be simply on the two traditional loci of Catholic eucharistic thinking (the elements and the priest as *in persona Christi*) but also on Christ's presence in the word proclaimed and in the gathered assembly. Seen in that way, it is suggested the notion of presence then gets subtly modified. Instead of the presence *of* Christ, we get his presence *to* the worshipper, or in other words a theology of encounter through various media rather than a theology of one static location.[2]

One recent work has sought to use literary theory in order to work out the implications of this change of emphasis in relation to preaching.[3] Since the 1980s the movement known as 'new historicism' had sought to ground the study of literature firmly in the context of the wider culture of its time: text requires context in order to be understood. One of its main advocates, Stephen Greenblatt, demonstrated how the theatre of Shakespeare is so much better understood when set against the backdrop of a Renaissance culture where theatricality in general played a large role.[4] Although most of such writing would be highly critical of any attempt to introduce a transcendent dimension, such a parallel with theatre is potentially illuminating. Understanding a text requires locating it in its original wider context just as much as in that of its immediate, present performance. Similarly, the words of the liturgy can have no trans-historical privilege: whether they

[2] The terminology and contrast comes from David Power, *The Eucharistic Mystery* (New York: Crossroad, 1992), 321–2.

[3] Paul Janowiak, *The Holy Preaching: The Sacramentality of the Word in the Liturgical Assembly* (Collegeville, Minnesota: Liturgical Press, 2000), esp. pt. II.

[4] In his *Shakespearean Negotiations* (1988) Greenblatt argues that pageant and public ceremony were crucial in negotiating power relationships in Elizabethan England and that this is carried over into the plays where economic and political realities are not only reflected but sometimes also subtly changed.

effect encounter or not will also be a matter of the overall context of their performance. The earlier literary theory known as reader-response (particularly associated with Stanley Fish) could also be used to raise similar pertinent questions. What effect the sermon has is a function not only of the listener and his specific situation but also of the wider interpretative community of which both preacher and listener are part.[5]

Critical questions can certainly be raised regarding such a line of argument, not least respecting the perils of assuming that presence is mediated in sermon, liturgy, and sacred elements all in the same way or without any having priority over the other. Seeing grace in terms of encounter and so of a presence *to* has its undoubted strengths. But, as in our own human interchanges, presence *to* remains parasitic on presence *of*, that the individual encountered exists in their own right, whether that be a hand's breadth away or at the end of a telephone line or computer message, for example. So more conventional discussions of eucharistic presence cannot, I believe, be entirely circumvented by such terminology, nor have I attempted to do so when discussing eucharistic presence.[6] None-theless, this should not be used to undermine the undoubted importance of the points being made. However objectively true it is that Christ has guaranteed to be present under the eucharistic elements in any validly performed mass, subjectively the sense of that presence will inevitably be inhibited for the believer, the more the rest of the liturgy, including the sermon, seems to run counter to that sense of presence. Put more positively, there is no reason why we should not speak of the other aspects of the liturgy, including the sermon, carrying that presence in their own right, even if in a different way. But how exactly?

In Catholic circles the sermon is now quite commonly spoken of as an area of 'sacramental encounter'.[7] This is not a narrowly Catholic idea. If anything, the notion is more frequent in Protestant writers than in Catholic, not least perhaps because it offers an obvious way of stressing the importance of the sermon. So, for

    [5] Janowiak notes the various changes in Fish's position over the years: *Holy Preaching*, 129–59, esp. 144–7.

    [6] See *God and Grace of Body: Sacrament in Ordinary* (Oxford: Oxford University Press, 2007), esp. 390–423.

    [7] e.g. Janowiak, *Holy Preaching*, 159.

example, in providing a guide to sermon writing in the 1950s one leading evangelical of the day chose to entitle his book: *Royal Sacrament: The Preacher and his Message*. Justifying the title, he observes: 'The ultimate aim of preaching is to give Christ. He is offered in words; He may be received in Person. Thus preaching is a sacrament.'[8] In similar vein Evelyn Underhill observes that 'the word is for Evangelical worship something as objective, holy and given as the Blessed Sacrament is for Roman Catholic worship. Indeed, it is a sacrament; the sensible garment in which the supra-sensible Presence is clothed.'[9] If the language chosen betrays that Underhill was not herself an Evangelical, her intuition is exactly right. As a more recent writer observes, a sacramental view of the sermon dominated Calvinist understanding of the sermon in Scotland, even if the term was seldom used.[10]

For some such talk will undoubtedly be to exalt the sermon one stage too far. Surprisingly perhaps given his high doctrine of the Word, Karl Barth would be among their number. For him the sermon like the actual fallible words of Scripture should never be confused with Christ himself. So at most the sermon mediates a possibility of encounter, but is not itself that encounter as such.[11] That may seem a wise thing to say in the light of the present practice of preaching which seems almost deliberately to set itself at one remove from such an encounter. Wildly generalizing, contemporary English sermons may be broadly divided into two main categories: the short homily that begins with a secular illustration before branching out into some aspect of morals or doctrine, and biblical exposition where the details of a specific passage are pursued at rather more length. While both types have their place, it is a great pity that the Church has artificially narrowed its options. What is thereby ignored is Christian theology's earlier deep engagement

[8] R. A. Ward, *Royal Sacrament: The Preacher and his Message* (London: Marshall, Morgan & Scott, 1958), 22. For similar views from Bishop S. C. Neill: 'the Word once more becomes flesh' (quoted, p. 23).
[9] E. Underhill, *Worship* (Guildford: Eagle, 1991 edn.), 211.
[10] D. Read, 'The Scottish Tradition of Preaching' in D. Forrester and D. Murray eds., *Studies in the History of Worship in Scotland* (Edinburgh: T & T Clark, 2nd edn., 1996), 149–57, esp. 150.
[11] Principles enunciated by Barth in a number of different places. For a helpful summary, B. Lang, *Sacred Games: A History of Christian Worship* (New Haven: Yale University Press, 1997), 180–9, esp. 181–2.

with the classical traditions of rhetoric and thus with the type of means that might be employed to help an audience inhabit the same world as the text, and so ultimately also that of the God who lay behind it. If that suggests only a looking to the past, it needs to be noted that such narrowing also represents a failure to confront contemporary culture. Successful communication demands that the two worlds meet, and so the need also to measure the sermon against effective forms of communication in our own day.

To appreciate the value of that earlier engagement with rhetoric, something needs first to be said on where as a culture we now stand. It is commonplace to be told that society has once more returned to being a visual culture, bombarded as we are now by a constant stream of images in advertising and on our television and computer screens.[12] Thinkers of a more Protestant slant often lament this fact, seeing in the phenomenon a return to the temptations of idolatry. Jacques Ellul, for example, informs us: 'The *invisible* God came as *word*. He cannot be recognised by sight. Nothing about Jesus indicated divinity in a visual way.'[13] That is an objection that I will attempt to answer later in this chapter. Suffice it to say here that any appeal to Paul's declaration that 'faith comes by hearing and hearing by the word of God' can not only easily be balanced by matching scriptural quotations on the other side but also by the fact that, as I have been seeking to emphasize throughout this work, the language of the Bible is itself heavily dependent on visual imagery.[14] Barth himself was notorious for objecting to any help from visual aids in the construction of church buildings. He successfully opposed the installation of stained glass in Basle Cathedral. Much admired by him was one modern German church that might be most naturally characterized as more like a lecture hall than place of worship.[15] Yet Barth was concerned to use in his preaching both

[12] For an unusual and challenging argument for its appropriate impact on preaching through an examination of how radio has adapted to this new world (including the Radio 4 programme *Thought for the Day*): J. P. Mitchell, *Visually Speaking: Radio and the Renaissance of Preaching* (Edinburgh: T & T Clark, 1999).
[13] J. Ellul, *The Humiliation of the Word* (Grand Rapids, Mich.: Eerdmans, 1985), 56.
[14] Rom. 10.17 (AV); Ellul, *Humiliation of the Word*, 80–1. 1 John 1.1–2 mentions not only hearing but also sight and touch.
[15] Lang, *Sacred Games*, 185–7. Included is a photograph of the interior of this church that Barth so admired: the Reformed Christuskirche at Eiserfeld.

the latest biblical scholarship and his deep knowledge of the history and theology of the Church. Where, however, like many others, he drew the line was in translation exercises, attempting to put inherited concepts into more modern images. The Bible must in some sense be allowed to speak for itself. Otherwise, it is another gospel that is being proclaimed.

That this is sometimes the result can hardly be denied. Dietrich Bonhoeffer was profoundly shocked at the results of such a strategy in the famous Riverside Church in New York where H. E. Fosdick was the celebrated incumbent minister.[16] But, equally, some contemporary applications of the alternative approach scarcely fare any better. It is only necessary to recall how often obscure passages of Scripture have been read in church without any form of introduction. Indeed, not uncommonly readers continue to fail to supply the identity even of a 'he' or 'she' in the assigned passage, for no other reason than that this has not been supplied within the relevant verses. Again, to give a more specific example, think of how seldom the meaning of 'Immanuel' is provided when Isaiah 7 is read in church. Yet Matthew had no hesitation is so doing when he quotes the passage in his Gospel.[17] In effect, under such circumstances the text is being treated with the same kind of superstitious reverence that such readers would no doubt unequivocally condemn, if applied to statues or relics of saints. Nor are such faults confined to the relatively unlearned or to the parish clergy. The modern penchant for accuracy above all else means that, when read in modern translations, the text sometimes comes across as little more than a poorly wrought and uncouth piece of work.[18] In this such translations contrast markedly with the principles behind the 1611 Authorized Version. Not only is Paul's poor sentence structure gone and the Book of Revelation's mistakes in elementary grammar, but also in their place a real attempt is made at a dignified literary style.

---

[16] For Fosdick's ministry and principles in preaching, Lang, *Sacred Games*, 189–96. For Bonhoeffer's negative comment, 196.

[17] Matt. 2.23: 'Emmanuel, which means God with us.'

[18] This is not an argument against modern translations as such but rather for the need to consider carefully the use to which they are being put. Using repeatedly the same word in English for the same Hebrew word is useful to a student of the text, but in a language as rich as literary English it jars when read, bordering almost on the trite.

The Bible is in fact like any other text in being dependent for its effectiveness on the way in which it is presented. This does not make it any less a divine instrument. But it does mean that, just as the biblical writers had to reflect on how best to communicate in their day, so does the contemporary Church in its own quite different circumstances. That is why Kierkegaard's injunction that the Bible is best read on one's own and in private seems so ill-conceived.[19] Of course, if some preliminary guidance has been sought, it can be done. But the natural tendency of the human mind to wander down familiar tracks will usually prevent profound challenges from being heard. Instead, powerful external stimuli are needed to draw us from where we currently are to where under God's grace we might be. That is one reason why C. S. Lewis thought imagery so integral to the sermon. His powerful wartime analogy for the incarnation, for example, was not intended to substitute for Scripture but it was meant to awaken or heighten the sense of its potential relevance.[20] Some recent writers have suggested borrowing from the techniques of cameramen and film makers: presenting a parable, for example, from a series of different angles, or structuring the sermon like a movie plot with an element of reversal, or the unexpected kept till the end.[21] Such strategies might well sometimes be successful in generating an appropriate imaginative response. Certainly, they should not be despised simply because it is a secular source from which such ideas come.

Yet, surprisingly among those acquainted with the history of the sermon, it is more likely the amateurishness of modern discussions that will be most noticed, when compared with the professionalism that once marked such debates. Perhaps that is just an inevitable

[19] Stressed in his *For Self-Examination* of 1851: 'he who is not alone with God's Word is not reading God's Word'; *For Self-Examination and Judge for Yourselves* (Princeton: Princeton University Press, 1941), 55. In his *Journals* he even criticizes Peter's Pentecost sermon for attempting the conversion of 3,000 individuals at one go (Acts 2.14–41).

[20] God is described as 'landing in this enemy-occupied world in disguise and starting a sort of secret society to undermine the devil': *Broadcast Talks* (London: Geoffrey Bles, 1942), 61.

[21] The second example comes from E. L. Lowry, *The Homiletical Plot: The Sermon as Narrative Art Form* (Nashville: Abingdon, 1980), esp. 22–3. The former is suggested by D. Buttrick, *Homiletic: Moves and Structures* (Philadelphia: Fortress, 1987), 55–6; R. L. Eslinger, *Narrative and Imagination: Preaching the Worlds That Shape Us* (Minneapolis: Fortress, 1995), e.g. 145.

result of the relative brevity of the modern sermon. When previous generations had to endure one or even two hours, strategy and content were matters of no small moment. Not that sermons in the past were without their problems. The prints of Hogarth and others of sleeping congregations alert us to a phenomenon as old as the New Testament itself. Eutychus set an early precedent when he fell asleep during a sermon of St Paul.[22] Even in more believing times preachers were also not above lamenting the tedium of their task: 'What pleasure is there in addressing plebeian ears and yawning circles of females about some trite biblical histories in long and lifeless periods?'[23]

But there was another side. Despite the remarks just quoted, Caussin pursues at length how best to communicate, as does his contemporary George Herbert, who recommends, as well as earnestness as a way of gaining the congregation's attention, a careful fixing of the eye on each of one's auditors in turn: 'letting them know', as he puts it, that the preacher observes 'who marks and who not'. Due attention is also given to various specific techniques such as storytelling, apostrophe, and dramatic figures.[24] In such high regard did another seventeenth-century figure, John Donne (Dean of St Paul's), regard the sermon that he even insisted on getting up from his deathbed to deliver his final oration, regarded by many as his best.[25] If deemed too severely intellectual in content, auditors had the choice of walking along to Paul's Cross instead. There they could hear an outdoor sermon, where the preaching often lasted as long as two hours and yet was heard by upwards of six thousand spectators.[26] 'Spectator' is used advisedly, as it was not just a matter of words. There could also be some dramatic actions, such

[22] For Eutychus, Acts 20.9. For two versions of Hogarth's *The Sleeping Congregation* (from 1728 and 1736), M. Webster, *Hogarth* (London: Studio Vista, 1978), 16, 17. Cranach the Elder could be used to provide examples from Germany.

[23] Translated from N. Caussin, *De eloquentia sacra et humana* (Paris, 3rd edn., 1630), 889–90 in D. K. Shuger, *Sacred Rhetoric: The Christian Grand Style in the English Renaissance* (Princeton: Princeton University Press, 1988), 156.

[24] G. Herbert, *The Country Parson*, in *The Country Parson, The Temple* (New York: Paulist Press, 1981), 62–4, esp. 62.

[25] The story is retold in B. Crockett, *The Play of Paradox: Stage and Sermon in Renaissance England* (Philadelphia: University of Pennsylvania Press, 1995), 141–3. The relevant sermon is 'Death's Duell'.

[26] For further details, Crockett, *Play of Paradox*, 38–41, 77–8. For the penitent sometimes outwitting the preacher, 73–4.

as the exposure of allegedly miracle-working relics or the public humiliation of a notorious sinner.

This might suggest undue preoccupation with technique. Certainly, the danger was that aesthetic pleasure in the performance would take priority over whatever was intended to be mediated through that performance. Repeated reminders, however, were given throughout Christian history of such potentials for corruption.[27] So, as pagan studies of the strategies of rhetoric were appropriated, they were also significantly modified.[28] It is not impossible that Luke himself had had some such training.[29] His own life coincided with the very beginnings of the great rhetorical movement known as the Second Sophistic (*c.*60–230 AD).[30] Although now largely forgotten, it was a time when the most prestigious form of literary activity in the ancient Greek world became identified with oratory. As a result rhetoric became an indispensable element in the ordinary educational curriculum, and technical terms such as epideictic and ekphrasis part of common parlance.[31] Examples both good and bad of Christian appropriation are not wanting. Contemporary with the movement's flowering, the Apologist Tatian is found, ironically, using the techniques of rhetoric to denounce its practice, while Melito of Sardis' famous Easter Sermon is as elaborate as the style Plato had denounced in the sophists generations earlier. Nor did its influence cease once its most famous advocates were dead. The Cappadocian Fathers had studied under the pagan Himerius, some of whose rather stilted declamations

[27] It was by no means only a Christian concern. Both Aristotle and Quintilian had warned that drawing attention to skill could only detract from the primary purpose of the oration: Aristotle, *Rhetoric* 3. 2. 4; Quintilian, *Institutio Oratoria* 9. 3. 102.

[28] For a general survey: G. A. Kennedy, *Classical Rhetoric and its Christian and Secular Tradition* (Chapel Hill: University of North Carolina Press, 2nd edn., 1999).

[29] For a study of possible influences from rhetoric on the Gospels, B. L. Mack and V. K. Robbins, *Patterns of Persuasion in the Gospels* (Sonoma, Calif.: Polebridge, 1989).

[30] The term was coined by Philostratus in his *Lives of the Sophists*. The largest surviving corpus comes from Aelius Aristides, who, significantly for Christianity, begins the practice of including hymns to the gods.

[31] The former gained early currency. Contrasted with judicial and deliberative forms of oratory, it delineated speeches of praise or blame. Ekphrasis is detailed literary description of any object, real or imaginary, such as the oft-quoted example of the shield of Achilles from the *Iliad*, or, a millennium later, Paulus Silentarius on the church of Hagia Sophia.

survive. While the sermons of Gregory of Nyssa and of Basil on the Psalms suggest a primary interest in the exposition of Scripture, quite different is Basil's *Hexaemeron* (on the six days of creation) or Gregory Nazianzen's surviving works.[32] The latter's famous Five Theological Orations are heavily indebted to the techniques of forensic debate, while the influence of the panegyric is to be seen in his festal sermons. Although sometimes disparaging about rhetoric, his comments, like Tatian's, seem mere ploy.[33] More moderate in style than Himerius, his addresses must at times have been highly effective in engaging the attention of his audience.[34] Even with John Chrysostom ('Golden mouth'), although most of his sermons are exegetical, others (such as the twenty-one Sermons on the Statues) do disclose the deliberate employment of some of the central established principles of oratory (among them variety) as a means of engaging his audience.[35]

It was Augustine, however, who was to make the decisive difference in insisting that reason or argument in itself was never enough. He himself had been a professor of rhetoric, and so he knew the power of oratory.[36] Admittedly in his only extended discussion there is some equivocation, with him at times appearing to suggest that all that matters is prayer and dependence on the divine will.[37] But on the whole, as with his treatment of medicine, he assumes the principle of multiple causation. So, if God remains the ultimate cause, the specific methods of rhetoric may also play their part.[38] This is not least because the will has also to be moved, and for that an emotional commitment in love is necessary.[39]

[32] For an analysis of Basil's debt, H. O. Old, *The Reading and Preaching of the Scriptures* (Grand Rapids: Eerdmans, 1998), ii. 45–61.

[33] J. McGuckin, *Saint Gregory of Nazianzus: An Intellectual Biography* (Crestwood, NY: St Vladimir's Seminary Press, 2001), 42–3.

[34] As with the watchtower image that opens an Easter sermon: *Oration* 45. 1.

[35] Others include parallelism, antitheses, chiasmus, apostrophe, and so on. See further, T. E. Ameringer, 'The Stylistic Influence of the Second Sophistic in the Panegyrical Sermons of Saint John Chrysostom', *Patristic Studies* 2 (Catholic University of America, 1922); H. M. Hubbell, 'Chrysostom and Rhetoric', *Classical Philology* 19 (1924), 261–76.

[36] For a helpful discussion of this influence, Kennedy, *Classical Rhetoric*, 171–82.

[37] His major discussion occurs in Book IV of *De doctrina Chistiana*. For everything depending on God making possible a good speech: 4. 63.

[38] *De doctrina* 4. 33.

[39] A theme throughout Augustine's writings: e.g. *De doctrina* 4. 27; *De civitate Dei* 14. 6–7; *Confessions* 13. 9. Arguably, Book IV of *De doctrina* was intended to be set against the backdrop of Book I, where love is made central.

So persuasion was just as integral as argument to the preacher's task. In this, imagery was of special importance, as the divinely appointed means of drawing the distant and strange close.[40]

Thanks to New Testament usage *pistis* is now automatically identified in our minds with faith. In Greek, however, *pistis* means suasion as much as faith. *Kerygma* or proclamation was thus not enough. The suasion of rhetoric is also necessary if subjectively this is to become faith. It is perhaps, therefore, not surprising that in the early centuries of our era Greeks in particular continued to explore how the classical rhetorical tradition might be modified in a religious direction. What might be meant by an elevated style suitable to a subject that evokes awe was explored at some length by both pagan and Christian writers, with numinosity, wonder, and sublimity now all common themes.[41] It also becomes a theme of literary criticism, most famously perhaps in Longinus' work *On the Sublime*. Once dated to the third century, the work is now commonly assigned to the first.[42] Of particular interest to Jewish and Christian readers is the author's inclusion of the opening of Genesis as an example of good style.[43] More relevant here is the general argument that sublimity needs to be supplemented by a strong emotional component.[44] If the medieval period shows less interest in rhetoric, the Renaissance demonstrated a return to such concerns.[45] Both Protestant and Catholic writers produced textbooks, and that practice continued well into the nineteenth century.[46]

---

[40] *De doctrina* 2. 1–3.

[41] Shuger, *Sacred Rhetoric*, 38–41.

[42] For detailed discussion of the issue, D. A. Russell, '*Longinus' On the Sublime* (Oxford: Clarendon, 1964), xxii–xxx.

[43] At 9. 9. Although set in the midst of examples from Homer, there is no reason to suspect an interpolation or doubt that the choice comes from the original author.

[44] Something that had been denied by the first-century BC 'Attic' rhetorician Caecilius of Calacte (in Sicily), to whom Longinus sees himself as responding.

[45] Although textbooks were produced in the Middle Ages, the focus moved to content rather than its ability or otherwise to convert an audience: Kennedy, *Classical Rhetoric*, 196–225, esp. 225. So expository sermons were the norm, even in contexts where one might have expected more care in addressing a specific audience, as with the Franciscans: Old, *Reading and Preaching of Scriptures*, iii. 341–86, esp. 352–6.

[46] The last important British textbook primarily on the rhetoric of preaching was Richard Whateley's *Elements of Rhetoric* of 1828.

Among the Reformers Calvin is conservative in following the medieval principle of unadorned expository preaching. It is Luther who is the more innovative, not least because of his own engagement with writings on rhetoric. Quintilian was apparently his favourite author.[47] His successor Melanchthon actually wrote a textbook on the subject.[48] Given my earlier reference to theatre, particularly fascinating to observe are the parallels drawn by a number of writers, especially for the period from 1550 to 1650. The point is not that the preacher has become a sort of actor with corresponding histrionic gestures (though there is some of this), but rather (and more interestingly) that there are certain parallels in aim. The theatre is concerned not only to allow spectators for a brief space to inhabit a different world but also by thus changing perspectives to open up the possibility of a permanent change of perspective. So too is the sermon on this view a theatre of the ear, as it were. The theatre uses a combination of visual and verbal imagery to engage and challenge its audience, in which the acting can, fortunately, still produce an impact even where the words float far above the hearers' intellect. The preacher, however, must rely on the words alone, and so an intensification of the actor's skills is required. What could be both in the field of vision and before the mind's eye must now be conjured before the mind's eye alone.

That parallel may still seem tendentious until it is recalled that both play and sermon began to exercise a larger role in society about the same time, and that by no means all Christians saw them as opposed. Indeed, even some who might be labelled Puritan admitted the stage's potential, among them John Foxe of *Book of Martyrs* fame.[49] So it is perhaps not surprising that some writers on rhetoric explicitly draw the analogy. The preacher should declaim 'as in a theatre' and 'introduce God and Christ commanding'. The congregation's eye should be 'surrounded with various striking details and circumstances' such that 'carried outside itself, it seems to behold the event as if placed in its midst'.[50]

---

[47] For Luther's use of rhetoric, U. Nembach, *Predigt des Evangeliums, Luther als Prediger, Pädagoge und Rhetor* (Neukirchen-Vluyn: Neukirchener Verlag, 1972), 124–72.

[48] His early *Elementorum rhetorices*. It exercised a continuing influence on his own thought, as well as that of others.

[49] Crockett, *Play of Paradox*, 7, 163 fn. 20.

[50] Translated from B. Keckermann, *Rhetoricae ecclesiasticae* (1616); quoted in Shuger, *Sacred Rhetoric*, 91.

Major figures of the time endorsed such a view of the sermon in which a distinctive use of imagination, literary figures, and emotion set it apart from the ordinary lecture form. Agricola's work of 1480 and Erasmus' of 1535 set firm precedents in insisting that such concerns did not mean a loss of structure, reason, and order. Rather, these were to be integrated into a larger whole.[51] Their subordinate place, however, did ensure that such forms came under increasing suspicion during the Enlightenment. Thereafter two extremes tended to dominate: the purely rational and the largely emotional. That was to be regretted, as both have obvious faults. If a simple appeal to the emotions did sometimes produce converts, the negative side was the way in which cool reflection afterwards led some to detect a crude manipulation of their feelings, with cynicism the inevitable result. A comment by Oliver Goldsmith in one of his *Essays* well encapsulates the problem with the other alternative, sermons based solely on appeal to reason: 'Such are indifferently acquainted with human nature . . . reason is but a weak antagonist . . . We should arm one passion against another.'[52] Not that the carefully reasoned sermon of the eighteenth century was entirely unsuccessful. Before the advent of Dr Johnson's *Dictionary of the English Language* one of Goldsmith's fellow essayists, Joseph Addison, had even planned such a dictionary entirely based on the language of sermons, so widespread were they consumed and admired.[53]

None of this is intended to argue for a return to the period of rhetoric's greatest flowering in the Renaissance sermon. To state the obvious, historical conditions have changed. If those are correct who have investigated the sermons of the period in some detail,

---

[51] Agricola, *De inventione dialectica libres tres*; Erasmus, *Ecclesiastes sive concionator evangelicus*. Apparently, Erasmus was responsible for introducing *concio* as the new name for a sermon (Shuger, *Sacred Rhetoric*, 261). For their stress on emotion, passion and delight, Shuger, *Sacred Rhetoric*, 61–4.

[52] O. Goldsmith, 'Some remarks on the modern manner of preaching' (1760) in A. Friedman ed., *Collected Works of Oliver Goldsmith* (Oxford: Clarendon, 1966), iii. 150–5. esp. 151.

[53] Johnson's own preference was for the language of poets and dramatists. Addison's project was by no means as foolish as it might seem today. The first dictionary of English pronunciation (by Thomas Spence) was likewise based on the language of the pulpit, not surprising perhaps in the days when all clerics had been educated at Oxford or Cambridge.

they had, like contemporary drama, a structure especially suited to the tensions of the time.[54] Part of the aim was to enable listeners to inhabit the paradoxes of life and faith that then so dominated discussion. Our own postmodernist age is of a different kind. An age less familiar with the details of Christian belief needs different forms of engagement. While an apologetic approach might well lead individuals to experience a sense of the presence of God in other contexts, actually to generate a sacramental encounter through the sermon itself, a somewhat different method would seem required. One option might be to try to enable the congregation to experience anew an incident from the Gospels, or Jesus telling a parable from the inside, as it were; that is to say, so tell it that hearers find themselves reliving the encounter and thus the possibility of the experience itself. A quite different technique would be to start from where people now are, in their ordinary experience, and gradually dress this in religious categories such that the ordinary can now be seen in a new light: life, for example, as a graced, undeserved benefit from the Creator.

I chose not to pursue such possibilities any further here not because I regard them as unimportant. On the contrary, on my view they merit detailed consideration as one way of returning the sermon to the seriousness the study of rhetoric once gave it. But my aim here has been much more limited: to illustrate the way in which the Church did once take seriously the sacramentality of the preached word and could do so again.

Illuminated Manuscripts

In numerous places I have sought to guarantee a sacramental role for the visual arts similar to what I have just defended for the sermon. Here I want to attempt a narrower focus, and examine that claim in contexts where text and image were actually placed alongside one another, in illuminated manuscripts. Such an investigation will, as we shall see, provide a natural transition to the final question I shall tackle in this chapter, whether one type of medium (verbal or

---

[54] The central theme of Crockett's *Play of Paradox*. He suggests, for example, that this is the way to understand Shakespeare's 'problem' plays: *Measure for Measure*, 104–8; *The Winter's Tale*, 113–20; *Richard III*, 148–53.

visual) is inherently more liable to the corruption of idolatry than the other.

In trying to understand the world from which such manuscripts come, the work of Mary Carruthers in her two books, *The Book of Memory* (1990) and *The Craft of Thought* (1998), is especially helpful. In the medieval world, she suggests, reading is best understood as an essentially architectural exercise, the building of interconnections in the memory that would help sustain certain patterns and ways of thinking.[55] The *inventio* that preceded commitment to memory was thus not just a matter of 'discovery' but also of the creation of a sort of catalogue system, an 'inventory' more in the modern sense.[56] Seen in that light, some of the more puzzling features of medieval (and earlier) habits of reading take on a quite different character. So, for instance, the arrangements of the stars into mythological constellations should not be seen as the arbitrary imposition of pleasing pictures in the sky. Instead, they become mnemonic devices for relocating the stars. Again, the composition of *centi* by Ausonius, Prudentius, and others ceases to be a pastiche of half-remembered lines of Vergil and instead the sustained attempt to incorporate the poet's images into the Christian tradition. In the past Bernard's florid prose style has been viewed as running counter to the hostility he displays towards the more elaborate elements of Romanesque architecture. What it really amounts to is the attempt to ensure that only one form of constructed memory (the interior) should hold sway over the minds of his contemporaries.[57] *Curiositas* or promiscuity in the cultivation of imaginative interrelations was the forbidden alternative. The Christian ideal thus becomes a memory entirely organized towards the pursuit of salvation. If the objection is raised that reading seems altogether too gentle an activity to conjure up the requisite commitments in a disciplined life, on the other side need to be set the dynamic metaphors applied to reading itself, not least the already noted image of chewing over

---

[55] Among others Hugh of St Victor actually uses this analogy: quoted in *The Craft of Thought* (Cambridge: Cambridge University Press, 1998), 20.

[56] Ibid. 11.

[57] Ibid. 24–7, 57–9, 84–7. Less convincing is her belief that St Peter's necessarily enjoyed the people's affection more than St John Lateran (41) because of the memory of Peter's martyrdom. The relics in the Lateran's Sancta Sanctorum pulled in the other direction, and anyway the papacy did not finally move to St Peter's till the thirteenth century.

its contents, and the harsh use of the scraper in the preparatory work of writing.[58]

A prominent theme of Carruthers' earlier book is that ancient and medieval writers did not sharply distinguish between verbal and visual images. The page as a whole functions visually, with decoration and letters alike an aid to memory. In her second book she observes how it is probably no accident that an image of the tabernacle is placed at the front of the Vulgate text known as the Codex Amiatinus. The temple was often so used to suggest spiritual pilgrimage, and that was what the reader was about to begin.[59] However, in what follows I want to consider not the impact of such a book as a whole, but the impression made in combining just a few words and image together on the same or facing pages. Most of those who write professionally in our times about manuscript illustrations regard them as essentially works of art. Of course they are that much, and quite often extremely beautiful. Little wonder, then, that, as techniques of reproduction have improved, increasingly these works have been made more widely available to a fascinated public. The danger in that popularity, however, is that important issues are side-stepped. Most of these illustrations are religious. So the question needs to be faced as to why this way of proceeding came to such prominence in the first place. The result was after all a still greater cost to producing the books involved. As this was not by any means marginal, clearly some major underlying principle must have been at stake.

Of course, as with most human motivation, almost certainly motives were multiple and mixed. The desire for ostentatious display of wealth certainly sometimes must have played its part. Indeed, kings and emperors were not slow to see how appropriate books and illustrations might bolster their own authority.[60] By the

---

[58] Rough patches on the vellum give clear indication of the widespread use of a scraper, although alternative forms of correction were available, e.g. underlining dots or 'va . . . cat' at the beginning and end of the words or passage to be omitted. For Anselm on 'chewing', see this volume, 71–2.

[59] This codex, the earliest surviving copy of Jerome's Vulgate and now in the Laurentian Library in Florence, was originally produced for Ceolfrith at Jarrow *c.* 700.

[60] For a helpful chapter on the subject, C. de Hamel, *A History of Illuminated Manuscripts* (London: Phaidon, 2nd edn., 1994), 42–73. For Charlemagne (d. 814) 'manuscripts written in gold on purple had a promotional value in symbolising imperial culture' (48). Only much later with someone like Henry II (d. 1024) were emperors at ease in being portrayed in missals (63–4).

turn of the first millennium some examples of such practice were already quite close to blasphemy.[61] But the general pattern had its origins in the monasteries, and so different forms of motivation might reasonably be expected there. However, it would be naive to posit a simple purity that contrasts markedly with secular decadence. Even Augustine speaks of key words from St John's Gospel acting as a talisman against headaches. So it is not implausible to suppose that ancient copies of that Gospel (such as the Stonyhurst Gospel) were valued precisely because they were seen as a prophylactic against illness and disease.[62] Again, taking such books on missionary endeavours where the sight of such splendour and the further mystery of reading could be combined must have acted as a powerful tool in advocating the superiority of the new religion. If that suggests relatively subtle techniques of persuasion, the fact that Columba's Psalter was known as the *Cathach* or 'Battler' returns us once more to the image of the book as a semi-magical instrument or talisman.[63]

Even with all these qualifications, however, there remains the essentially religious impact that such books must have had. Although illustrations in texts such as the Codex Amiatinus indicate that even in earliest times such books were sometimes just kept in cupboards, a more reverential attitude is evident elsewhere. So, for example, at St Augustine's, Canterbury, four were lined up on the altar itself, and no doubt this must have happened quite often in other places as well.[64] The Gospels on which successive Archbishops of Canterbury make their inaugural oaths were probably once permanently displayed in that same monastery in this way (rather than locked away as they usually are in their present home in

[61] Otto III allowed four women to represent the different races bringing him gifts, in much the same way as the Magi adore Christ: cf. ibid. 62, 67.

[62] Augustine, PL 35. 1443. The Stonyhurst Gospel, once kept at the Jesuit school of the same name but now on deposit in the British Library, is perhaps more properly called the St Cuthbert Gospel of St John, as it was buried with him and kept at Durham till the Reformation. The chronicler, Reginald, tells of a Durham monk suffering terrible swellings as a result of interfering with the manuscript.

[63] In all this one underlying utilitarian aim should not be forgotten. Colour and pictures would make a codex easier to use in a world before clear chapter divisions. Perhaps an analogy with the headlines in modern newspapers might not be altogether inappropriate.

[64] For an illustration of the practice from the early fifteenth century, de Hamel, *Illuminated Manuscripts*, 16, ill. 5.

Corpus Christi Library, Cambridge). Perhaps the clearest example of such attitudes comes from within the Armenian tradition, where an illustrated Gospel is always placed next to the cross on the altar. Even objects as apparently boring as illuminated canon tables are described as 'baths of sight and hearing for those approaching the soaring peaks of God'.[65] The sacramental intention of aiding a sense of divine presence could scarcely be clearer, as also the desire for the book to exercise more than some merely private aesthetic delight.

The illustrations were thus available to make their impact at large. That impact might well have been more like that of relics, or chalice and paten rather than how books are now viewed, in essentially utilitarian terms. The manuscript itself functioned as a vehicle of God's presence rather than only the words spoken through it. It had acquired a sort of holiness by extension as it were, as became likewise true of the altar and its accoutrements in due course. If in earlier centuries the number of such books directly susceptive to such a transformation was still relatively small, the expansion of book production through the foundation of universities and still more so through the popularity of devotional Books of Hours meant that by the late Middle Ages their impact was not just on monks but on the population at large.[66] Indeed, it is probable that by the time of the invention of printing it had become the norm for every moderately wealthy home to possess at least one such a book, its status augmented by being quite commonly still the only book in the household. For the educated layperson text and illustration or illumination now effectively combine in such Books of Hours to preach a common message. They helped make the biblical scenes come alive, transposing the reader to that other world but also mediating God's presence from that world into the reader's own.

In the case of the earlier insular tradition, it is now widely acknowledged that much of the design element was borrowed

---

[65] See further V. Nersessian, *The Bible in the Armenian Tradition* (London: British Library, 2001), 67–78, esp. 74, 75. The quotation is from Nerses Shnorhali. Before Stephen Langton introduced chapters into the Bible in 1228, complex comparative canon tables were the only easy way of identifying Gospel parallels.

[66] Books of Hours took a standard form in the thirteenth century and continued to be highly popular until the sixteenth. There are 300 or so in the British Library alone.

from earlier paganism. In the estimate of some that might be held to count decisively against it.[67] But to be set on the other side is the way in which such incorporations functioned as a wise recognition that not all that had preceded the new religion was in itself bad. This might make its own legitimate contribution. It was a sacramental way of drawing into Christian life what might initially seem most alien to it. Some elements in this approach continued deep into the Middle Ages. As a consequence some ways of presenting the Christian faith must appear otherwise puzzling, unless set within that wider context.[68] God had once been found in cormorant and deer and in intricacy of pattern, and was once more. That such applications continued might be deemed subversive of the Christian message, were its central elements somehow compromised. But it is an implausible claim in a situation where such illustrations were actually used to enhance the significance of the new faith. Again and again, it is texts that are seen as central to Christian self-understanding that are selected for illumination. Consider a possible exception, Matthew 1.18, where the text is preceded by seventeen verses of genealogy. Highlighting 'Christ' in that verse in effect makes a profound incarnational and sacramental claim. Christ is positioned in our world by the genealogy but also declared present in the words of the actual text through its visual illumination. The visual thus twice over supports and reinforces the value of the words on the page.

One intriguing feature of such early books is the focus given to each of the four evangelists. A cynic might postulate that this is only the contemporary scribe or illustrator celebrating the key role of his own profession. However, the real reason lies in the desire to suggest supernatural presence, whether through the august character given to the evangelists themselves (as in *The Book of Kells*) or

---

[67] For others it may be the human figures that are problematic. Sir Edward Sullivan, for instance, while conceding their pagan origins, praises spiral and serpent. But he calls the figures 'rudely expressed travesties'. The Virgin, for example, was given two right feet: *The Book of Kells* (London: Studio Editions, 2nd edn., 1920), 9, 42, 104, 122–3.

[68] *The Book of Deer* from ninth-century north-east Scotland is an interesting case in point. The way in which the holy figures raise their hands remains puzzling until parallels are drawn with the Celtic gods on the pagan Gundestrup Cauldron: so R. Ellis and P. B. Ellis, *The Book of Deer* (London: Constable, 1994), 67. For deer, ibid. 66–7.

(as with the more common pattern of *The Lindisfarne Gospels*) through the addition of the mysterious creature with which each writer came to be associated. The aim was to celebrate the presence of God himself, somehow mysteriously inhabiting the text.[69] Not that all such attempts were uniformly successful. In the much later *Winchester Bible* Mark is rather incongruously given the head of a lion, which makes him slightly comic. Again, in that same work the artist charged with illuminating Isaiah's reception of his commission makes of it a poor, matter-of-fact exchange that could scarcely be in more marked contrast to how Jeremiah is treated by the so-called Leaping Figures Master. In that latter case the prophet reels, as an angel touches his mouth with a scroll. Heaven and earth are thus effectively linked, an idea that is reinforced by the artist's decision to place the angel's feet firmly beyond the upper frame, and so presumably within heaven itself.[70]

That Bible beautifully attests to the greater range and quality of illustration that occurred as the centuries passed. What, however, also changed but is not reflected by *The Winchester Bible* is the increasing numbers of a lay public to whom such books were now available. Although Books of Hours had certain constant elements such as the Little Office of Our Lady and the Office for the Dead, as well as shortened versions of the monastic offices (hence their name), there were also other aspects that varied between owners, both textually and visually. That suggests some degree of reflection on how such books might be most appropriately used by any one particular owner. While contemporary Christians are likely to recoil from the theology of some recurring aspects such as Bernard's eight lucky verses or 'Egyptian days', some beautiful prayers have also been preserved as a result.[71] Shakespeare has probably made it impossible for Richard III ever to recover from his

---

[69] For the three surviving evangelist portraits in *Kells*, Sullivan, Plates V, VII, XVIII; for their symbols (treated separately), Plate IV. For the quite different treatment in Eadfrith's work: J. Backhouse, *The Lindisfarne Gospels* (Oxford: Phaidon, 1981), 40, 46, 50, 54.

[70] C. Donovan, *The Winchester Bible* (London: British Library, 1993), 41–2, 61. *The Winchester Bible* dates from the late twelfth century.

[71] The legend was that in an encounter with the devil Bernard had been told that, if these particular verses (all from the Psalms) were recited daily, the petitioner was bound to escape hell. A complicated formula was used to work out which days of each month were held to be unlucky or 'Egyptian'.

sullied reputation. Nonetheless, the king's notoriety cannot but be softened, once attention is paid to the distinctive features of his own particular set of Hours. It may not finally settle whether he was a monster or not, but it cannot but succeed in raising doubts as to whether Shakespeare's picture is entirely fair.[72]

Such richly illustrated personalized texts make it likely that quite a complex dynamic is occurring between text and illustration. In the *Sforza Hours*, for instance, the inclusion of the child challenging Augustine on the incomprehensible character of the Trinity suggests that that picture is there, at least in part, to moderate the apparent simplicity of the text alongside of which it is placed: a not implausible thought, since the illustrator in this case was also a priest.[73] More commonly, however, illustrations are there to enhance rather than qualify reading of the text. Their aim is to help the biblical stories become experiential realities and not remain mere bare records of now long-distant events. So successful was the pursuit of these objectives that, when printing did come along, for some time the printed page continued to resemble a manuscript, with accompanying illustrations and so forth. There were even attempts at Protestant versions of Books of Hours, but in the end suspicion of implicit popery proved too strong.[74]

Aspects of such treatment of books continued even as late as the nineteenth century, as in the custom known as fore-painting where the side of a book opposite the spine was painted. Held tightly closed and nothing of interest is apparent; held loosely and a painting becomes visible, spread over the edges of the connecting pages. Prince Albert owned just such a Bible (still at Windsor), in which scenes from his native Germany were depicted.[75] If it is hard to see any deep religious significance in this (the aim was surely to give pleasure by the reminder of an earlier life), the almost

---

[72] The most recent editors of his Hours are more cautious: 'Richard III still eludes us': A. F. Sutton and L. Visser-Fuchs, *The Hours of Richard III* (Stroud: Alan Sutton, 1990), 85. While Bernard's verses and Egyptian days are included, so too is a rather beautiful personal litany: 44, 50, 67–78.

[73] This particular piece was created in the late fifteenth century by the earlier of the book's two illustrators, Giovan Pietro Birago, who was himself a priest; Augustine's attempts to explain the mystery of the Trinity are compared to the child's attempt to empty the sea into a small hole: M. Evans, *The Sforza Hours* (London: British Library, 1992), 17, 41, 45.

[74] E. Duffy, *Marking the Hours* (New Haven: Yale University Press, 2006), 171.

[75] I am grateful to Bridget Wright for drawing my attention to this phenomenon, and for showing me some fine examples held at Windsor Castle Library.

complete cessation of such practices does pose the question of whether something important has not been lost in the process. If the danger of illustration is that it focuses, at least for the lazy, on only one way of imaging the situation, its absence carries a more serious threat—that the reader ceases to imagine at all. The picture at least brought the divine into the words on the page, whereas the words on their own could so easily set their world over against the reader's. Contrast and even alienation might then be the net impact rather than the merging of two different worlds. In short, without the illustrations the danger is that the world of the text would become distant and unreal or even mythical rather than sacramentally once more made present.

So far from such illumination being a corruption or a mere lazy alternative to more detailed attention to the text, what I would like to suggest is that this tradition did at least seek to encourage readers to a lively imaginative engagement with what was therein described. In modern biblical discussion the text is most frequently placed over against the reader, with its world one reality and ours quite another, whereas in this tradition the requirement was already being fulfilled that the world of the text should actually enter the world of the reader and so exercise its power by being seen as a continuing present reality, not just an account of some distant past. The difference, if I may put it like this, is rather like exploring family history through registers of births, deaths, and marriages on the one hand and on the other bringing out an old family album. It is the album that starts the process of experiencing real connections, noting family resemblance, for instance. In a similar way Mary may be seen to pray in a posture just like the reader of a Book of Hours, King David to sit enthroned on a chair not unlike a contemporary chieftain or king. Of course, such depictions are seldom historically accurate but they could help spark a process whereby not just two different material realities were united, but more importantly their spiritual equivalents. So it would be quite wrong to suggest that there was no element of challenge in such a methodology.

Idolatry in Visual and Verbal

This modern distancing, with its associated tendency to treat the text as a series of isolated facts rather than a world waiting to be

entered, provides a natural transition to the third and final focus in
this chapter, the question of whether the visual is inherently more
idolatrous than the verbal. The question is pertinent because so
much of contemporary Christianity sees itself as a religion of the
word, and as such marginalizes the visual. To my mind this is a
fundamental error that does harm not only in how the Christian
responds to the visual in the art and architecture round about them
but also no less in attitudes to the word itself. If words contribute to
religious belief most effectively when they are nearest to the visual,
that is, in metaphor and analogies, then inevitably their impact will
be distorted unless the rules appropriate to such forms of language
are properly appreciated.

In the first section on sermons I sought to indicate that in the past
homilies were seen essentially as concerned to bring the content of
the text before the mind's eye, with rhetoric used in a manner not
dissimilar to the stage, with scene-setting, powerful imagery, and so
forth. Thus, however much scholarly endeavour might go into its
preparation, the natural comparison for performance was not primarily with the study but with the theatre and so with a visual art.
To those obsessed with the idea of the fixity of the visual image, and
so with its inherent temptation towards idolatry, that might suggest
a closing of options. But even with illuminated manuscripts
I suggested that it appears as though options were opened rather
than closed, as readers were thus enabled to experience the biblical
world as their own. What I want to suggest here is that to talk of
automatic closure with images, whether visual or verbal, is to
misunderstand both. Great art in both media should open possibilities, not close them. It will therefore discourage idolatry rather
than lead to the absolutizing of what is interim and transient. My
suspicion is that theologians think the danger greater with the visual
simply because they misconceive how artists work, and so look
only to the surface. To do so, however, is as foolish as to stop at the
surface of the biblical text.

Perhaps the best way to introduce the issue is to examine a text
where metaphor is used extensively but set in deliberate opposition
to the visual. The Book of Revelation turns out to be a good
test case to take. In his second chapter (2.12–17) the author takes
up once more an image he had used earlier, of Christ wielding a
two-edged sword (1.16; 2.12; 2.16). It is used to indict the people of
Pergamon (the administrative capital of Asia Minor) with the sin

of idolatry. They are apparently ready to eat meat, even though it has been offered formally in sacrifice before statues of the deified emperor or other deities. Such temporizing Christians (called Nicolaitans in the text), John suggests, are really like the Israelites of old who succumbed to the wiles of the pagan prophet Balaam.[76] The people of Pergamon have been compromised not by anything they have said but by where the meat has been, within sight of pagan deities. The plot is thus a familiar one. For most of its history, Christianity has identified idols with artistic objects—statues and so forth—and seen these as the greatest dangers to belief. By comparison words have in effect been treated as a fairly safe medium. Sometimes music has incurred the same suspicions as the visual arts in its capacity to beguile and lead astray. More commonly, however, it has been protected by the help it gives to words (in singing) or been allowed to shelter under the characteristic it shares with words, that of being non-visual.

To class John among those suspicious of the visual will undoubtedly to some seem odd, given that there is so much imagery in this book. Yet closer inspection, I suggest, confirms precisely that estimate. His imagery, when pursued, altogether collapses, if measured in purely visual terms. Take the one to which allusion has already been made, that of the two-edged sword in Christ's mouth. Now try to visualize it. As the average such sword in the ancient world was between sixteen inches and three feet, no human mouth could possibly easily bear that weight. The result is that any attempt to visualize Christ in this way presents the Christian with a dilemma. However much reverence for Christ might make one hesitate, the attempt inevitably tends towards the comic. That is what I suggest in general happens with John's imagery.

The two most famous examples of detailed exploration of the possibility of the visualization of the book as whole, the late medieval Angers tapestry and Dürer's sixteenth-century woodcuts, are both magnificent failures.[77] The more they are studied, the less

---

[76] As in Num. 22–5.

[77] The Angers artist tries to disguise the sword in the Father's mouth by allowing it to be obscured by the seven candlesticks behind. The greater realism of Dürer produces its own set of problems. The seven-headed beast is comic rather than frightening: for illustration, W. Kurth ed., *The Complete Woodcuts of Albrecht Dürer* (New York: Dover, 1963), 115.

inclined one is to believe in John's version of the end of all things. Such a judgement is confirmed, even if attention is confined to the more generally acceptable elements in John's work, such as his vision of the heavenly Jerusalem. Attend to the details in chapters 21–2, and the reader finds a city dwarfing Manhattan at 1,500 miles high, but with surrounding walls of only 140 feet; again, a great tree arching over its solitary street that has a river flowing through its middle but yet is able to sustain the tree's roots on either side. Little wonder that modern translations—rather than confronting us with the absurdity of the project—in general seek to maintain the obscurity of the original by providing measurements in the original stadia, cubits, and so forth!

There is of course a way out, and that is to concede, as many commentators do, that John after all lacks a visual imagination.[78] What he is really doing is drawing metaphors from the Old Testament and reapplying them, somewhat indiscriminately, to the new dispensation. So the two-edged sword is no more intended to be visualized than is the reference to Balaam, or for that matter the new city of Jerusalem. The two-edged sword is John's way of alluding to Daniel's vision of God in judgement, mention of the story of Balaam his way of ensuring that what his opponents are up to is taken with maximum seriousness.[79] Again, the dimensions of city and tree do not really matter. It is just John making sure that we revisit the story of the Garden of Eden and the new Jerusalem promised by the prophets: the new future, we are being told, will reverse the fate of the former and fulfil the promise of the latter.

Certainly, if there is good reason to be suspicious of the visual, John has achieved something quite remarkable. Even when using metaphors and symbols, the need to visualize is circumvented, since that is not really the point. Rather, it is the strength of the embedding of his message in the Hebrew scriptures that is being asserted. But at a price. What in effect John does by acting in this way is to narrow our options. The meaning of his images is in fact not yielded through our own imaginative, far less visual, explorations

---

[78] 'It was inspired and meditative, more verbal than strictly visionary': A. Farrer, *The Revelation of St. John the Divine* (Oxford: Clarendon, 1964), 23–9, esp. 28. For an account more sympathetic to a visionary reading: I. Boxall, *Revelation: Vision and Insight* (London: SPCK, 2002), 27–47.

[79] Rev. 1.14–15 is based on Dan. 10.5–6.

but rather by their literary relationship to the Old Testament. They are thus, as it were, controlled and controlling metaphors, means of dictating to us how we should read the community of faith's past and future. And what is idolatry, if not the assigning of absolute significance to what is merely provisional, replacing the one absolute God by what is created and subordinate? Now of course John's metaphors may not have been intended in this absolute way, but the fact that they are more like rules for reading than images for exploration does suggest that he is not as far distant from idolatry as might initially have been supposed.

I want to pursue that thought a little further in a moment. First, however, let me turn to art and music, and ask whether these media are necessarily more constrictive than words, more subject to the temptation to absolutize. Obviously, sometimes this is so. The evangelists leave open what happened at the precise moment of resurrection, whereas all too often art offers us a constricting, not to say pedestrian, alternative. The familiar image of Christ standing on the open tomb is surely as pedantic an absolute as one can get—all very literal, and very unbelievable.[80] Calvin was right to protest that, whatever Easter's message is, it was surely not this. So the more extreme Reformation's reluctance to admit such imagery as a part of faith becomes quite understandable.

But art need not resort to such crude literalism. Contrast Titian's interpretation of the resurrection in his great painting of the appearance of Christ to Mary Magdalene in the garden, usually entitled *Noli me tangere*.[81] Admittedly, he too was tempted initially to literalism. In the painting's first version Titian gave Christ the gardener's hat to which John's Gospel alludes. But his final version is quite otherwise. If I can put it like this, viewers have to work at seeing in order to discover the meaning, but eventually this does emerge. Mary is kneeling at Christ's feet, her body bent at an angle that encourages the eye to trace the shape it takes. As the eye follows the arch of her back, the viewer's gaze is drawn up through

---

[80] Even as great a painter as Piero della Francesca fails to carry it off: B. Laskowski ed., *Piero della Francesca* (Cologne: Könemann, 1998), 65. Even so, a degree of awe is preserved, which cannot be said of most who adopt the same scheme, e.g. Schongauer. For Calvin's general view of images, *Institutes of the Christian Religion*, I. xi–xii.

[81] In the National Gallery in London. For illustration, M. Kaminski, *Titian* (Cologne: Könemann, 1998), 24.

Mary's eyes into Christ's own, and then through him to a tree that
stands between them both, and then on heavenwards. Our salvation, we are being told, comes like Mary's through penitence and a
longing to follow Christ wheresoever he may lead. It is one of the
great paintings of European art. It achieves its effect, however, not
by force but by invitation and exploration: the provisional, the
open uncertainty, eventually leading viewers towards the transcendent and absolute.

There are quite a few references in John to music in the worship
of heaven.[82] Christianity has on the whole tended to see music as
inherently less dangerous than the visual arts. I cannot help won-
dering, though, whether Plato was not after all right in thinking
music potentially the more seductive of the two, for the inevit-
ability of its temporal sequence means that it normally has to choose
to direct us along one path rather than another.[83] In *God and Grace
of Body* I considered the ending of Bach's *St John Passion*.[84] There
I drew attention to how much more difficult it is for the composer
to present John's text as it stands. The great cry of triumph from the
cross that the Christ of that Gospel utters (John 19.30) would sound
false and artificial in a musical context without more time first
devoted to death's agonies. So Bach really had no choice but to
direct our emotions in a particular way and so build up gradually to
such a triumph. That contrasts markedly with the numerous Johan-
nine visual representations of the crucifixion that exist.[85] There
divinity and humanity are set side by side on the cross, with viewers
left to themselves as to how and when either is appropriated. A good
example of such interplay between life and death, and divinity and
humanity (precisely because it is not too obvious), is Zurburán's
Crucifixion of 1627.[86] As the eye moves from one side of Christ's

---

[82] 'The Apocalypse is an extremely noisy book' accounted for in part by the
fact that 'music . . . permeates'. For comment and references, Boxall, *Revelation*, 5.

[83] *Republic* 398–400.

[84] *God and Grace of Body*, 254. Also discussed in more detail in my article
'Images of Redemption in Art and Music' in S. T. Davis, D. Kendall, and
G. O'Collins eds., *The Redemption* (Oxford: Oxford University Press, 2004),
295–319, esp. 312–13.

[85] The dominant way of representing the crucifixion during the first
millennium.

[86] Now in the Art Institute, Chicago. Illustrated in J. Brown ed., *Zurburán*
(London: Thames & Hudson, 1991), 54–5.

body to the other, slowly partly hidden visual clues help with assessment of significance. If the play of darkness and light is perhaps a little too obvious, the meaning behind the opposing of angular deadweight to gentle curve only dawns more slowly; the stark reality of death of the one side is conquered in the light, smooth body of the other illumined, as it is, by an internal divine light. That freedom in presentation can also of course be paralleled in the writing of the evangelists. My point is therefore not that the visual artist has a natural superiority, only that it is not the case that the composer has a freedom that the literary or visual artist lacks.

So, in hearing the author of Revelation, we must, I believe, also hear his limitations. In unequivocally condemning those who ate meat offered to idols, John is much less generous than Paul in 1 Corinthians, who found nothing wrong with such conduct.[87] He is also much less generous to Balaam than was many another contemporary Jew, for whom Balaam was not only an honourable pagan but also something of an honorary Jew.[88] That lack of generosity also meant, I suggest, that he proved incapable of perceiving any of the open potential of art. There may be an allusion to the architecture of Pergamon in his passing mention of Satan, since one of the city's great temples was dedicated to Asclepius, whose sign was the serpent.[89] That was at the foot of Pergamon's main hill that had a great temple to Zeus on top, many of whose magnificent carvings are now on display in Berlin. It was a city of spectacular visual beauty, one of the great ordered and planned cities of the ancient world, with careful zoning practised as one ascended the hill to that impressive temple of Zeus.[90] Of course with Christianity a threatened, tiny minority it would have been hard for John to see any merits in such architecture. He saw only the temptation to apostasy. Such limitations have extracted their inevitable price.

[87] 1 Cor. 8.

[88] *Sifre* on Deut. 34.10. Even to this day Balaam's words are part of the synagogue's morning service.

[89] It was a great pilgrimage centre, known for its healings. Pergamon was the birthplace of the doctor Galen. For the symbol of the serpent in medicine, see *God and Grace of Body*, 395–9.

[90] Achieved mainly under Eumenes II in the second century BC. For an illustration of this 'tour de force in the adaptation of urban planning to the configuration of the land': J. Boardman, J. Griffin, and O. Murray, *Oxford History of the Classical World* (Oxford: Oxford University Press, 1986), 502.

He in turn absolutizes his own opinions no less fiercely and
fanatically than any follower of Zeus or Asclepius might have
done. All who disagreed with him were assigned to perdition,
even those holding views not dissimilar to Paul's. Ironically he
does so through means invented in Pergamon itself, the parchment
that was once so essential for writing.

I hope that some readers have found the focus on a specific
example helpful. Others, however, may wish to object that what
is thereby lost is a more rounded view. In particular, it might be
observed that hitherto I have paid no attention to the root meaning
of the word. In the original Greek 'idolatry' means simply 'the
worship of images'. So the problem is clearly identified as lying
essentially with the visual. Historically, that is no doubt right. Gods
came to be virtually identified with the statues that represented
them. As a result the statue was treated as though it contained in
itself a divine power that, because easily available, could therefore
be made subject to human control. That this has often happened in
human history cannot of course be denied. Indeed, it may well have
been the treatment of icons as relics, as preserving something of the
historical Christ, that led to the first iconoclastic controversy.[91] But
equally it surely also needs to be admitted that this is not an
inevitable consequence of visual imagery. Indeed, an objector
would be hard-pressed to point to conclusive evidence of this
happening anywhere in a church in modern Britain, whatever the
denomination.

So the more interesting question is really the comparative one,
whether there is really any good reason to be more suspicious of the
visual than of the verbal. In a world in which Islam, the least iconic
of the world's major religions, now makes the headlines most
frequently for fanaticism, the contention is surely odd to say the
least. Muslim fanaticism is most naturally analysed as in part at least a
function of treating particular texts as absolute, and so can be
construed as idolatry of the text. If conceded, the point might
equally be applied to Christian fundamentalism. Even so, to many
readers the greater danger may still seem to lie with the visual.
Those unfamiliar with art have a tendency to think of its role simply
as illustrative and so derivative and fixed, and thus inherently
constrictive of the divine in a way that words are not.

---

[91] Cf. my *God and Enchantment of Place*, 40–51, esp. 51.

I have already made a preliminary attempt to dislodge such a prejudice against the visual. As Titian's *Noli me tangere* illustrated, the visual can be just as effective as the verbal in inviting exploration and so in avoiding the risk of idolatry: imposing on the interim and provisional a fixed and absolute meaning. That, it should be stressed, was no isolated example. Statues are often thought to be most at risk in encouraging idolatry. So it will be salutary to consider a couple of examples from Christian art. Take the most famous Christian statue of them all, Michelangelo's Pietà in St Peter's in Rome, with the Virgin Mary cradling the dead Christ on her lap. The theme seems obvious, but it is of course not in Scripture. So in that fact already there is encouragement towards further reflection. Then again Michelangelo has made Mary the same age as her son. The intention is more than simply aesthetic. It would remind Michelangelo's fellow Italians of Dante's familiar description of Mary in the *Divine Comedy* as 'Vergine Madre, figlia del tuo Figlio' and so also of her role as disciple of her son and thus as an example to us all.[92] Nor is this by any means an isolated example. Forty years or so later Michelangelo began his Rondanini Pietà, and was still at work on it more than twenty years later, six days before his death in 1564. Although some have seen it as marking a real decline in powers, for others it is one of his greatest achievements, and one can see why.[93] Despite the anatomical abnormalities, it offers a powerful sense of Christ's flesh retreating into another world. So far therefore is the statue from encouraging focus on a single element in Christ's story (his dead corpse), it pulls the viewer through death into life and so into another kind of reality.

Again, to take a quite different but almost equally famous case, Donatello in making Mary Magdalene thin and haggard could

---

[92] 'Virgin Mother, daughter of your Son' (*Paradiso* 23. 1). In 1500 the theme was still unusual in Italian art, although it had existed in France and Germany since at least the fourteenth century. As well as Dante, sermons of Bernadine of Siena may also have played a part: Bernardine speaks of Mary dreaming of herself once more holding her baby in her arms. For illustration, K. Bradbury, *Essential Michelangelo* (Bath: Parragon, 2000), 26–8.

[93] Contrast the negative judgement of Howard Hibbard with the enthusiastic endorsement of Anthony Blunt: H. Hibbard, *Michelangelo: Painter, Sculptor, Architect* (London: Octopus, 1979), 190; A. Blunt, *Artistic Theory in Italy, 1450–1600* (Oxford: Oxford University Press, 1962), 77. For illustration, Bradbury, *Essential Michelangelo*, 250–1.

easily be seen as merely alluding to the legend of how her life ended in strenuous fasting in the south of France.[94] But anyone who studies the statue for any length of time could not possibly finally concur with that judgement. The statue itself speaks of a real nobility and depth of character refined through suffering, and so not merely of a false story of a self-mutilated body. Rather, it opens up the possibility of sanctity coming to us all through a life disciplined by prayer, whatever hardships may also come.

Each of my examples so far has taken off at a tangent from Scripture. Even where tentativeness and exploration in the sculptural text are conceded, it might still be questioned whether greater openness could be achieved in a situation where text and artwork are trying to portray exactly the same event. Do not words have a more natural openness than a picture frozen at a particular moment in time could ever possibly have? Such claims could, I think, only be made by someone who has given little thought to art, for great artists again and again invite us into a meditative exploration of their theme rather than offer a simple retelling. Let me return once more to Titian's *Noli Me Tangere* and make a direct comparison with the narrative in John's Gospel. The phrase is a difficult one to translate adequately, and a number of competing interpretations are on offer, among them the Vulgate's 'Touch me not' and the more popular contemporary option 'Stop clinging to me.' So, although many ordinary readers no doubt interpret the phrase as just a matter of Jesus being in transition from one world to the next, the Greek original, if not the English translation, does at least encourage further reflection.[95] Is it, for example, a particular type of clinging that is being rejected, or is it the superiority of faith to sight that is being underlined, or what? In the latter case Mary's need for evidence is by implication being unfavourably contrasted with the beloved disciple's and others' lack of such a requirement for

---

[94] The statue is in the Museum of the Opera del Duomo. For a couple of illustrations, G. G. Bertéla, *Donatello* (Florence: Scala, 1991), 70–1. An illustration and commentary also accompanies my *God and Grace of Body*: Plate 5.

[95] For the great range of interpretations that have in fact been offered: R. E. Brown, *The Gospel According to John* (New York: Doubleday Anchor Bible, 1970), 992–4, 1011–17. Brown's opting for a single dogmatic answer seems to me unfortunate. That might of course be how John's mind worked, but the richness of the passage lies for me in its openness to multiple, varying strands of possible lines of interpretation.

proof.[96] So I am certainly not denying that the words here have the power to initiate further thought.

But so also do some paintings of the scene, like this version of Titian's. Christ's right hand drawing back his shroud is used to convey the verbal distancing, but intriguingly the art, unlike the words, allows a further possibility, that the distancing is also a way of drawing close, for the angle of Mary's body forces us to traverse the space between, first meeting Christ's eyes before we are carried further by the angle of the background tree into the heavens beyond. The reader like Mary thus discovers the possibility of a new relationship with Christ that can gain the believer's access to heaven along with the ascended Christ. So Titian, I suggest, allows more than the Gospel words. Of course, Titian's perspective can be grasped from the message of the Gospel overall. My point is that when the two media are compared as isolated units it is not always the purely verbal that is necessarily the more open or more adventurous.

None of this is intended to make the Christian revelation after all primarily visual, nor is it to claim that the imagination always works most effectively through what can be seen with our eyes. Verbal metaphors and analogies can be just as powerful as the work of the visual artist. As I have tried to indicate in this and earlier chapters, the sadness is that Christians have not always conceded them their proper power. Biblical metaphors thus become as much entrapments of the spirit for some contemporary Christians, as sculptures once were for the ancient world. Just as the verbal once rightly acted as a critique of the visual, so perhaps in our own age the visual needs now to return the compliment, and encourage greater openness in appropriating the verbal.

To see such a potential for the visual in practice we need to step outside our own particular religious tradition, and consider the very different role accorded the visual within Hinduism. That idolatry of the most superstitious kind is sometimes present can hardly be denied. But more educated Hindus have a legitimate case when they insist that the visual functions quite differently within their own religion from the way it does in Christianity. In effect it acts as

[96] For the former, John 20.8; for others, 20.29. The fact that these verses encase Mary's story almost compel that particular reading, and so make the verbal less free than the visual.

guardian of the transcendence of deity in much the same way as we westerners commonly think can only be achieved by words. The riot of imagery in Hindu temples actually protects against precisely the possibility of any one in particular being seen as definitive. Equally, when worshippers enter the *garbha griha* or inner shrine, the single image they encounter is not only sometimes aniconic (as in Shiva's *linga*) but also, even where representational, so shrouded in flowers and worn down by anointing as to be no longer easily legible. Hinduism is thus frequently misread at a key point in its practice, most obviously perhaps in the false supposition that because the *linga* was phallic in origin that is how it now functions rather than as symbol. Again, just as westerners contend that words preserve the otherness of divine address, so Hindus make the same claim for the visual. In looking at images they talk of the importance of *darshan*, of being observed by the divine rather than a purely human initiative in actually looking at the deity.[97] That way the absolute priority of divine grace is maintained. Some modern reformers even argue for a return to the priority of the visual in a religion now in their view altogether too corrupted by words; so even in reforming zeal there are parallels.

Of course in a religion like Christianity so heavily committed to doctrinal definition few are ever likely to concede parity for the verbal and visual. But that the reductionism associated with words is perhaps Christianity's greater danger does, I think, need to be conceded: that is, the temptation to suppose that definitive articulation has now been reached. Too often in the past analogies and metaphors have been reified and set in complete opposition to one another, whereas a more realistic option might have been to see them as complementary. A hopeful sign of changing attitudes is to be found in a recent report of the Doctrine Commission of the Church of England. There eight types of approach to atonement with their corresponding images and stories are treated as complementary rather than, as in the past, set in opposition to one another.[98] Likewise, despite having written a book favouring one particular analogy for the Trinity (the social), I would now

---

[97] *Darshan* is a repeated theme in T. R. Blurton, *Hindu Art* (London: British Museum Press, 1992). Another commentator finds 'grace' indispensable to his exposition: V. Dehejia, *Indian Art* (London: Phaidon, 1997), 137.

[98] *The Mystery of Salvation* (London: Church House, 1995), 102–19.

be inclined to say that the other (the psychological) also has its merits, and should not therefore be entirely jettisoned.[99] To speak in that way and thus recognize that the metaphorical and analogical in doctrine allow greater complementarity than has been appreciated hitherto is to draw words closer to images. Neither verbal nor visual would then instantiate reality exactly as it is.

Perhaps, in conclusion, what happens in the eucharist may be used to present the more complementary approach I am seeking to advocate here. Calvin spoke of the sacraments as enacted preachments, thereby giving priority to word.[100] But truer to our experience would be the fact that neither verbal nor visual work entirely on their own in such contexts. How the service is seen to be conducted matters no less than what is said. Each needs the other to produce the typical rounded experience. Yet even that is not quite true, because other senses such as touch and taste also play their part. In effect, we have what the Germans call a *Gesamtkunstwerk*. My plea for proper acknowledgement for the role of the visual is thus not an attempt to supplant one exclusivity with another, but rather a plea for a more rounded view of the totality of the types of senses that contribute to the reception of divine revelation. God after all made us with five senses and not one. So it would seem not unreasonable to suppose that the whole gamut of which God is creator would be used to communicate with us and thus, centrally, the visual no less than the verbal.

It is that integration of the aural and the visual that I want to explore further in the second part of this book, as I turn to consider some of the ways in which drama might open us up to the possibility of experiencing the divine, and the implications this might have for how the eucharist is celebrated.

[99] My earlier position is to be found in *The Divine Trinity* (London: Duckworth, 1985), esp. 272–80.

[100] e.g. *Institutes of the Christian Religion*, IV. xiv. 3–4.

Experience through Drama

As in the first part of this work, I shall be concerned here also to progress towards worship from a much wider context in what would now be regarded as the secular sphere. So, just as, in Part I, I began with the significance of words, and of metaphor in particular, before proceeding to consideration of congregational singing and preaching, so here it is only after an initial examination of ordinary drama and its connections with religion that I propose moving towards examination of choral music and liturgy more generally. Such a progression reflects my conviction that much has been lost in modern liturgical developments by treating liturgy as a discipline in its own right that can function entirely adequately without regard to its most obvious natural partners. Some liturgists might agree at this point, but suppose that I mean academic theology more generally (biblical and doctrinal). While such an alliance could bring advantages, that is not my point here. While worship is a duty we owe to God irrespective of what it offers to us, that presumption provides no excuse for ignoring the sort of impact it actually has on worshippers, not least on their immediate experience. If it fails to evoke a sense of the presence of God, something has surely gone badly wrong. The question then arises where the fault lies, and for that question to be adequately answered, I suggest it is not sufficient to look to the liturgy itself. Instead, it is necessary to examine parallels with how human experience is handled elsewhere under related, if not exactly parallel, conditions.

Even so, to some, drama will seem quite the wrong category with which to associate worship. The root meaning of the Greek word is human 'action', whereas for them Christian worship is essentially a matter of a divinely given word and our response to

it in adoration and praise. It is only thereafter in our action outside
the building that a more active response becomes appropriate, in
working towards the establishment of Christ's kingdom. But, while
some may find the quiet recitation of the daily offices enough to
sustain and direct their thoughts, most of us need help in focusing
those thoughts. At the very least, in order to avoid engendering
monotony or boredom, this will entail variations in emphasis as
something is read, and probably also some form of contextualiza-
tion for the passages in question. Sermons are also quite likely to
send us to sleep, unless there is some element of performance about
them. But the issue is not just one of communication. Equally
pertinent is how we conceive of God's self-communication to us.
Not only was the incarnation a downward movement from the
divine into the totality of human experience, the eucharist also
seeks to continue that process by enabling us to join with Christ in
his self-offering to his Father. So it would be odd, to say the least, if
the offering of our bodies were held back and only our minds
brought into play. As the 1662 Prayer Book puts it: 'Here we
offer and present unto thee, O Lord, ourselves, our souls and
bodies, to be a reasonable, holy, and lively sacrifice unto thee.'[1]

Even so, the comparison with theatre and stage may still seem a
step too far: the sacred reduced by comparison with the secular.
However, as I have been concerned to argue throughout this book,
such contrasts are essentially modern and necessarily result in a
marginalization of religion. All of life was once seen through the
prism of the divine, and could be once more. Although contested
by some scholars, it seems to me that the association of ancient
Greek drama with religion ran deep. It was by no means just a
matter of accident that the performance of both tragedy and
comedy took place in the context of a religious festival. Not only
were the themes frequently religious, so too, as we shall see, were
the aims. Nor do such associations between dramatic performance
and religion cease with Christianity. Admittedly, that relationship
began in hostility, but when theatre was at last allowed to re-
emerge, it began an association that has lasted much longer than is

---

[1] From Holy Communion, first of two concluding prayers; cf. Rom. 12.1.
Unfortunately, most modern translations (e.g. RSV) render the AV's 'reasonable
service' as 'spiritual worship'. But *logikon* carries no such contrast with the material
world or body.

commonly appreciated. In view of common assumptions about the universal and inevitable advance of secularism, it will be intriguing to observe in due course how several major theatre directors of the twentieth century were actually concerned to restore to theatre just such a spiritual focus.

While such issues will be the focus of the first chapter that follows, the next then explores the tradition of liturgical and choral music. Here I explore the often tumultuous relations between the Church and its musicians, from the Middle Ages onwards. One key theme that has persisted throughout has been the concern of reformers to ensure at the very least that the words were clearly heard and that the experience of the music should remain firmly subordinate to the liturgy as whole. That concern has often expressed itself in the exclusion of certain types of music as essentially secular, or too difficult.[2] In those recurring arguments what is usually ignored is any consideration of how different forms of music are supposed to achieve their effect, and so the need for education and induction into certain ways of hearing. Were that task taken with proper seriousness, the role of music as a legitimate element in the overall drama would be more enthusiastically accepted by congregations. Instead, for many it is to the concert hall or to their CD player that they turn for an experience of God through such music. Any such possibility is of course sometimes precluded from church by shortage of resources but just as commonly the real fault is a lack of imagination over what might be permitted.

In the final chapter 'Performance, Costume, Staging' I explore more directly the liturgical setting itself. In Part I, I have already identified some key issues about the sort of language that is required, especially a richness in allusion and metaphor that allows the mind to return again and again for fresh stimulation and reflection. So here the focus is rather on the theatrical props, as it were. While my concern with the ritual of bodily expression continues themes that were prominent in this volume's predecessor, the focus on staging takes up a concern of the first of these three volumes, the architectural setting.[3] The discussion of liturgical costume has,

---

[2] Mozart and Schubert Masses might be used to illustrate the former, medieval and some twentieth-century compositions the latter.

[3] For body, *God and Grace of Body* (Oxford: Oxford University Press, 2007), esp. chs. 1–4; for architecture, *God and Enchantment of Place* (Oxford: Oxford University Press, 2004), esp, chs. 5 and 6.

however, no precedent. What that discussion well illustrates is how even something as apparently recondite and trivial as what clergy wear in church has never, and can never, stand apart from the wider society of which the Church is indissolubly part. Clothes have always had a symbolic import, and continue to do so.

The result is that the book will end as the project began, by pleading for the setting of religious experience in the much wider framework that it has borne through most of human history. Its current narrowing in so much theological and philosophical writing does not exempt the Church from the impact of such symbolic mediation as exists outside its doors. Sadly, it simply means that most flee outside in order to renew their experience of God under more favourable conditions.

5
Drama and Religion

IN this chapter I want to explore the history of the theatre and drama and its varying relationships with religious belief. As my ultimate aim in this second half of the book is to draw implications for the performance of liturgy in our own day, I shall begin in the ancient world where the term 'liturgy' had its origins and where one such liturgical act was the staging of drama. Thereafter, I shall trace the revival of religious drama after its initial suppression by Christianity, not only in medieval mystery plays but also in now largely forgotten Reformation and Counter-Reformation drama. Then I turn to baroque poetry and explore how disputes about ritual often reflected wider cultural change that is indebted to notions of theatre. Finally, something needs to be said about our present situation. In particular, I shall draw attention to the ways in which, to the surprise of many, a relationship with religion continues, especially in the various theories that have been proposed about the value and purpose of drama.

Liturgy and Classical Drama

As some readers will know, the term 'liturgy' has deep roots in dramatic performance. Before examining these, a brief note on how present usage originated may be of some help. Although the word was in continuous use throughout the centuries in eastern Christendom, it only returned to common currency in the west in the eighteenth century. With its endorsement by the Second Vatican Council it has quickly once again become the most widely used term for services of worship. This has meant a return to how the word was used in the Septuagint, where the term occurs over a hundred times. It is used mostly of the worship of priests and Levites in the tabernacle and temple, though occasionally it is also employed of pagan worship.[1] Use in the New Testament is much less frequent. Here it mainly refers back to the Jewish cult.[2] However, at one point Christ is called by analogy a minister of the sanctuary, while twice Paul applies similar terminology to himself.[3] The Greek literally means 'a work done on behalf of the people'. Clearly the New Testament continues that representative meaning, but on the whole finds such representation in what would now be understood to be non-liturgical contexts. There is one possible exception.[4] More characteristic is Paul's identification of the collection for the poor in Jerusalem in this way: it is something done on behalf of others.[5]

In view of the modern stress on congregational participation in the liturgy it might be thought hazardous to hark back to those roots, in stressing representative roles. It would be more accurate, however, to observe that much modern liturgy has merely widened the range of representatives rather than secured universal, corporate participation. Readers, intercessors, and so forth are no longer drawn exclusively from the clergy, but on the whole they continue to come from a small select band within the congregation. It is in any case worth pondering whether the congregation even when acting corporately does not still fulfil a representative role, in that it seeks to do something on behalf of humanity as a whole, and perhaps the whole creation. Certainly, there was a strong current in ancient Judaism that thought of liturgy in precisely those terms. Although not explicitly stated within Scripture itself, the later assumption was that menorah, basin, and so on were all intended to allude to the Temple's key role in preserving creation in existence and the need to present it as an offering back to God.[6] That assumption may well date much further back than is usually accepted.[7] If such attitudes are without direct parallel in fifth- and

---

[1] For typical examples, Exod. 28; Ezek. 40; for worship of idols, Ezek. 44.12.
[2] Including cognates, 15 times.
[3] Heb. 8.2; Rom. 15.16 and Phil. 2.17.
[4] Acts 13.2: 'Set apart Barnabas and Saul for the work to which I have called them.'
[5] For the collection in this role, Rom. 15.27 and 2 Cor. 9.12.
[6] A recurring theme in the extracts gathered in C. T. R. Hayward ed., *The Jewish Temple: A Non-Biblical Sourcebook* (London: Routledge, 1996).
[7] Consider Exod. 40.16–33, where eight times it is stressed that Moses arranged the tabernacle as the Lord had commanded him. B. S. Childs presupposes an allusion to the sabbath command, but it seems to me more likely that the seven days of creation are directly in play, not least because that is the ultimate basis of the sabbath command in Exod. 20.8. For Childs's view, *The Book of Exodus* (Louisville: Westminster, 1974), 634, 638.

fourth-century BC Athens where the term 'liturgy' had its origins, most of the other elements mentioned can also be detected.

In Greek thought (especially Athenian) *leitourgia* was a service offered by the wealthy on behalf of the citizenry as a whole. Although usually secured under implicit compulsion, it seems mostly to have been regarded as an honour, despite the resultant burdens.[8] The form such service could take greatly varied. In case of a trier-archy, it involved not only paying for all the maintenance and repair expenses of a rowing trireme but also captaining the vessel, an onerous business that was eventually shared between two indivi-duals.[9] The sporting facilities in Athens' three gymnasia were sup-ported annually in a similar way, as were the annual dramatic competitions. From surviving inscriptions we know that great pride was taken in victories at the latter, for integral to the dramatist's success was not just the intrinsic merit of the plays but also the quality of the chorus employed, the richness of scenery and costumes, rehearsal facilities, and so on, all furnished by the *choregos* or individual who had undertaken this particular liturgical task.[10] If all this seems far removed from any element of religion, it is worth recalling that Athens' wars were fought under the protection of her gods (hence the trireme as liturgical), while even gymnasia were given a sacred character by being set by a river and grove dedicated to the gods.[11]

Nor was the theatre any different. Admittedly, there are some contemporary scholars who have claimed that religion was purely incidental to the famed dramatic performances of fifth-century Athens and later.[12] In part this may be a reaction against the so-called Cambridge Ritualist School that at the beginning of the twentieth century had used now almost universally rejected arguments to advocate intimate links with fertility and puberty

[8] Nomination was by turn through magistrates, but one could volunteer, or argue the case for someone better placed. For mention of volunteers, Lysias, *Speeches* 21. 1–6. The adoption of the practice more widely in the Greek East explains its application in the Septuagint.

[9] The boat itself was provided by the state. Sharing of the responsibility between two citizens was introduced in 411 BC.

[10] For a mean *choregus* ruining a play, Aristotle, *Nichomachean Ethics* 4.2.

[11] The Lyceum was on the banks of the Cephisus, the Academy and the Cynosarges by the Eridanus and the Illisus.

[12] O. Taplin, *Greek Tragedy in Action* (Oxford: Oxford University Press, 1978); I. C. Storey and A. Allan, *A Guide to Ancient Greek Drama* (Oxford: Blackwell, 2005), 24.

rituals.[13] The root meaning of the term 'tragedy', for instance, was connected not with the award of a goat as prize but rather with an analogous use to the English 'kid' in speaking of children on the verge of puberty. What survives uncontested from that earlier discussion is the close link with festivals of the god Dionysus, in particular the city Dionysia and the rural Lenaia.[14] As with the world of politics, this meant that cultic sacrifices were an integral part of the celebrations.[15] More importantly, the choice of the god Dionysus as patron seems more than just fortuitous. The connection of aspects of Dionysus' own legend with liminal experiences legitimated the performance of dramas that also themselves explored areas of uncertainty and otherness.[16]

That feature of uncertainty and openness has been taken by some to indicate contrasts rather than parallels with religion. Certainly, what was on offer in no way resembled an exposition of religious doctrine or even a simple appeal to faith. But this is very far from conceding, as some have claimed, that the dramatic content was really therefore a very human wrestling with life's dilemmas, in terms of which the gods became mere ciphers. On that analysis they functioned as symbols for the issues rather than themselves being constituent players in the way in which the drama unfolded. So, for instance, for one critic Aeschylus' real interest is in justice not Zeus, and Sophocles is more concerned with heroes than with treating the gods in a way consistent with his reputation for conventional piety. Only Euripides is taken to evoke something like traditional attitudes, and that despite his reputation for the opposite.[17] While it

[13] Seen especially among classicists in the writings of Francis Cornford, Jane Harrison, and Gilbert Murray. For a brief resumé of their theories and their relation to those of Burkert and Girard, S. Goldhill, 'Modern Critical Approaches to Greek Tragedy' in P. E. Easterling ed., *Cambridge Companion to Greek Tragedy* (Cambridge: Cambridge University Press, 1997), 324–47, esp. 331–6.

[14] The authoritative reference work is still A. Pickard-Cambridge, *The Dramatic Festivals of Athens* (Oxford: Clarendon, 1953; 3rd edn. 1968).

[15] Every Assembly began with a blood sacrifice and prayers. The sacred procession or *pompe* into the theatre is described by S. Goldhill in Easterling, *Greek Tragedy*, 55. For sacrifice as part of a 'performance culture', Cartledge in ibid. 5–6.

[16] A prominent argument in J.-P. Vernant and P. Vidal-Naquet, *Myth and Tragedy in Ancient Greece* (Cambridge, Mass.: MIT Press, 1988).

[17] J. D. Mikalson, *Honor Thy Gods: Popular Religion in Greek Tragedy* (Chapel Hill: University of North Carolina Press, 1991). For Aeschylus, 210–13; for Sophocles, 39, 217–25; for Euripides, 6–7, 225–30.

is true that there is little deference to the gods and much incon-
sistency in doctrine between plays, care needs to be exercised in
imposing modern assumptions about attitudes to divinity.[18] Perhaps
a parallel with the Psalter might be drawn. The plaintive, accusatory
tone of some of the psalms also no longer finds an echo in modern
Christian piety, while there are similar inconsistencies in theology.[19] All three of Athens' major dramatists seem to me better
viewed as using the stage to explore tensions in religious experience, but without themselves necessarily giving any specific
answers. The nearest biblical parallel might therefore be the Wisdom
literature of the Old Testament, especially the book of Job, rather
than the Hebrew history books or even the Gospels.

In the work of Aeschylus and Sophocles we find myth and story
being continuously adapted (within appropriate limits) to new
forms that more easily facilitate fresh exploration of certain key
issues.[20] Sophocles' treatment of Oedipus, for instance, is quite
different from that of Homer, but different too from that apparently
accorded by Aeschylus: the 'facts' change, as well as the moral
implications.[21] Again, in the one case where three plays from
each of the three major dramatists survive dealing with the same
theme (Electra), it is interesting to observe how changing the
location of the play's action enables Euripides also to alter profoundly the implicit evaluation of the various figures involved.[22]
Part of the motivation for such change is undoubtedly different
theologies. Aeschylus is convinced of cast-iron laws operating that
secure some justice between cause and effect. Sophocles, though no
less pious, thinks the workings of divine justice hidden from us;

---

[18] He notes that blaming of the gods is more frequent than it seems to have
been in ordinary life: 18. While right to suggest that popular religion was more
concerned with honour than love or faith (202), Mikalson surely goes too far in
reductively suggesting that 'in popular religion a god existed primarily to perform
his functions' (77).

[19] There are conflicting theories about suffering, the existence of other gods,
how creation is upheld, and so on.

[20] 'Appropriate limits' are not easy to specify, but some had to be maintained, if
it was still to constitute the same story.

[21] *Odyssey* 11. 271–80. For differences from Aeschylus, Storey and Allan, *Greek
Drama*, 234.

[22] P. Burian, 'Myth into *muthos*: the Shaping of Tragic Plot' in Easterling, *Greek
Tragedy*, 178–208, esp. 179–80, 196. The relevant plays are the *Electra* of Sophocles
and Euripides and *The Libation Bearers* of Aeschylus.

so all we can do is face our fortunes heroically.[23] Euripides is different again. Although the most radical questioner of the three, he is more prepared to adopt a conservative strategy to secure his end. So, for the most part he leaves myths about the gods unchanged.[24] It is almost as though he wanted the dilemmas posed by their anthropomorphic character presented as starkly as possible.

That pattern of change is by no means only a Greek phenomenon. Numerous parallels can be quoted in the changing character of biblical narratives both within the canon and subsequently.[25] Nor did such changes in narrative occur only in the ancient world. Turn to dramatists of the Christian centuries such as Racine or Goethe, and similar processes will be found to be at work, as further modifications are made to the inherited form of ancient myths.[26] Not only that, pagan myth and Christian story continue to interact in creative and dynamic ways. Take, for example, the changes Goethe made in his *Iphigenie auf Tauris*. These neatly parallel Handel's decision (in the case of a biblical story) to save Jephthah's daughter from her father's pyre (in his oratorio *Jephtha*).[27] Indeed, the name chosen for the anonymous girl (Iphis) makes explicit precisely that interaction.[28] Both Handel and Goethe were concerned to portray human life as no mere plaything of the gods, and so ensure that self-sacrifice continued to be regarded as the highest religious ideal.[29]

---

[23] The contrast is nicely summarized in H. D. F. Kitto, *Greek Tragedy* (London: Methuen, 3rd edn. 1961), 148–9.

[24] Quite compatible with major changes in what happens to the human figures involved, e.g. in his two versions of *Hippolytus*: Burian, 'Myth into *muthos*', 201–2.

[25] Explored in my two volumes *Tradition and Imagination* (Oxford: Oxford University Press, 1999) and *Discipleship and Imagination* (Oxford: Oxford University Press, 2000): e.g. in the infancy narratives and sacrifice of Isaac in the former (72–105, 237–60); on Job in the latter (177–225).

[26] For changes in Racine's *Phèdre* and in Goethe's *Iphigenie auf Tauris*, P. Burian, 'Tragedy Adapted for Stages and Screens' in Easterling, *Greek Tragedy*, 228–83, esp. 235–8.

[27] Judges 11.29ff.

[28] The initial decision may have been made by Handel's librettist (Morrell), but Handel did endorse the change.

[29] For further discussion of the influence of the story of Iphigenia on that of Isaac, see my *Tradition and Imagination*, 200–2.

It could be argued that such questioning was rendered safe by being set in the distant past, and that this was the rationale for the mythological setting. Perhaps, but it was by no means always the case that the events depicted were so obviously remote. Although given a mythic colouring with dreams, portents, and so on, Aeschylus' *Persians* is almost contemporary with the events it is describing. Again, comedy in particular did not hesitate to raise political issues of the day. So too did tragedy, if usually more indirectly. The high value Euripides accords the opinions of women and slaves is an obvious case in point, something of which both Plutarch and Origen complained.[30] In any case in a culture where theological issues were being raised elsewhere (as in the poetry of Pindar or the philosophy of Xenophanes), it is unlikely that the audience would have left the questions embedded in the safety of the myth. More plausible is the contention that the overall religious context of the performance allowed issues to be raised without this being seen as undermining civic and personal religion as such. Not only were such exploratory dramas presented in the context of a religious celebration, the final play of the traditional four was by convention a satyr play in which a more confidently optimistic note could be struck, of harmony in relations between human and divine.[31]

If this account is anywhere near correct, the whole process may have something to teach the Church of our own day. Instead of questions controversial to its life being raised (as at present) overwhelmingly outside the church building and its liturgy, they could after all find their focus at the heart of worship. Clearly this would not be possible in corporate and communal parts of the liturgy such as the creed or other recurring parts in the Ordinary of the mass, but from this it by no means follows that only the sermon is available as a possible forum. Song or short dramatic presentations are also possibilities. Under such a scenario not only would the liturgy provide a restraining context of love in mutual recognition of the other in which to hear opinions and ideas from which the majority demurred, but also advocates of new positions would be forced to locate their views more explicitly in relation to the traditions of the

[30] Plutarch, *De Aud. Poet.* 28a; Origen, *Contra Celsum* 7. 36. 34–6. For two examples of plain speaking from slaves, *Andromache*, 186–90; *Helen*, 728–31.
[31] The normal pattern, as noted by Easterling, 'A Show for Dionysus' in Easterling, *Greek Tragedy*, 36–53, esp. 39.

Church. It is all too easy to posit indifference to theological matters in the ancient Athenian audience. Of course the nature of their communal bond was significantly different from that alleged to hold in the Church. Even so, it does look as though it gave them a freedom to explore in dramatic performance precisely because that performance was also in some clear sense an act of worship. So, despite initial appearances, Greek religion may have provided a confidence that contemporary Christianity lacks. Of course, the possibility of such exploration came in part through its lack of a formal creed. Equally, however, modern Christians are far too ready to assume any critique to be a threat to faith's foundations.

Apart from religious content there were other major differences from modern conventional drama. Aeschylus had to operate with a chorus of between twelve and fifteen and only two actors, expanded under Sophocles and Euripides to three.[32] Since theatres might hold ten thousand spectators or more, the experiential 'feel' of the event must have been quite different. Actors would appear tiny to the back rows. While masks offered some basic clues, gestures of a strongly rhetorical kind would be needed by way of supplement.[33] Even so, these might not always be noticed.[34] This is no doubt one reason why, rather than providing original information, the chorus on the whole comments and supplements.[35] Fortunately, acoustics were excellent. But in a sense they had to be, since so much would have depended on hearing the words. At the same time added complications were introduced by the fact that actors had to play multiple roles. Male and female, good and bad characters, were adopted indifferently by the same actor.[36] So in determining who was now speaking the audience could not rely on voice alone but also needed the help of what was being said. That is no doubt why in stichomythia (short exchanges) the convention of

[32] The dithyrambic chorus (or hymn) to Dionysus had many more (probably, 50). It is sometimes argued that the same was also true of some plays: Pickard-Cambridge, *Dramatic Festivals*, 234–5.

[33] For Quintilian and a scholia on Euripides' *Orestes* pointing in the same direction, P. T. Arnott, *Public and Performance in the Greek Theatre* (London: Routledge, 1989), 69–70.

[34] For the contrast with the possibility of more intimate gestures in modern acting, Arnott, *Public and Performance*, 112.

[35] The sung lyric metres would be more difficult to understand. In the main iambic metre was used for dialogue, anapaests for recitative.

[36] For examples, Arnott, *Public and Performance*, 165.

single-line responses was maintained, to leave the audience in no doubt as to whose turn it was now to speak.

Precisely because of the quality of the acoustics, a further important consequence followed. Not only were the actor's words easily heard but also the reactions of the audience throughout the auditorium. So personal responses could not help but be affected by how others were reacting. The drama was thus essentially a communal experience, accentuated by the key role given to the chorus. Because its members were local volunteers, they were in effect already an extension of the audience onto the stage. But the process also worked in reverse. The responses given to the chorus by the dramatist helped shape those of the wider audience. Here once again modern liturgy is perhaps not as far distant from the ancient model as is it is from more recent staged performance. With the lights down in the contemporary theatre, each one of the spectators in effect retreats into his or her own private world, whereas with the ancient stage that was impossible. Similarly, in a church service the tendency is for gestures and style of response to spread and eventually through repeated practice become uniform across a congregation. Uniformity in charismatic gestures comes to mind. The rise or demise of genuflection within a particular congregation might equally be a case in point.[37] All this suggests that parallels with the ancient audience are not wanting.

Some readers may find such comparisons objectionable. It seems to me that they are ignored at our peril. Christian liturgy is like ancient drama a 'mythic' act. It strives to explore the nature of the human relationship to the divine through the retelling of canonical stories that have been given different slants, as need arises. No doubt what will reinforce resistance in some to such a comparison will be recollection (keen or otherwise) of Nietzsche's portrayal of the cult of Dionysus in essentially reductionist terms: it was really all about the human, not the divine.[38] Increasingly, however, classical scholars are insisting that this was simply untrue of ancient practice and belief. The cult of Dionysus was itself integral to what appeared on the stage.[39] Even his wild female followers, the Maenads, should

[37] Not only charismatic gestures becomes ritualized but even the order and form of such services: D. Stancliffe, *God's Pattern* (London: SPCK, 2003), 38.

[38] As in his *Birth of Tragedy* (1871) and elsewhere.

[39] A repeated theme of the contributions to T. H. Carpenter and C. A. Faraone eds., *Masks of Dionysus* (Ithaca: Cornell University Press, 1993).

be seen more as supernatural nymphs acting on his behalf than as ordinary human beings.[40] The religious experience implied may be more chaotic than Christianity has usually been prepared to contemplate, but it is not without parallel in other major contemporary religions. If the severe bearded figure of the cult seems at first sight totally at variance with the playful youth of the drama, Vishnu's avatar, Krishna, and his various 'comic' turns suggests a not dissimilar dichotomy.[41]

From Rejection to Medieval and Reformation Sacred Drama

Sadly, Christianity's initial response to the stage was almost uniformly hostile. So it comes as no surprise that it took till the later Middle Ages before such presentations eventually returned in full flood in the mystery plays. Conventional wisdom suggests fresh hostility from Protestants at the Reformation. The truth is more complex, and needs to be noted both for what it says about the human condition and for how such insights might be applied to stage and liturgy in our own day.

It is one of the great ironies in the history of drama that our best evidence for its continuing vitality in the last days of the Roman Empire comes from its fiercest opponents, Christian bishops and theologians. Eusebius relates how ostentatiously enthusiastic or otherwise audiences could be in their reactions, Gregory of Nyssa how spectacular the scenery might be.[42] But it is John Chrysostom who provides us with most details. Despite his hostility, it has even been suggested that some of his own homilies may have been 'performed', with the bishop as 'actor' commenting on a particular tableau. Although this seems unlikely in view of prevailing Christian attitudes and his own savage critique of the stage, there is no doubt about the

---

[40] Argued persuasively in R. Schlesier, 'Mixtures of Masks: Maenads as Tragic Models' in Carpenter and Faraone, *Masks of Dionysus*, 89–114. Supported by the artistic evidence in T. H. Carpenter, *Dionysiac Imagery in Fifth-Century Athens* (Oxford: Clarendon, 1997), e.g. 82–4, 121.

[41] Such as stealing butter or the clothes of the *gopis* (cow maidens).

[42] Eusebius, *Ecclesiastical History* 7. 30; cf. Lucian, *De saltione* 76. Gregory of Nyssa, *Epistles* 9. 1 (*ad Stagirium*).

impact of the theatre on the oratory of the time.[43] Sermons might even be applauded, judged according to their success or otherwise as good rhetorical performance.[44] Chrysostom's critique is still commonly equated with objections to the licentious nature of the plots and the low life of actors and actresses.[45] While that was undoubtedly a contributing element, it is probable that he had wider considerations in his sights. Despite its effect on him, in his eyes the stage prevented the right kind of religious experience: a humble, graced life led under the all-seeing eye of God. Rather, plays encouraged the desire for ostentation, display, and pure entertainment, and with that the vainglory that he saw as at the root of original sin.[46] For him there could be no such thing as innocent laughter at the pantomime and burlesque of the day, as that was implicitly to sanction unacceptable moral behaviour.[47] Yet the very attractiveness of the medium is acknowledged not only in the rhetorical character of his sermons but also in the way in which he deploys analogies with theatre to parody views within the Church to which he is opposed, among them spiritual or celibate marriage. Men pretending to such a relationship were like comic actors emasculated in their assumed role, women like tragic figures waiting to be seduced.[48]

The surprise is that no attempt was made to intervene in stage performances through providing alternative more acceptable themes. Instead, the nearest the theatre came to Christianity was in jokes at its expense, with pagan stories continuing to provide some residual justification for rather different attitudes to the divine.[49] So censorship and eventual abolition was perhaps

[43] Suggested by George LaPiana at the beginning of the twentieth century. For the extent of Chrysostom's borrowing from the theatre, including dialogue, soliloquy, and choral interludes, S. Longosz, 'I germi del drama cristiano nella literatura patristica', *Studia Patristica* 31 (1997), 59–69.

[44] E. Hatch, *The Influence of Greek Ideas on Christianity* (New York: Harper, 1957 edn.), 88–115, esp. 96–7.

[45] Still the tendency in J. N. D. Kelly's biography, *Golden Mouth* (Grand Rapids: Baker, 1995), e.g. 78–9, 135. Women were by this time performing, at least in mimes.

[46] Well developed in B. Leyerle, *Theatrical Shows and Ascetic Lives* (Berkeley: University of California Press, 2001), 44–60.

[47] He appeals to the Beatitudes: *Hom. in Matt.* 6. 6 (PG 57.70).

[48] Leyerle, *Theatrical Shows*, 100–182.

[49] For some examples of such jokes, Chrysostom, *Hom. in Eph.* 17. 2 (PG 62.120); *Hom. in Heb.* 15. 3–4 (PG 63.121–2). As an example, consider the following: 'Woe to you, Mammon,—when you haven't got enough of it!'

inevitable, with the nearest surviving equivalent now in the Christian liturgy itself. There is no need to rehearse here the various dramatic moments the liturgy provided, except to note not only their expansion as the centuries advanced but also the introduction of seasonable elements that helped recapture some of the power of the abandoned art form, most obviously at first in the liturgy of Holy Week. The elevation of the host is an obvious piece of drama from medieval times.[50] Notable for their comic character were the ceremonies of the Boy Bishop around Christmas, usually on Holy Innocents Day, when at various churches and cathedrals across western Europe a boy was elected bishop for the day. Dressed in full pontificals, he was allowed to preach, as well as preside in other ways.[51] Holy Week and Easter provided more solemn moments, with the symbolic burial of Christ and the visit of the three Marys to the tomb among new medieval enactments.[52]

It used to be thought that the medieval mystery plays of the fourteenth century and later had their origin in these liturgical rites. Nowadays, they are more commonly seen as an independent tradition, not least because they were performed for the most part in the vernacular and out of doors. Of the numerous English cycles that once existed, four have survived: those from York and Chester and two others commonly known as Towneley and Coventry but probably to be associated with Wakefield and East Anglia.[53] They were performed at the relatively new feast of Corpus Christi, itself only introduced in the western calendar in 1264 by Pope Urban IV.[54] What is telling about the pope's words of justification is their oft repeated theme of joy. Maundy Thursday is too crowded he suggests with other reflections, set as it is on the eve of Good Friday.

[50] The earliest injunction requiring elevation after consecration of the host comes from the Bishop of Paris in 1210.

[51] The Boy Bishop ceremonies have been revived (in part) at Hereford and Salisbury. For a detailed description of the former (restored in 1982), P. Iles, *The Boy Bishop Ceremony* (Hereford, 1992).

[52] The earliest example of the three Marys ritual to survive comes from tenth-century Winchester.

[53] The most easily accessible selection is P. Happé ed., *English Mystery Plays* (London: Penguin, 1975).

[54] As Jacques Pantaléon he had been archdeacon of Liège when Blessed Juliana had her vision urging such a feast. Despite Aquinas' composition of the liturgy of the day, it seems to have made slow progress until the decree was reissued by Pope John XXII in 1317.

So what is wanted is a day that can be given over to what he calls a 'glorious act of remembrance, which fills the minds of the faithful with joy at their salvation and brings them tears mingled with a flood of reverent joy'. And so 'there will sound forth from the mouths and lips of all, hymns of joy at the salvation God has wrought for us'.[55] Little wonder then that the joy of drama came to be associated with this feast.

On a more practical level the timing of the feast was highly appropriate. From Advent to Ascension and on to Pentecost, the Church calendar is firmly controlled by a temporal sequence that focuses on specific incidents in the history of salvation. Corpus Christi (together with the preceding Trinity Sunday) is the first period in the year to break free from such a rigid pattern. So it offered the possibility of something more, the ability to look back over the story that had been told in the preceding nine months and say something about its significance overall. The plays therefore run all the way from the Creation to the Last Judgement, with two principal recurring themes: God's compassion for his people (however often we may let him down, he never reciprocates), and the way in which all of history culminates in Christ. To underline the latter point, typology is repeatedly used. Spectators are encouraged not only to see the story of Abraham's sacrifice of Isaac as a pointer towards that greater offering made by the Son but also a similar anticipation in Abel. Similarly, Noah's ark is treated as a figure of the Church, the Red Sea of the waters of baptism, and so on.

Details, however, are less important than the overall theme, that God was working out a plan for his people, including contemporary folk. So, all of this must bring joy. It is into such a context that the plays' rough and sometimes earthy humour needs to be set: Mrs Noah, for instance, scolding Noah, the shepherds fighting among themselves (the thief and rogue Mak among them), Joseph teased for having been cuckolded by his wife, and so on. Some have suggested that these traits are the first signs of secularization, of a less reverential and so less religious approach. I do not believe it. Equally, however, I am unpersuaded by those who want to find a serious and devout purpose after all in the humour. For them it is the dramatist's way of accentuating the key role of divine

---

[55] For Latin text, V. A. Kolve, *The Play Called Corpus Christi* (Stanford: Stanford University Press, 1966), 45.

grace: grace operating even where human beings seem muddled and incompetent, with values reversed.[56] Far more probable, it seems to me, is that it is simply a case of the authors rejoicing in the presence of God in the everyday, in situations like the audience's own lives, where precisely the same sort of mix could be found. Although there is no connection between the two types of drama, it is surely interesting to observe that the comedies of Aristophanes were no less constitutive of Greek religious feasts than were the tragedies of Aeschylus and Sophocles. No part of life could be excluded from divine concern.

It is perhaps by thinking further along such lines that the obsession of the plays with the miraculous side to the events might become more relevant to our own day. Medieval Latin drama had been quite restrained. Not only was there no humour, nor God ever appearing on stage, even Christ was more likely to be represented by a wafer or Mary by a statue, lest too crude understandings of their identity should develop.[57] Admittedly, some have interpreted such moves in precisely the opposite direction, as premised on a crude realism, with the statue actually identified with Mary, for example. That I think unlikely. With other parts acted, it was a way of maintaining awe and distance.

In the English drama such restraint was thrown to the winds. What became possible as a result was ability to stress the wonder of God appearing in the most ordinary and everyday: amid a badgering Mrs Noah, shepherds complaining of poor wages, or youngsters wrestling even in the presence of the Christ Child.[58] Numerous anachronisms also helped to give a sense of events that might just as easily have taken place in the England of the time. In the Chester play the knights who slay the Holy Innocents compare themselves to 'the kinge of Scotis and all his host', in Towneley Cain is buried at Goodybower quarry just outside Wakefield, and so on.[59] Even so, realism was not the result. As with ancient drama, lack of continuity in actors' parts and the artificiality of the staging (in

[56] Kolve's argument in the relevant chapter, ibid. 145–74, esp. 173–4.

[57] The host represents the buried Christ and a statue Mary in the eleventh-century Rouen *Pastores*.

[58] In the Chester play Trowle wrestles with each of the shepherds in turn and successfully throws them all.

[59] For these and other examples, Kolve, *Corpus Christi*, 101–23, esp. 112.

this case guild carts) prevented forgetfulness on the audience's part of their present situation. It was more the meeting of two worlds than the substitution of one for the other.

Even so, the practice was fiercely criticized by some Lollards and not simply because of its association with Corpus Christi. It was seen as participating in precisely the sort of symbolism that for them led inevitably to idolatrous confusion of the pointer with the reality itself. Only the Word could bring Christ himself. 'For the Word is God and God is the Word. And therefore whosoever receives devoutly God's Word he receiveth the very body of Christ.'[60] As I observed in the previous chapter, such remarks bring in turn their own real danger of idolatry. Such rejection of more conventional sacramentalism appears in any case to have elicited its own contemporary response. The Towneley cycle in particular is full of implicit counter-attacks on Lollard ideas. Like the Lollards, the murderer Cain is seen as attacking clerical tithes. Again, Noah anticipates a eucharistic feast, while the shepherds learn how to be good priests at Bethlehem itself, suitably translated as 'the house of bread'.[61]

Such allusions, however, need to be set against surprisingly few explicit references to the sacrament. Even the Last Supper play has its main focus elsewhere, in the act of betrayal.[62] If that is a pattern often repeated in art of the time, it contrasts markedly with the *autos sacramentales* (sacramental plays) of sixteenth- to eighteenth-century Spain.[63] Here such plays usually find their culmination in strong advocacy of a high doctrine of eucharistic presence.[64] Perhaps this contrast might be taken to indicate two rather different ways of conveying the experience of a sacramental world. In Counter-Reformation Spain what is on offer is an exploration that seeks to

[60] John Whitehorne in 1499; quoted in M. Aston, *Lollards and Reformers: Images and Literacy in Late Medieval Religion* (London: Hambledon, 1984), 66.

[61] Some of the examples considered in L. Lepow, *Enacting the Sacrament: Counter-Lollardy in the Towneley Cycle* (Cranbury, NJ: Associated University Presses, 1990), 57, 71, 81–4.

[62] Even in the liturgy, John 13.1–15 was set for Maundy Thursday, not an institution narrative as such.

[63] *Auto* is a somewhat unusual word that can mean judicial decree, document, allegory, or mystery play.

[64] As in the conclusion of Valdivielso's *Bandit Queen* and Calderón's *King Belshazzar's Feast*: R. G. Barnes, *Three Sacramental Plays* (San Francisco: Chandler, 1969), 70, 103.

deepen eucharistic devotion through appropriating other related, often fairly abstract ideas, whereas the English tradition starts at the more worldly end only to culminate in the ecclesiastical. Sometimes the Spanish plays provide vivid and strongly sympathetic characterization as in Lope de Vega's treatment of Joseph, or are daring as in Valdivielso's comparison of Christ to Cupid.[65] But for the most part they are fiercely didactic, as in Calderón's long discourse on creation. [66] Yet, however earthy the humour, the English mystery plays did at least end in church. So at Durham, for instance, the plays concluded in a solemn procession of the host from St Nicholas, the church in the market place, to the cathedral, where a Te Deum was sung.[67]

I have already mentioned Lollard hostility. In the one surviving tract on theatre from this group, however, there is nothing of the venom that comes later.[68] Even then, that later material seems more concerned with context than content.[69] Thereby appears confirmed a recent trend in scholarship that suggests a more complex dynamic. Just as hard-and-fast distinctions between Puritan and establishment Anglicans have increasingly been called into question, so also it has been noted that the strongest advocates of Reform need not necessarily be seen as uniformly hostile to drama.[70] Not only was the stage itself sometimes used as an instrument of Protestant propaganda, but also even where the theatre was condemned the alternative media deployed were to be found adopting very similar kinds of strategy to the stage.

[65] For Lope de Vega: Barnes, *Three Sacramental Plays*, 24–5; for Valdivielso, 66.
[66] For Calderón on creation: ibid. 78–83.
[67] J. T. Fowler ed., *Rites of Durham* (Surtees Society 107, 1903), lvi. 107–8. The Durham plays do not survive. For an attempt to reconstruct them from a surviving cope, J. McKinnell, *The Sequence of the Sacrament at Durham* (Papers in North Eastern History 8, 1998).
[68] *A Tretise of Miraclis Pleyinge* in C. Davidson ed., *A Middle English Treatise on the Playing of Miracles* (Washington: University Press of America, 1981).
[69] As in John Northbrooke's *Treatise against Dicing, Dancing, Plays and Interludes* (1577) and William Prynne's *Histriomastrix* (1635).
[70] For attacks on any rigid distinctions, P. Collinson, *The Elizabethan Puritan Movement* (Berkeley: University of California Press, 1967); ibid., 'A Comment concerning the Name Puritan', *Journal of Ecclesiastical History* 30 (1980), 483–8. Contrast J. F. H. New, *Anglican and Puritan: The Basis of Their Opposition* (Stanford: Stanford University Press, 1964).

Take first the question of actual performance. The situation in the Spanish Netherlands under Charles V proves an interesting test case. The major towns had literary guilds that took responsibility for the annual staging of plays, the great bulk of which were religious.[71] Irrespective of whether the author was Protestant or Catholic, recurrent themes are critiques of the clergy and a readiness to indulge in somewhat coarse humour.[72] Modern analyses of content suggest that Protestants were no less willing to write plays of that mix than Catholics, provided they were free to give the tale an appropriate Protestant slant. The result was quite a number of Lutheran plays and even occasional Anabaptist ones. There is even one example of a Catholic counterblast to the Anabaptist position.[73] Such plays were seen as an effective means of carrying on Reformation debates, even if increasing political instability meant that Protestant arguments had eventually to become much more covert.[74]

England provides fewer examples, but these are not insignificant. Under the patronage of Henry VIII's minister, Thomas Cromwell, John Bale composed and produced quite a number, all religious in character bar one where the hero is King John.[75] Exiled to Ireland as bishop of Ossory, he continued to secure their performance there.[76] Although singing, dancing, and jesting are all brought on stage, they are treated with such suspicion that the move may well have been counterproductive even in its own day.[77] Nonetheless, it does witness to a felt need to come to terms with the kind of religious experience that could be generated by the stage.

[71] At Antwerp, for example, there were three such rhetorical guilds: the Gillyflower, the Marigold, and the Olive Branch. For some details, G. K. Waite, *Reformers on Stage* (Toronto: University of Toronto Press, 2000), 51–62.

[72] For Catholic attacks on clergy, ibid. xx, 101; for humour, 73.

[73] For Lutheran examples (at Antwerp), ibid. 66–71; for Anabaptist (at Amsterdam), 81–96; for anti-Anabaptist, 119–21. Calvinist influence only comes later (176).

[74] As did Carnival in Germany: cf. R. W. Scribner, *Popular Culture and Popular Movements in Reformation Germany* (London: Hambledon, 1987), 100–1. There was a revolt in Amsterdam in 1535, another in Ghent in 1539.

[75] For a discussion, R. T. Kendall, *The Drama of Dissent: The Radical Poetics of Nonconformity, 1380–1590* (Chapel Hill: University of North Carolina Press, 1986), 90–131, esp. 101–22.

[76] At Kilkenny: ibid. 122.

[77] Even God spends his time telling the audience what he is not: ibid. 101.

More commonly observed, however, is the application of the strategies of drama to other more acceptable forms of presentation. Three general types may be distinguished. First, there is the persecution narrative, which is frequently given dramatic form. A good example is the Lollard *Examination of Master William Thorpe*, where Archbishop Arundel is represented as himself resorting to personal violence, one suspects more for the purposes of the narrative than out of any loyalty to the truth.[78] In the most famous, Foxe's *Book of Martyrs*, one such individual even ascends the scaffold with the preparatory words for the mass now put to a new sacrificial use: Introibo ad altare Dei.[79] Secondly, there is satire. Here the writings of the anonymous Martin Marprelate are perhaps best known. Scathing in his treatment of Elizabethan bishops, he was later to be identified by the distinguished literary critic Dover Wilson as 'a Puritan who had been born a stage clown . . . his style . . . that of a stage monologue'.[80] Finally, there is the form of argumentation adopted in both preaching and tract, where the sort of emotions once associated with the stage now perform a key role. Thomas Cartwright, for instance, condemns permissive use of set homilies in preaching. He urges instead emotional identification with the congregation in a style that refuses to be confined by formal argument.[81] The new ideas of the French Calvinist, Petrus Ramus, on logic were also to become influential in England. In brief, Ciceronian dichotomies were to replace Aristotelian syllogisms.[82]

This is not to claim that such conduct was without its stresses. Not only did advocates of the new approach employ the creative imagination that they condemned in others in order to advance their own views, those same views were in an obvious sense themselves dependent on just such a creative freedom. Although claiming total subordination to Scripture, in effect each was his

[78] Kendall, *Drama of Dissent*, 58–67.

[79] 'I will go unto the altar of God.' G. Townsend ed., *The Acts and Monuments of John Foxe* (New York: AMS Press, 1965), v. 646.

[80] J. Dover Wilson, 'The Marprelate Controversy' in A. W. Ward and A. R. Waller, *The Cambridge History of English Literature* (Cambridge: Cambridge University Press, 1909), iii. 383–4.

[81] For detailed discussion especially in relation to his dispute with Archbishop Whitgift, Kendall, *Drama of Dissent*, 132–72.

[82] W. S. Howell, *Logic and Rhetoric in England* (New York: Russell & Russell, 1961), 140–230.

own final arbitrator. Despite their declaration to the contrary, some Protestants in effect continued the imaginative engagement that had been such a prominent feature of the stage. Not that all of this was done in total ignorance. Some writers at least were acutely aware that precisely the same kind of objection that had once been made against the visual image, of equating the surrogate with the real thing, could now also be laid against its verbal equivalent, in metaphor. The verbal was not after all immune from idolatry.[83] Metaphor might itself turn into a form of linguistic transubstantiation: wherever the hearer is tempted towards a literal reading.[84] The resultant tension can be seen in poetry of the seventeenth century.

Ritual and Poetry of the Baroque Age

Since his death George Herbert has been continually exposed to contradictory readings. Even among his contemporaries this was so. For Izaak Walton and Henry Vaughan he is a supporter of Archbishop Laud, while the Puritan Richard Baxter found in him a supporter of his own stress on an intensely personal and private experience of grace.[85] Such disputes continue. It will be more helpful here to set him against wider currents in the age, not least because attitudes to ritual were part of a much wider phenomenon that affected the Baroque age as a whole. In effect, dilemmas over the religious side to drama found a new voice in the poetry of the age.

   Herbert claims to write without artifice. In one poem he rejects 'invention', and in another 'sweet phrases' and 'lovely metaphors' are identified as sources of temptation.[86] Yet it is precisely his

---

[83] Martin Marprelate is a good example of sixteenth-century mistrust of metaphor. Even biblical metaphors are avoided.

[84] Kendall, *Drama of Dissent*, 37; cf. also M. M. Ross, *Poetry and Dogma: The Transfiguration of Eucharistic Symbols in Seventeenth Century Poetry* (New Brunswick: Rutgers University Press, 1954).

[85] See further G. E. Vieth, 'The Religious Wars in George Herbert Criticism: Reinterpreting Seventeenth Century Anglicanism', *George Herbert Journal* 11 (1988), 19–35.

[86] 'Jordan (2)' and 'The Forerunners' : J. Tobin ed., *George Herbert: The Complete Poems* (London: Penguin, 1991), 94–5, 166–7.

selective use of symbol and metaphor that gives his poetry its
peculiar power. For the more Protestant reader these should only
ever point elsewhere, to an inward conversion of the heart. But,
while sometimes this is the most natural reading of his poetry, at
other times it does look as though symbol is integral to expressing
an ideal in which body and mind form an integrated reality, and so
act is no less important than word for him. Take, for instance, his
marvellous evocation of prayer in 'Prayer (1)', from which the
subtitle of this book's predecessor was derived: 'Heaven in ordinary, man well dressed.'[87] Here Herbert bombards the reader with
metaphors in a way that suggests that his real concern is the
integration of two realities rather than the substitution of one by
another. So his criticisms of discord between inner heart and outward bodily gesture should probably not be taken as rejecting
external expression in ritual altogether but rather as emphasizing
its pointlessness unless there is such a harmony.[88] 'Well-dressed'
thus endorses coming before God with one's bodily best (including
Sunday-best clothing) rather than the alternative scenario of clothes
as a symbol of the Fall and so of what sets us apart from God.

Certainly, that concern for integration was the view adopted by
some of Herbert's contemporaries who were also fellow poets. For
John Donne, for example, 'God hath made us of both body and
soul . . . we understand all things . . . by benefit of the senses.' So, just
as the soul depends on the body, spirituality must be mediated
through material worship. Herein lies the motivation behind John
Cosin's dispute with Peter Smart while both were canons of Durham Cathedral, movingly illustrated by the concluding act of
Cosin's life.[89] Throughout most of his adulthood he had been in
acute pain from a kidney stone. Indeed because of it he seldom
achieved more than two hours of sleep a night. During the day pain
was often so severe that he had to get out of his coach and be carried
by sedan chair. On 15 January 1672, feeling his end was near, he
asked to receive Holy Communion one last time. Unable to kneel,
he knelt in the only way of which he was still capable, by taking off

[87] Tobin, *George Herbert* 45–6. Rather than direct quotation, my subtitle to *God and Grace of Body* adapted Herbert's phrase to 'Sacrament in Ordinary'.
[88] As in poems such as 'Aaron' and 'Lent': ibid. 164, 79–80. This is not to deny the existence of other poems that appear consistently anti-ceremonial: e.g. 'Sion' in ibid. 98.
[89] For some brief reflections on Cosin's actions, see my *Through the Eyes of the Saints: A Pilgrimage Through History* (London: Continuum, 2005), 117–21.

his cap as it were, the bandage round his head that was easing his pain. And with the words, 'Lord I bow the knees of my heart,' he died.[90] For Cosin internal piety had to be acted out in corresponding external actions. That explains in part the two hundred or more candles for Candlemas 1628 that so infuriated Smart, and the 'frequent and profound duckings and prostrations' that now went with the liturgy. Relevant too was Cosin's conviction that ceremonial was integral to the Church's corporate identity. At any rate that could explain the fierceness of his objection to 'lazy sows' who sat through the Creed. Indifference to public actions meant retreat into competing individual subjectivities.[91]

Cosin's concerns can be neatly paralleled by another poet, Robert Herrick. Although he is sometimes dismissed as superficial in his attitudes, this strikes me as grossly unfair.[92] Some may find offensive his apparent endorsement of pagan customs and of 'Roman' ritual, but such endorsement is based in a generous spirit that sees ritual as natural to the human condition.[93] At the same time he is very concerned not to advocate ritual merely for its own sake. As with Herbert there is an insistence on corresponding internal dispositions, as in his fine poem on Lent.

> Is this a Fast, to keep
> The larder lean?
> . . . .
> No: 'tis a Fast to dole
> Thy sheaf of wheat
> . . . .
> To show a heart grief-rent;
> To starve thy sin,
> Not bin,
> And that's to keep thy Lent.[94]

[90] For further details, R. H. Osmond, *A Life of John Cosin* (London: Mowbray, 1913), 299–301.

[91] For that particular dispute, Appendix A in *Durham High Commission Court* (Surtees Society 34, 1858); *Correspondence of John Cosin* (Surtees Society 52, 1869). The two quotations are from the latter, 165, 174.

[92] For a helpful defence, A. Guibbory, *Ceremony and Community from Herbert to Milton* (Cambridge: Cambridge University Press, 1998), 79–118.

[93] For his defence of May Day and Christmas season customs, ibid. 84–5; for his positive allusions to 'Roman' ritual, 87, 91–2. There is no need to posit a secret 'papist'.

[94] Perhaps most easily accessible in H. Gardner ed., *The Faber Book of Religious Verse* (London: Faber & Faber, 1972), 115–16.

More interesting, perhaps, is continued evidence of tensions within those who took the opposing view. Milton's hostility to ceremonial is well known. So privatized did his attitudes become later in life that the home became for him the most appropriate venue for worship.[95] Even so, some of his poetic descriptions of ritual are so sensual and engaged that it is hard not to think of him being attracted by one part of himself, even as another is repelled. Comus may be condemned as a 'foul enchanter' but his ritualist behaviour is given some of the finest lines in the poem.[96] Again, in *Paradise Lost* sometimes the metaphors are so developed as to suggest delight not only in the imagery but also in the picture conjured up as well. For instance, when Christ as intercessor takes up the fallen pair's prayers, they are said to rise like incense to heaven.[97] Christ declares on their behalf:

> See Father, what first fruits on Earth are sprung
> From thy implanted Grace in Man, these Sighs
> And Prayers, which in this Gold'n Censor, mixt
> With incense, I thy Priest before thee bring.[98]

Perhaps it is just the poet in him at work, but the image is laboured over so many lines that it suggests a fascination in Milton, almost despite himself. So, it is intriguing to ask the source of such ambivalence in those times.

At one level one might speak of ritual as natural to the human condition. It is after all something we share with the rest of the animal creation. Certainly, those with domestic pets soon become familiar with a whole range of actions that communicate in a formalized way what their dog or cat wants, without any need on their part for a bark or purr. Gestures of deference are also integral to the animal kingdom. So the bow or kneel in worship can scarcely be dismissed as merely the product of aggressively hierarchical societies. It is a natural way to admit dependency and thus the need for divine grace. So it is unsurprising that the Bible never

---

[95] His likely practice after the Restoration. But already defended in *De Doctrina Christiana*, I. xxviii.

[96] For 'foul enchanter', *Comus*, line 645.

[97] *Paradise Lost*, XI. 14–21.

[98] *Paradise Lost*, XI. 22–5: H. Darbishire ed., *The Poetical Works of John Milton* (London: Oxford University Press, 1958), 242.

condemns such gestures, except where wrongly directed.[99] Indeed, prostration in worship is seen as especially appropriate, and adopted by, among others, Abraham, Joshua, Job, and Ezekiel, and by the Israelites in general at the dedication of Solomon's Temple.[100]

But there may well be reasons unique to that particular time that explain why the theatre generated such strong responses in the sixteenth and seventeenth centuries, extending its influence far beyond the stage itself. It is after all the period in which the Renaissance gradually gives place to the Baroque world, and, if there is one thing that characterizes baroque, it is the pre-eminence of the stage. Churches were even designed to look like theatres, while the art and sculpture of the time also took on the mantle of the theatrical.[101] Bernini's *Ecstasy of Saint Teresa* is an obvious case in point. It is not only the sensuousness of the saint's reaction to the spear that suggests movement but also the patron's family represented in theatrical balconies above, looking on.[102] A revolution had in fact occurred in European thought. The physics of Aristotle had made rest the natural condition of things, whereas Galileo and Newton had established that it was in fact motion: first, motion in the earth and then motion in all things. With that rise of science also went a new forward-looking conception of human existence. Myths of an original perfection were replaced by the possibility of progress into the future.[103] Human identity thus lay not in an ideal static form but in self-creation, in movement from one type of being to another, in an acted drama of existence. In the same way new concepts of infinity led to church ceilings that sought to open themselves through *trompe l'oeil* to the heavenly realms, while threats to harmony in landscape paintings no longer need suggest

---

[99] e.g. Exod. 20.5; 2 Kgs. 17.16.

[100] Gen. 17.3; Josh. 5.14; Job 1.20; Ezek. 1.28; 2 Chron. 7.3.

[101] Perhaps most obvious in the Rococo churches of the following century: e.g. Church of the Virgin, Birnau, and St John Nepomuk, Munich: illustrated in R. Toman ed., *Baroque* (Cologne: Kőnemann, 1998), 228, 234.

[102] For illustrations of this famous 1652 work: Toman, *Baroque*, 286–7. For an illustration of the entire ensemble, H. Hibbard, *Bernini* (London: Penguin, 1965), 132–3.

[103] As in Eden and in the Golden Age of Saturn. It is true that Christianity in theory had a forward-looking earthly eschatology. But by this time such a vision was no longer being interpreted as in any sense continuous with our present reality.

defeat but a harmony about to be realized.[104] The new perspective runs deeply through the culture of the time. Shakespeare's familiar image may, therefore, provide something rather more than just a passing thought.

> All the world's a stage,
> And all the men and women merely players.
> They have their exits and their entrances;
> And one man in his time plays many parts.[105]

It is an idea that permeates this culture. Action rather than stasis has become integral to human self-understanding and as such constitutive of the acted drama of human lives.

The Catholic Counter-Reformation whole-heartedly welcomed the innovative vision that seemed implied for liturgy and its accompanying buildings.[106] Protestant churches of the time failed to respond, apart from such weight as now fell on the rhetorical power of the sermon as verbal drama. Possible implications for church buildings were ignored until the nineteenth century when Protestant churches began to adopt models not too far distant from those earlier baroque principles. Banked seating for large audiences became quite common along with a stage that no longer had the pulpit as its exclusive focus. In 1820s and 1830s New York the evangelist Charles Finney initially had a theatre adapted for his large congregations, only eventually to have a purpose-built theatre/church.[107] If his primary focus remained the pulpit and the need to maintain eye contact with his congregation, later churches in this style were to place an almost equal emphasis on a prominent position for choir and organ.[108] Inevitably, neo-Gothic pulled in a rather different direction, not least towards a more sacramental

[104] Usefully explored in L. F. Norman, *The Theatrical Baroque* (Chicago: University of Chicago Press, 2001), esp. 13–19, 58–67. The latter passage helps to explain why Claude and Poussin include drama (and so change) in their idealized landscapes.

[105] *As You Like It*, II. vii, lines 138–41.

[106] The theatrical aim is already obvious in what is often regarded as the first baroque church, Il Gesù in Rome: V. H. Minor, *Baroque and Rococo* (London: Laurence King, 1999), 79.

[107] First in his adaptation of Chatham Theatre and then in the specially constructed Broadway Tabernacle. For the story and illustrations of the two buildings, J. H. Kilde, *When Church Became Theatre* (New York: Oxford University Press, 2002), 22–55, esp. 30, 44. For eye contact, 50.

[108] Ibid. 112–45, esp. 121–3, 132–7.

understanding of both building and the worship that went on inside.[109] However, the late twentieth century has witnessed a return to some of those more theatrical forms, especially among more conservative evangelical congregations.[110] So it would be quite wrong to conclude that such perceptions are exclusively Catholic. Whether conscientiously intended or not, the experience of worship is often of life as theatre.

Readers, however, may protest that we now live in a quite different culture, one in which churches with plain, simple interiors defy any interest in or from the theatre. I am unpersuaded. Those plain, simple interiors seem to me to be one more instance of the Church only actually catching up with secular culture when it was already moving elsewhere. Modernist architecture was already showing some signs of disintegration as the Fathers of the Second Vatican Council gathered in the mid-sixties to make their momentous decisions. Modernism's concern with function and simplicity was soon to give place to postmodernism in which the element of play has once more come to the fore.[111] Even parallels with baroque are not without some plausibility. We are also now a much more visually preoccupied culture. But even if all this were not so, twentieth-century 'secular' reflection of the role of the theatre has continued to wrestle with religious issues. So it is to these that I now turn.

Modern Theory and its Application

One possibility at this point might have been to survey the more recent history of the stage, pinpointing key dramas that are of potential relevance to Christianity. But that would have necessitated as detailed an analysis as was accorded to 'secular' music in *God and Grace of Body*.[112] More feasible might have been an examination of the revival of religious drama in the twentieth century.

---

[109] Seen not least in dedication ceremonies for Protestant churches, with the use of passages such as 1 Kings 8 and Revelation 21: ibid. 109.

[110] Crystal Cathedral and Willow Creek Community Church are two obvious examples. For description and illustrations: ibid. 215–20.

[111] Other kinds of parallels have also been drawn, e.g. C. Jencks, *Ecstatic Architecture* (Chichester: Academic Edtions, 1999), where the title is used to bring together postmodernism and baroque.

[112] *God and Grace of Body* (Oxford: Oxford University Press, 2007), chs. 5–7.

Although sometimes treated as a narrowly English phenomenon (perhaps because of the importance of some of the figures involved such as T. S. Eliot, Christopher Fry, and Dorothy L. Sayers), it was actually pan-European in character.[113] In France Paul Claudel (d. 1955) had a marked impact, while also of significance were Ugo Betti (d. 1953) in Italy and Alfonso Sastre (b. 1926) in Spain. Claudel was only eighteen when he converted to Catholicism (in 1886) as the result of an intense mystical experience. Nonetheless, that experience, combined with admiration for Aeschylus and Rimbaud, can be said to have influenced all his writing. Its influence is still detectable in his greatest play *Le Soulier de satin* (1928), where his favourite theme of humanity running from God only eventually to be embraced by the divine is once more taken up.[114] While Betti insisted that his plays were written to prove the world's need for God, this is argued without much explicit reference to God or church doctrine. In what is commonly regarded as his greatest play *Frana allo scalo nord* (1932) he explores evil and guilt but without in any obvious sense reaching a 'solution' to the problem of evil.[115] Equally, the younger Sastre (who was influenced by him) pursued a subversive agenda in favour of the underprivileged, but not in a way that compels religious belief.[116] Dorothy Sayers is now best known for her radio play *The Man Born to be King* (1941–2), a landmark in broadcasting since it was the first time that an actor had been allowed to voice Christ's words on the new medium of the wireless. However, she had already made her mark in the previous decade with her first play (for Canterbury Cathedral), *The Zeal of thy House* (1937), a more accessible composition than Eliot's earlier rather cold *Murder in the Cathedral* (1935) written for the same festival.[117] The contributions of several others

[113] For a survey of some key plays, W. V. Spanos, *The Christian Tradition in Modern British Verse Drama: The Poetics of Sacramental Time* (New Brunswick, NJ: Rutgers University Press, 1967).

[114] Best known in an abbreviated version produced by the distinguished director, Jean-Louis Barrault, to music by Arthur Honegger.

[115] Available as *Landslide* in G. H. McWilliam ed., *Three Plays on Justice* (San Francisco: Chandler, 1964).

[116] His plays were banned under Franco. For key articles on the relation between the two dramatists, M. Carlson, *Theories of the Theatre* (Ithaca: Cornell University Press, 1993 edn.), 417–18.

[117] If that judgement on Eliot's play is thought unfair, it would be hard to resist on what came later, e.g. *The Family Reunion* of 1939.

ought not to be forgotten, among them John Masefield and Charles Williams, and the unjustly neglected James Bridie.[118]

While the more explicit English treatments are subject these days to much criticism and seldom performed, such decline in interest may say more about present culture than it does about the quality of the work as such. The dramas were written at a time when most audiences could still be expected to have some basic sympathy with their religious themes, whereas today the advance of secularism has meant that it is much harder to persuade an audience to enter into the spirit of what is set for their reflection. At any rate that is one explanation widely canvassed. But there may be another, quite different in its implications: that the topics of the plays are not yet sufficiently distant. After all, classical and medieval drama, and even the drama of other cultures, seems to attract ready audiences. So the real problem may well be that the ideas are still too near to the bone, that spectators feel that they are 'being got at' rather than allowed to enter into a particular thought frame and then judge for themselves.

To look in any more detail at such work here would be to take me down a trail less directly pertinent to my overall theme. So what I have chosen to do instead is consider the relevance of the explosion of theory that occurred during the course of the twentieth century. This will provide some suitable points of contact with the following two chapters where liturgical questions are addressed more directly. Not that the twentieth century first saw reflections on what drama was trying to achieve. Sustained consideration of the issue is at least as old as Aristotle. Inevitably, much reflection from the Renaissance onwards was a response to what he had said, or was believed to have said.[119] But much, indeed most, of this reflection is incidental, and it is only really with the twentieth century that such questions are pursued at length.

One reason for this change is as a response to a much wider phenomenon, the explosion of academic study in the now leisured west that has resulted in quite new areas being adopted

---

[118] For an analysis of Bridie's work, W. Bannister, *James Bridie and his Theatre* (London: Rockliff, 1955).

[119] Even the precise meaning of Aristotle's key term in his *Poetics* (*katharsis*) has been subject to long dispute. If the root of the metaphor is medical, then probably it is the elimination of certain emotions that is being considered; if moral, their purification.

for exploration.[120] There may also be a deeper reason. Just as the invention of photography produced a crisis for painting, so also film generated similar dilemmas for stage performance. The crisis with photography of course occurred much earlier, but the issue was much the same: a new medium appeared better able to achieve what at the time was considered one of the main aims of the theatre, perhaps its primary aim, realistic portrayal.[121] The camera could now capture better what an individual looked like; film, the actual narrative course of events. All the artificialities associated with stage props and so forth no longer applied. Of course many a painter and many a dramatist of an earlier age would have refused such a characterization of the main aim of their art. But their wider vision had first to be recovered in an age that had moved increasingly towards realism or naturalism.[122] Modern staging had made this so much more feasible, as also the way in which actors were taught. So what I would like to examine here are four types of theoretical analysis that were generated in reaction to this crisis of identity, two concerned with the issue of identification and two with that of dislocation. In each case I shall attempt to highlight some potential implications for liturgy.

Perhaps the most widely known theoretical approach to emerge was what eventually came to be known as method acting. It is essentially an American adaptation of the teachings of the Russian K. S. Stanislavsky (d. 1938) through the teachings of Lee Strasberg and Elia Kazan. Ironically, thanks to the work of the latter it is now perhaps most commonly associated with the screen rather the stage. Two resultant performances that are likely to remain indelibly printed on the memory are James Dean's *East of Eden* and Marlon Brando's *A Street Car Named Desire*, both directed by Kazan, although the latter had in fact begun as a stage play. The approach, taught at the Actors' Studio in New York from 1947 onwards, had actually been intended by Stanislavsky as a means of reviving the theatre. Although he made his name initially in directing Chekhov,

<hr>

[120] English literature as an academic subject was for long resisted in universities like Oxford. Theatre studies is entirely a product of the twentieth century.

[121] I pursue some of the implications of Daguerre's invention of 1839 in *God and the Enchantment of Place* (Oxford: Oxford University Press, 2004), e.g. 90, 129, 208.

[122] As in the plays of Chekhov, Ibsen, and Strindberg, and strongly advocated in a famous preface by the novelist Emile Zola, in his *Thérèse Raquin* of 1867.

Stanislavsky gradually came to make the realism of that playwright subordinate to development of character. The aim instead should be for the actor so wholly to identify with the person he is playing that he conveys fully his inner life. Numerous devices and practices were advocated as a means of ensuring that possibility. Drama was thus less about the depiction of external events and more about the dynamism of an individual's internal psychology.

The most common objection made to method acting is that some degree of distancing is essential if the actor is not to be overwhelmed by particular moods of his subject, and so help spectators towards some sort of independent assessment.[123] However, with that qualification the need for deep engagement with character and narrative remains. That issue perpetuates itself into Christian worship. Coleridge spoke of how in any engagement with literature but drama in particular 'a willing suspension of disbelief' is sometimes necessary.[124] That seems no less true of what is heard in church. As I have noted several times over the course of earlier volumes, imaginative identification has been a recurring and important theme for Christian piety. Ignatius Loyola repeatedly observed that integral to a full appropriation of gospel stories is 'seeing in imagination and contemplating and meditating in detail the circumstances in which they take place'.[125] In my view such an approach is no less requisite for those aspects of Scripture where difficulty is experienced, such as with a dubious moral lesson or a difficult miracle. It is important for congregations first to hear such passages sympathetically conveyed, not carefully edited or even eliminated altogether. So, for example, Elijah on Mount Carmel or in the cave should not end with the offerings lit or with 'the still, small voice' but include the savagery of the subsequent slaughter.[126] Only then should a sermon or biblical discussion

---

[123] For an extended discussion with Diderot used as an early objector, D. Meyer-Dinkgräfe, *Approaches to Acting Past and Present* (London: Continuum, 2001), 38–54.

[124] The precise phrase is used in *Biographia Literaria* iii. 6. But the idea is pursued at length in his essay 'Progress of a Drama': W. G. T. Shedd ed., *Collected Works* (New York, 1853), vol. iv, esp. 73, 86–7.

[125] Ed. I. J. Puhl, *The Spiritual Exercises* (Chicago: Loyola University Press, 1951), § 122, cf. 112.

[126] So in the first case not at 1 Kgs. 18.39 but at v. 40, and in the second not at 1 Kgs. 19.12 but running on till v. 18.

call the legitimacy of such conduct into question. That way Christians will hear past struggles towards understanding as just that, inadequate attempts not without parallel in our own day. Again, disengagement too soon from what is viewed as an implausible miracle may well prevent any spiritually useful appropriation from the passage at all, since the symbolic so often builds on the literal. As possible examples, consider the Virgin birth, the turning of water into wine, or the raising of Lazarus. My point, I stress, is not that these stories necessarily only have symbolic and not literal meaning. Rather, it is that the former may well be lost, unless the unsympathetic reader is willing to suspend disbelief and engage with the totality of the text. So method acting's total absorption in the presentation is not misguided, provided, that is, it is taken only as the right guideline to an initial and not final response to the material.

Such close identification with what is being said could well generate precisely the same type of attitudes and experience that were present when the story was first being written. Even so, that should not be assumed to entail any automatic endorsement of the experience as being unqualifiedly of God. It may still be the case that cool reflection points towards an exclusively symbolic rationale for the miracle; the story of how God was perceived to act in Elijah's case deemed inadequate to how God should now be understood.[127] Reliving past experience thus does not always entail endorsing it.

Similarly, there are positive and negative aspects to the corporate side of drama and worship. As was noted earlier, response to drama is a function of how other spectators react no less than of one's own personal response. The same is no less true of liturgy. With such a focus in mind another quite different theory was being developed at the same time as Stanislavsky's work. This is the notion of drama as community experience, especially associated with the name of Max Reinhardt (d. 1943). Applied before the First World War to Greek drama in particular, it stressed its ritualist aspect, and so the way in which a community could work through the shared experience of a dramatic performance to a common view on contentious issues

---

[127] Such a claim is quite compatible with acknowledging that the inadequate account is still a legitimate part of the community's continuing search for a proper understanding.

such as the need for sacrifice.[128] One of the earliest applications of his ideas was in post-revolutionary Russia with its great pageants of the sacrifices involved in achieving the new order. Spectacles like *The Overthrow of the Autocracy* and *The Storming of the Winter Palace* were performed frequently between 1917 and 1920, with some-times as many as three thousand actors involved.[129] Later, such ideas were to migrate in two quite opposed directions, towards endorse-ment of Nazi ideology on the one hand and on the other into American Jewish attempts to galvanize opinion in favour of a Jewish state. Again, very large numbers of actors and spectators were encouraged to participate. Reinhardt himself became known in Germany for his Theatre of the Five Thousand. So anxious was the Nazi regime to keep his services that he was even offered honorary Aryan status. However, Reinhardt migrated to the Uni-ted States where under his influence pageants interpreting Jewish suffering as a means to a new political destiny attracted never less than tens of thousands and often into the hundreds of thou-sands.[130] In all cases there were extensive borrowings from religion, in the attempt to bolster a common view.[131] With huge numbers involved in such performances and them performed with such passion, it is perhaps scarcely surprising that ringing endorsements from the audience were often the result.

However, the very variety of purposes to which such drama was put illustrates its inherent dangers, not least in its focus on sacrifice for the common good. Christian liturgy might not seem to be in any danger of falling foul of a similar criticism, least of all more formal kinds of worship which seem at the furthest remove from any suggestion of mass hysteria. Nonetheless, there can be pro-blems. There can be a quiet form of exclusion that is no less oppressive than that based on emotion or hysteria. The desire to avoid 'fuss' undoubtedly sometimes entails that certain problems

[128] For a detailed description of his 1903 production of Sophocles' *Electra*, including its violence to the actress playing the principal role: E. Fischer-Lichte, *Theatre, Sacrifice, Ritual: Exploring Forms of Political Theatre* (London: Routledge, 2005), 1–14, esp. 9.

[129] For further details, ibid. 97–121. For religious aspects, 99, 101, 109.

[130] For Aryan status, ibid. 136.

[131] For influence of the Cambridge Ritualists, ibid. 38–44; for the use of religious themes in plays approved by the Nazis in the *Thingspiel Movement*, e.g. *The German Passion*, ibid. 123–30, *Play of Job the German*, ibid. 130–1.

are never faced. The result is that some individuals are left permanently on the fringes of the community, deprived of the possibility of any deeper engagement. Indeed, so strong sometimes is the pressure to conform that all doubts are suppressed. So, when these are first brought to the surface, a more radical reaction than might otherwise have been the case can occur, with belief rejected altogether. What is meant by sharing in a corporate experience and understanding, therefore, needs careful unpacking. The Creed, for example, may be for some a matter of highlighted haloes, as it were (perhaps reinforced by musical memories) rather than a totality endorsed or, if endorsed, properly understood.

While these first two types of theory were both concerned with issues of identification, my next two are more a matter of dislocation and shock. Marxism has been a major influence here. George Lukács's views are typical. While regretting the fall of theatre from its mythological and universal focus into mere entertainment, for him an acceptable substitute was a new social realism that depicts to the masses the nature of society as it is and as it might be.[132] More radically, the playwright Bertolt Brecht (d. 1956) thought this impossible. Instead, on his view the dramatist must deliberately set out to unsettle the audience's present perceptions and so alert them to the extent to which they and their society are in the grip of bourgeois ideology. So various techniques were to be employed to jolt them out of such complacency through what Brecht called *Verfremdung*, estrangement or alienation. In effect, both actor and audience are periodically reminded of the artificiality of the stage, and that some sort of independent judgement is required of them in respect of what is taking place. This may sound wholly negative, but it was not just a matter of breaking continuities. *Verfremdung* might also lead indirectly to the enhancement of the drama, through, for instance, a specific gesture being artificially universalized to imply something about the nature of class struggle in general, or characters not acting in ways the audience might have expected.[133] However, Brecht was too great a dramatist to allow

---

[132] For a brief exploration of Lukács's ideas, Carlson, *Theories of Theatre*, 328–35, 387–91.

[133] Brecht praises George Bernard Shaw for the way in which his characterization avoids stock associations: J. Willett ed., *Brecht on Theatre* (London: Methuen, 1964), 11.

theory to destroy the power of his presentation. So such devices work their effect for the most part indirectly, and his great characters like Mother Courage or Azdak retain all their fascinating complexity.[134]

A more recent example of this type of approach is in Augusto Boal's 'theatre of the oppressed' in South America.[135] As such it provides some immediate resonance with the attempts by liberation theologians to get Christians to become more aware of the radical political dimensions to the gospel. For precedent, appeal might even be made to the parables of Jesus. Their aim was after all to shake Jesus' audience out of their expectations. In that respect, Kierkegaard's use of story, irony, and multiple voices can be seen as similarly inspired.[136] Formal liturgy offers fewer possibilities. But this might happen. New emphases in familiar readings or pauses in unexpected places could, for example, make worshippers reflect anew on what has been repeatedly heard and now may seem jejune. Liturgical innovations might also sometimes prove effective. At the installation of the present bishop of Durham, for instance, for many the most memorable part of the service was the way in which children with local accents were assigned the task of reading the new bishop his duties, as he sat on his throne, the highest in Christendom: a Church now more prepared to serve.[137]

Finally, there is the dislocation advocated by Antonin Artaud (d. 1948). Here the aim is more psychological than sociological, to force spectators towards a true perception of their inner selves, both as they are and as they might be.[138] Artaud himself had originally planned to become a priest, and a religious dimension to drama remained a focus of great interest to him throughout his life. Although he does not appear to have always correctly interpreted the religious drama of other cultures, his basic insight

[134] Mother Courage is the indomitable survivor of the Thirty Years War in the play of the same name, Azdak the rogue turned judge of *The Caucasian Chalk Circle*.
[135] His approach is inspired by Brecht. For his own theoretical and wide-ranging discussion, A. Boal, *Theatre of the Oppressed* (London: Pluto, 2000 edn.).
[136] Those unfamiliar with Kierkegaard's aims can find a short exposition in J. D. Mullen, *Kierkegaard's Philosophy* (New York: Mentor, 1981), 34–40.
[137] Especially pertinent in a see that historically had a prince bishop.
[138] There is so much stress on the dark side of our natures that he has been accused of really being a Gnostic.

seems correct.[139] It is a means of entering an alternative world, of providing, for example, in the case of Hindu drama some inkling of cosmic consciousness or with Japanese Zen a hint of the universal Buddha-nature that is believed to underlie all reality. Western drama he felt should have similar august aims, acting like a plague in purging us of our more mundane desires and so elevating us to a new level of consciousness.[140] A 'theatre of cruelty' is therefore necessary first, before loftier aims can be achieved, the return of the 'metaphysical' and the 'mysterious'.[141]

The more negative side of Artaud's views were to influence playwrights such as Samuel Beckett and Eugène Ionesco with their 'theatre of the absurd', in which psychological dislocation unites with dislocated plots to create an overwhelming sense of the pointlessness and absurdity of the world. For a more positive vision it is necessary to turn to the British director, Peter Brook. In his brief but classic work *The Empty Space* he distinguishes between four basic types of theatre—'deadly', 'holy', 'rough', and 'immediate'. Of the four it is clearly the holy that fascinates him the most.[142] Seeking to sweep away all that is inessential to performance, he stressed how important absence was to the imagination, in particular the absence of distracting props. So, for instance, someone saying 'Mr Livingstone, I presume' 'might well be all that is necessary for an audience to conjure up the continent of Africa'.[143]

What such minimalism also makes more easily perceptible in his view is the invisible, an alternative spiritual world.[144] In his highly esteemed 1970 production of Shakespeare's *Midsummer Night's Dream* Brook sought to illustrate how this might emerge out of

[139] In the case of Balinese theatre he assigned the main role to the producer, whereas much is in fact improvised: Meyer-Dinkgräfe, *Approaches to Acting*, 69–71.

[140] 'Theatre and the Plague' in A. Artaud, *The Theatre and its Double* (London: Calder, 1970), 7–22. The image that Augustine had used to attack the theatre is turned against him, 17.

[141] A repeated theme in *The Theatre and its Double*, e.g. 33, 47, 54, 56, 60, 77.

[142] Each is given its own chapter in *The Empty Space* (Harmondsworth: Penguin, 1968).

[143] The example is drawn from another of his books, *There Are No Secrets* (London: Methuen, 1993), 26.

[144] Holy theatre is in fact defined as 'the Theatre of the Invisible Made Visible': *Empty Space*, 47. For a psychologist making his approach central to the importance of ritual: B. Shorter, *Susceptible to the Sacred* (London: Routledge, 1996), esp. 108–21.

even so apparently flippant a tale. With 'scenery' consisting of only a plain white wall and the actions of the fairies indicated through simple conjuring tricks, the real focus of the play now became more readily apparent, in conjuring up an alternative spiritual world.[145] More commonly, such ideas were pursued through adaptation of explicit religious dramas from other cultures, such as the Shi'ah Iranian Ta'ziyeh or Shabih tradition, or the better-known Hindu *Mahabharata*. Both productions have met with some severe criticism, effectively that Brook altered too much in order to appease western secular sensitivities. Certainly, that is the verdict of one recent book on the Muslim drama.[146] Equally with the *Mahabharata* it is ironical that its most significant religious element in the *Bhagavad Gita* is assigned by Brook only a relatively small role as compared with more traditional performances.[147]

In Hinduism creation is itself an acted drama, and so there is much more readiness to use the whole body to reflect the divine than is the case within Christianity where logos and verbal reflection remain all too dominant.[148] Even as limited a tradition as Islamic drama may have something to teach Christians about the imagination. 'Just as a Catholic can imaginatively transform a wafer of unconsecrated bread into the body of Jesus Christ, so a spectator at a Ta'ziyeh play can imaginatively transform a pot of water on the stage into a roaring river.'[149] The comparison is scarcely a happy one, in terms of what is believed in the two cases. But the Muslim author is right to this extent, that engagement with Christ in such a context is fundamentally an imaginative exercise.

Although sometimes closing possibilities, drama more commonly opens them. Shakespeare's *Measure for Measure* may or may not turn out to be a profound Christian drama, depending on how it is acted.[150] It is often claimed that Christianity is incapable of

---

[145] In Brook's view, for Shakespeare 'in essence, his theatre is religious': *No Secrets*, 85.

[146] J. Malekpour, *The Islamic Drama* (London: Frank Cass, 2004), 157.

[147] His 1980 production is available as a British Film Institute DVD. The 15-hour Hindi Arrow/Freemantle version (2003) provides an interesting contrast.

[148] For Indian theory, Meyer-Dinkgräfe, *Approaches to Acting*, 94–123.

[149] Malekpour, *Islamic Drama*, 115.

[150] M. Harris, *Theater and Incarnation* (Grand Rapids: Eerdmans, 2005 edn.), 22–3, 99–101. Contrast David Edwards's negative judgement, one suspects based on reading alone: *Poets and God* (London: Darton, Longman & Todd, 2005), 66.

endorsing tragedy as a genre because of its postulation of Christ's triumph in the resurrection and still greater triumph at the end of time. But this too is to ignore performance. A distant end hardly makes the acts of the immediate moment any the less tragic.[151] So Scripture and the liturgy alike can acquire quite different meanings, depending on how they are performed. As I noted in Chapter 4, Bach deliberately chose not to follow John too literally in his *St John Passion*, precisely because only that way could he ensure full significance for the fact of crucifixion. That too is why the liturgical year makes sense. The annual re-enactment of Holy Week ensures that it is the totality of Christ that is encountered and not just some favoured aspect.

The four theories discussed here have usually been treated as rivals rather than as complementary, but there is no reason why insights should not be drawn from them all, and indeed from others besides.[152] Content is of course important. But Aristotle was quite wrong when he suggested that as much might be gained from reading a tragedy as from watching it.[153] It is precisely through performance pulling us now in one interpretative direction, now in another, that possibilities old and new can be most easily accessed and developed. That way significant encounter is most likely to occur.

A liturgical performance that has secure boundaries but also opens up unexpected avenues as well ought, therefore, it seems, to be the aim. Although far from easy to get the right balance, the disconcerting can have its positive value no less than the predictable. Readers may object that this is said too lightly. What diverts must necessarily distract from a sense of the presence of God. I disagree. Unusual stimuli can sometimes deepen engagement rather than undermine it. In Part I, I noted how the inexhaustibility of metaphor could help rather than hinder where words might otherwise come to feel barren of fresh insight. In a similar way the introduction of new liturgical acts or unfamiliar music can challenge and encourage. Resistance to innovation in liturgy can exist for both good

---

[151] A repeated theme in Donald Mackinnon, e.g. *The Problem of Metaphysics* (Cambridge: Cambridge University Press, 1974), 122–35.

[152] For such a wider range considered, J. Roose-Evans, *Experimental Theatre: From Stanislavsky to Peter Brook* (London: Routledge, 1989 edn.).

[153] Aristotle, *Poetics* 26, esp. 1462a 11–13.

motives and bad. For as many as there are who find in an unchanging liturgy a symbol of the unchanging steadfastness of God there are those for whom it has become a psychological prop against their aversion to living in an insecure world.

Changes in liturgical music are often where such feelings come most to the fore. Just as in architecture for some Gothic is, and was, the only proper architecture, so for some the singing of the liturgy must be based on Gregorian chant or, if ranging more widely, still within firm limits. While attempting to set such attitudes in their historical context in the chapter that follows, I also want to challenge such constraints.

6

Enactment in Music

THE form of song that I am about to discuss, the repeated pattern that characterizes liturgical singing, is for some Christians an entirely secondary or minor matter while for others it is absolutely indispensable to worship. In the mass there is the Ordinary (those elements that recur week by week) and the Propers (or seasonable elements), with a similar format repeating itself in non-eucharistic rites. Choral contributions are also evident in anthems, introits, and motets, as well as in the longer oratorio. Although often expressed in terms of a contrast or conflict between congregation and choir, this of course need not be so. Contemporary congregational settings of the Ordinary abound, while in the more distant past monastic communities, if not others, would in general have participated throughout. My focus here, however, will not be on that debate as such. Rather, what I want to explore is the role exercised by such music in generating or deepening human experience of God, however the music is performed. So my focus will be on musical enactment, on how such music might help to create a sense of drama, of a story relived: most obviously Christ's life, death, and resurrection, but other aspects of the biblical story and subsequent church history as well. That story is most obviously told as a whole in the words of the Creed. So I might have devoted much of the chapter to assessing the various alternative strategies composers have used to bring that narrative to life. But given the range of uses to which music is put in the liturgy, it seems best instead to offer here a more rounded picture of music's contribution.

I shall begin by considering the medieval situation and the ideals on which it operated. Thereafter, I explore the attempt to reform the principles under which Gregorian chant and polyphony were sung (the latter in the sixteenth century, both in the nineteenth), before going on to examine how Protestant and Catholic traditions interacted to produce the situation we now find ourselves in. That will lead naturally into where my discussion will end, in consideration of what kind of contribution the Church might expect from such music today.

Medieval Music, Symbolism, and the Rise of Polyphony

Given the distinctive and even idiosyncratic character of so much medieval music, one is somewhat surprised to discover so many of the issues to do with religious experience already implicit within it. Three in particular might be mentioned as an opening. First, the absence of any early reflection on how God might be mediated through such music is often taken to argue that the medieval concern was really with making an offering to God and not with some human-orientated experience. The latter, it is often claimed, is only really a modern preoccupation. Secondly, the way in which Counter-Reformation no less than Reformation censured late medieval obfuscating of the words is commonly used to endorse the view that singing should never properly be anything other than a mere adjunct to the words, enhancing certainly but no more. Finally, the recent huge rise in the popularity of purely secular uses for such music (particularly Gregorian chant), it is said, suggests that there is nothing intrinsically religious in the medium in any case; it can serve quite other ends. All of these issues are ones to which I shall return in due course.[1]

A brief historical sketch will be of help. Although the basic structure of the mass was set quite early, it is important to note that developments continued throughout the first millennium, and indeed well into the second.[2] Although hymns early gained a fixed place in the daily offices, conservatism ensured that this was not to be so with the mass.[3] So for some considerable time the Ordinary retained its role as the people's main contribution.[4] This took the

[1] The third is not treated till the next section.
[2] e.g. the *Agnus Dei* did not arrive till the seventh century, and the Creed was not officially authorized at Rome till 1014. Propers continued to develop throughout the second millennium.
[3] Considering the thousands of potentially suitable poems that were written, very few made it even into the daily offices. Such attitudes contrast markedly with attitudes in the East where new hymns continued to be introduced into the liturgy until the eleventh century: E. Wellesz, *A History of Byzantine Music and Hymnography* (Oxford: Clarendon, 1961), esp. 146–70.
[4] The assigning of parts of the Ordinary to a choir probably did not begin until the eighth century. Throughout the Middle Ages settings of the Creed remained rare. For further details, R. H. Hoppin, *Medieval Music* (New York: Norton, 1978), 130–41, esp. 131–2.

form of simple unison plainchants, though as early as Ambrose we know that psalms were being performed antiphonally.[5] Although the Roman order was eventually to dominate, it is important to realize how weak Rome was after the collapse of the Roman empire.[6] Gregory the Great (d. 604) may possibly deserve some credit for establishing order among the chants. But there is little historical substance to justify the way in which such forms of singing came eventually to be known as Gregorian chant as though his was the major role. Moves towards greater elaboration in liturgical song probably came first from northern Europe. It was almost certainly the Carolingian empire that made the decisive contribution rather than Rome itself, just as earlier the *Kyries* and *Agnus Dei* had come from the East.[7] Pope Gregory's main role seems to have been in providing an iconic justification for music's divine origins.[8]

Until Guido of Arezzo's invention of a simple form of notation in the eleventh century, all chants had to be committed to memory, and were passed on in that way.[9] This obviously severely limited the possibilities for new or more elaborate compositions, which explains why developments were relatively slow. This is not to say, however, that earlier monodic chants lacked interest. Melismas, for example, at the end of lines could add greatly to the dignity and ingenuity of pieces.[10] Polyphony first arrived in the form of what is

[5] Hoppin, *Medieval Music*, 35.

[6] Other rites included the Gallican, Celtic, and Mozarabic or Spanish (our knowledge of the latter only narrowly survived thanks to the work of Cardinal Ximenes in the fifteenth century).

[7] Hoppin, *Medieval Music*, 42–9. Jungmann stresses the Frankish love of the dramatic: J. A. Jungmann, *The Mass of the Roman Rite* (New York: Benziger Bros., 1951), i. 77.

[8] Numerous images survive in which the dove of the Holy Spirit dictates chants to Gregory, to write down (an impossibility in his day). For an example, N. Bell, *Music in Medieval Manuscripts* (London: British Library, 2001), 7.

[9] He was also responsible for the do–re–mi system. Based on a Latin hymn to John the Baptist, do (dominus or Lord) eventually replaced an initial 'ut'. For details, K. L. Mée, *The Benedictine Gift to Music* (New York: Paulist Press, 2003), 104–10.

[10] Strictly speaking, melismatic refers to longer passages of music sung to a single verbal syllable, neumatic to those enjoying two to five notes, syllabic a one-to-one correspondence: so Hoppin, *Medieval Music*, 78. Such practices probably began with elaborations on concluding Alleluias.

known as parallel organum, that is to say, the same melody running parallel at two different pitches.[11] Thereafter came variations in other parts, with the primary tune usually being in the lower 'holding' or 'tenor' voice. The common four-part harmony with which we are now familiar, although appearing as early as Pérotin in the twelfth century, only became the norm relatively late. More pertinent to note here is the way in which secular motets may have helped to encourage their religious equivalents. Sung with alternative words in the higher register (often in the native language), these found their place in the Propers, especially in the tropes and sequences that increasingly had been added to dignify particular festivals and occasions.[12] But of course once such more complex settings had found their place in the liturgy, it was but a short step to similar techniques being applied to the Ordinary as well. Although protests were made long before the Reformation about the resultant inaudibility of the words, it was only with the Council of Trent that simplifications were effected.[13] Although well intentioned, much of such change was based on misunderstanding. So a second major reform took place in the nineteenth century. The Cecilian movement addressed the issue of religious music more generally, while the work of the Benedictines at Solesmes Abbey was devoted exclusively to reforming Gregorian chant.[14]

In trying to understand the underlying principles which helped to guide such changes, scholars must work almost entirely indirectly, by inference rather than direct evidence. Some with a particular axe to grind are likely to insist that the absence of any explicit comments on underlying rationale should be taken to demonstrate that the motive was entirely instrumental. The intention was to praise God and nothing whatsoever to do with the augmentation or

---

[11] Most commonly an octave apart, but sometimes at a fifth or fourth.

[12] A sequence is an addition to the Alleluia that introduces the Gospel reading, tropes additions elsewhere. In respect of the Ordinary, the *Kyries*, for example, might be given a trinitarian context by adding to each evocation an address to each of the three persons in turn. It was then but a short step for the additions to feed back on the unchanging text, to generate a more complex melody for the words as a whole.

[13] John XXII's decree of 1324, urging reform, seems to have been quite ineffective even at the papal court itself: Hoppin, *Medieval Music*, 375–7. For Trent's declaration, Mée, *Benedictine Gift*, 182.

[14] Situated in the Sarthe region of France, south-west of Paris.

enhancement of human experience. But arguments from silence are seldom very secure. To illustrate from a quite unrelated issue, nowhere in the New Testament is the common practice of the ancient world in exposing unwanted infants condemned, yet it would be foolhardy to deduce from this that first-century Christians were therefore in favour. In short, it is necessary to look at the wider context of contemporary assumptions, and draw inferences that way. So, to draw a closer parallel to this case, it by no means follows from the fact that Romanesque architecture found no justifying theoretician, that there was therefore no symbolism involved or that an equivalent to Suger could not have been produced.[15] It is just that no need arose to make shared, underlying assumptions explicit.

So a number of pointers may, I believe, legitimately be used. The first is the theoretical treatises on music that survive from the early period and whose ideas continued to be copied well into medieval times.[16] Within the seven liberal arts, music constituted part of the *quadrivium*, and as such was seen as a branch of mathematics along with arithmetic, geometry, and astronomy. Such a conception inevitably steered evaluation of music in certain directions rather than others, particularly towards order and harmony. So it is numeral ordering that lies at the heart of Augustine's analysis, with the instrumentalist who lacks understanding of underlying principles deemed no better off than a singing nightingale.[17] If Boethius devotes more attention to harmony rather than rhythm and metrics, for him also it is essentially mental understanding that is at stake in his comparison of instrumental music with *musica mundana* and *musica humana* (music of the spheres and the balance of

---

[15] For Suger's rationale for Gothic, see my *God and Enchantment of Place: Reclaiming Human Experience* (Oxford: Oxford University Press, 2004), 272–7; for my own attempts to provide a rationale for Romanesque, 263–72.

[16] To an extraordinary degree. For example, in the twelfth century Hugh of St Victor's threefold division of music in his *Didascalicon* comes straight out of Boethius, his comparison of the various senses of Scripture to a musical instrument from Isidore: ed. and trans. J. Taylor, *The Didascalicon of Hugh of St Victor* (New York: Columbia University Press, 1961), ii. 11; v. 2 (69–70; 202 fn. 47; 120; 219. fn. 2).

[17] Book 6 of Augustine's *De musica* is especially important in understanding his position. A further six books on harmony (*De melo*) were planned but never completed.

body and soul).[18] It is hardly surprising, therefore, that what emerged more generally was an intellectual rather than emotional appreciation of musical performance.[19]

It would seem no exaggeration to suggest that the whole direction of western music might have been quite different had those theoretical treatises not pushed western music towards some values over others. What was promoted was a rationalization vertically in harmony and horizontally in metrics rather than the focus on melody and rhythm that came much earlier to non-western systems: in other words a preoccupation with order over against freedom.[20] Nor should this be thought unrelated to religious questions. Harmony in music, as these treatises underline, was seen as part of a wider harmony to be found in divine creation as a whole, not least in the notion of the harmony of the spheres, the music produced by the movement of the planets, allegedly inaudible to our ears because continuous and so unnoticed. It is a topic which I have already considered in some detail in this volume's predecessor.[21] So little more needs be said here, except perhaps to underline that such ideas were by no means confined to the western world;[22] and that despite some obvious difficulties in the theory, most notably the so-called Pythagorean comma and the *diabolus in musica*.[23] So it seems not unreasonable to conclude that for the medieval mind to hear music was to participate in the more fundamental order and harmony that governs the divine creation as a whole, a position effectively mediated to the Christian world by Plato's decision to base his analysis of creation on musical principles.[24] Thus music did

[18] His *De institutione musica* was a youthful work. Some have suggested that his theoretical interest was so strong that by *musica instrumentalis* he meant not heard music but simply what capacities were inherent in the instrument.
[19] Frequently stressed by commentators; e.g. Hoppin, *Medieval Music*, 476.
[20] So W. Wiora, *The Four Ages of Music* (London: Dent, 1966), 125–30.
[21] *God and Grace of Body: Sacrament in Ordinary* (Oxford: Oxford University Press, 2007), 233, 239–40, 377.
[22] For similar ideas in ancient China, P. Vergo, *That Divine Order: Music and the Visual Arts from Antiquity to the Eighteenth Century* (London: Phaidon, 2005), 37–44.
[23] The Pythagorean comma is the name given to the phenomenon produced by the great cycle of fifths returning to its original at a slightly higher and so dissonant pitch. The horrible dissonance, at least to medieval ears, of the tritone produced by dividing an octave equally, for example C and F#, was known as the *diabolus in musica*.
[24] In his *Timaeus*. For further details, F. M. Cornford, *Plato's Cosmology* (London: Kegan Paul, 1937), 66–72.

help to enact a particular perception of the world and so open further possibilities of God being experienced under just such an aspect. Yet there was an irony in all of this. The theoretical tradition failed to engage adequately with the unison melody and metrical freedom of plainsong. Where order was most easily perceived, it was in the modal system as this was gradually developed.

Secondly, we may note the enhancement of the liturgy provided by music. Since readings were also chanted, all words were in effect given a musical dimension. There was thus a consistent dignity to the occasion that was lacking from the rest of life. Although offered as a way of glorifying God, it also suggested an encounter with a being who was majestic and awesome.[25] While chants were not usually adapted to provide specific meanings for different moments in the mass and indeed were often interchangeable, it is possible to detect some thinking along not unrelated lines. So, for instance, the Gradual and Alleluia chants (that became increasingly elaborate as the centuries advance) helped to add dignity to the simple chanting of the Gospel. In effect, they were the vocal equivalents of the bodily gestures that included a Gospel procession and the congregation standing for the reading. Polyphony too seems to have found its initial rationale in adding splendour to the great feasts of the Church. So, not surprisingly, our earliest evidence for its use at Chartres is for Easter.[26] That said, and we can also understand the pressure to ensure that polyphony occurred at the principal moments of the mass rather than on its margins. As one commentator observes: 'We must use our imagination, both to appreciate the liturgical context and also to understand the hierarchy of musical styles at whose pinnacle the polyphony stood: the simple tones of the prayers, lessons, and psalms; then the modestly inflected antiphons; the richly melismatic antiphons such as the alleluia and offertory; and finally the crowning glory of polyphonic music where the unison columns of plainchant, as it were, burst asunder into the multiple arches and ribs of church vaulting.'[27]

---

[25] This is not to deny the presence of more human motives, such as the desire to impress visitors, and musicians' own delight in greater sophistication.

[26] M. Gushee, 'The Polyphonic Music of the Medieval Monastery, Cathedral and University' in J. McKinnon ed., *Antiquity and the Middle Ages*, Man and Music Series (Basingstoke: Macmillan, 1990), 143–69, esp. 148–50.

[27] D. Hiley, 'Plainchant Transfigured' in McKinnon, *Antiquity and Middle Ages*, 120–42, esp. 138–9.

As that last quotation indicates, related to the liturgical context
was also the wider issue of how the singing might fit with the
architecture of the building as a whole. Human response to sight
and sound are of course not quite the same.[28] But equally it would
be odd if one artistic medium had no impact whatsoever on the
other.[29] If the intricate structure of a Gothic building suggests a
drawing of us heavenwards, might the same not also be suggested or
augmented by a complex polyphonic structure? Although any
direct application of architectural principles to music encounters
numerous difficulties, a parallel inspiration seems by no means out
of the question.[30] In the case of polyphony, for example, one could
argue that the popularity of the triplum form reflects the three-
storey Gothic construction pattern that builds from the ground or
'tenor' upwards.[31] But no less than a drawing heavenwards, there is
also a movement of God earthwards. In Gothic architecture the
heavenward thrust of pointed arch and glass seemingly effortlessly
supported was balanced by great attention to intricacy of detail and
a very obvious humanity in sculptures of scriptural and angelic
figures alike.[32] Correspondingly, in the music of the time one can
hear not only that layered order that draws one heavenwards but
also a sense of the immaterial made present. Thereby it strikes a
perfect balance with the medieval theology of the mass. It suggested
a dynamic whereby Christ is at one and the same time made a
sacrificial offering in heaven but also simultaneously present on the
altar in the worshipper's church.

So far as details are concerned, any suggestion of an anticipation
of Romantic concerns in word painting would of course be quite
misplaced. Equally wrongheaded is the assigning of particular
moods to the various modes or individual notes.[33] For the most

[28] For some writers who have investigated the contrast, Vergo, *That Divine Order*, 156–7.
[29] The architectural writers who have drawn parallels include Vitruvius, Alberti, and Palladio, and among modern writers Wittkower and Simson. For details, Vergo, *That Divine Order*, 11, 95–7, 147–63.
[30] For the arguments for and against a Dufay motet being modelled on Brunelleschi's double-barrelled dome at Florence, Vergo, *That Divine Order*, 163–70.
[31] Accepted by Vergo, *That Divine Order*, 120–7. Trinitarian symbolism might also be relevant.
[32] For this point in more detail, see my *God and Enchantment of Place*, 272–81.
[33] It is puzzling that Mée, while criticizing Solesmes for the former, herself insists on individual notes on any particular scale having definite emotional values: *Benedictine Gift*, 65, 85.

part, particular chants gained such meaning as they had by fre-
quency of association rather than through specific content. Nor,
with the possible exception of Guillaume de Machaut's *Mass of
Notre Dame*, was any overall unity given to the various elements of
the mass until the fifteenth century.[34] Even so, this does not mean
that symbolism was entirely absent. A good example is the hymn
Veni, Sancte Spiritus that became known as the Golden Sequence
because of the formal beauty of its composition.[35] It makes extensive and elaborate use of the imagery of seven (Pentecost falling on
the seventh Sunday after Easter). There are three sets of seven
syllables in every verse, with syllable seven and fourteen identical
in every verse and each verse ending on -*ium*.[36] Similarly, the last
Kyrie in one chant uses a different note from all the others to
indicate a final plea for help. Again, in the Creed reference to the
Ascension can lead to sweeping up an octave, while the lowest note
in one *Agnus Dei* is reserved for our sins (*peccata*).[37]

More contentious is the question of what might be said in
defence of the more elaborate polyphony that characterizes the
end of the medieval period. Here Protestant and Catholic often
unite in condemning the way in which the words were so intri-
cately absorbed into the music that they ceased to be distinguish-
able. The result, it is often said, must have been a purely aesthetic
rather than a religious experience. So the reforms of Trent and
Palestrina's model mass can only be seen as a welcome relief. There
is, however, something to be said on the other side. Certainly, in
tropes and sequences there was a problem since not even the
learned would necessarily be familiar with the words. But in the
Ordinary, memory of the familiar words was surely sufficient, and

[34] This mass by Machaut (d. 1377) is the first complete mass by an identifiable
individual to survive. Hoppin doubts its claims to an overall unity: *Medieval Music*,
418. Contributing to that doubt is the contrast between the *Gloria* and *Credo* (with
words fully audible and intelligible) and other parts which are quite otherwise and
where the strange phenomenon known as hiccupping or hocketing occurs (breaking up phrases with periods of silence).

[35] It may have been composed by Stephen Langton, Archbishop of Canterbury
(d. 1228).

[36] An example given by the Irish singer N. R. Riain in her *Gregorian Chant
Experience* (Dublin: O-Brien Press, no date), 80–3.

[37] Other examples from Riain, *Gregorian Chant*, 103, 120, 127. The relevant
musical score is provided.

indeed perhaps the general sense only, since for most worshippers the mass was in a language that in any case they could not understand. In other words, might it not have been enough to have been aware only of the basic difference of intention between, for example, the *Kyries* (penitence) and the *Sanctus* (awe before the divine majesty)? So it would seem a mistake to treat Palestrina's *Missa Papae Marcelli* as quite the revolution it is so often portrayed to be.

The issue is often in any case presented in a manner that suggests a false dilemma: clarity in simple chants or else obfuscation with complex music. What this ignores is that even with monophony it is not always possible to hear the words clearly. This is because languages in general, and Latin in particular, present a number of conflicting demands. Even in speech there are competing possibilities that can affect clarity of reception, and still more so once the demands of musical phrasing are introduced. On the former point, it is important to note that the pronunciation of Latin underwent a revolution between the patristic and medieval periods. By that I do not mean the move towards ecclesiastical Latin (with hard consonants sounded soft, and so on), although this also happened. More relevant here is the transition from primarily a quantity system of pronunciation to one based solely on stress and pitch.[38] That inevitably had a major impact on any material from the early period that continued to be used later. A case in point would be Ambrose's hymns, where the metre would now seem odd. Add to this where the new accentuation system runs counter to the natural demands of the music.[39] So even in the simplest chant some degree of compromise proved necessary, if audibility was not to be gained at the price of unnatural musical sounds or else strange pronunciation. Although there is little explicit evidence of such reflection within the medieval period itself, there are occasional exceptions. One such is the work of the French *concertor* Jean Le Munerat, who helped with the running of the choir at the College of Navarre in fifteenth-century Paris.[40] Perhaps in response to the Council of

---

[38] Any significance for long and short syllables gradually disappeared after the fourth century, with accents now invariably falling on the penultimate syllable or earlier.

[39] Melodic stress most naturally goes with higher notes or melodic peaks. Melismas inevitably conflicted, as they fell on final syllables. For further details, Hoppin, *Medieval Music*, 85–8.

[40] Available in Latin with English commentary in D. Harrán, *In Defence of Music* (London: University of Nebraska Press, 1989).

Basel that like John XXII in the previous century had demanded greater clarity of diction, he pleads for a balance between the demands of grammar and music.[41] The emphasis of Renaissance humanism on grammar helped to ensure that musicians felt obliged to accommodate themselves to Trent's demands, but the issue remained. That trend is already evident in Josquin des Prés (d. 1521), which is no doubt one reason why that particular composer earned Luther's admiration.

It is worth considering, therefore, whether in the light of such competing tensions there is any religious purpose that still might be served, where audibility is abandoned. An important dimension not so far noted is the way in which such music might contribute to a sense of the mysteriousness and wonder of God. It can scarcely be denied that some complex polyphony was purely secularist in its inspiration. The added words were sometimes even ordinary secular love lyrics or of a joking kind.[42] Indeed, it is thought that two of Pérotin's best-known compositions were deliberately introduced to Notre Dame in Paris in order to counter the infamous Feast of All Fools tradition.[43] Nonetheless, where the words were already well known, as in the Ordinary, it is not at all obvious why they had always to be heard on each occasion anew. The nadir in such an alternative possibility is often taken to be the silent reciting of the consecration prayer that was to become the norm by the later Middle Ages. Contrary to common assumptions, however, such suppression of the words could have good as well as bad motives. As a way of enhancing the power of the clergy, seeming to ascribe to them semi-magical powers, it was undoubtedly quite wrong. But as a way of motivating a deeper sense of divinity as something strange, mysterious and awesome, grounds for condemnation are surely much less clear. When one recalls that most of the population could not read, far less read or understand Latin, it is not clear

---

[41] For some examples, ibid. 53–60, 95–105.

[42] For an example on a CD that also includes Pérotin's *Viderunt omnes*, the anonymous *In sompnis mira Dei*, where the duplum is a secular love lyric while the triplum continues the Magi theme: *Alleluia Nativitas* (Metronome, 1992), tracks 7 and 9.

[43] So Gushee in McKinnon, *Antiquity and Middle Ages*, 158. The two works in question were *Viderunt omnes* and *sederunt principes*. Examples of the type of music being rejected survive from Beauvais, including that for braying at the donkey: Bell, *Music in Medieval Manuscripts*, 33–6.

what necessarily would have been gained by clarity of diction. The meaning of particular words would still have been just as remote. Even today one suspects that the personal focus of many worshippers at that point in the liturgy is not on the words being uttered by the priest but rather on their own particular relationship with Christ. Thus, what matters, I would suggest, in respect of both the consecration prayer and polyphonic singing is some awareness of the overall sense, and that could of course be taught, however unclear the words remained because of the nature of the singing or *sotto voce* enunciation.

So, in short, just because the Middle Ages offers little by way of reflection about connections between music and religious experience, and even obfuscates the words, nothing therefore follows about a general absence of such experience or even its presumed unimportance in the kind of presentation offered of the drama of Christ's life. Such theoretical reflection as did exist encouraged hearers to discover in music some sense of a divinely given order and intelligible structure: the Logos himself inherent, as it were, in the music. Even in the cloudy inaudibility of the words there might be found a heightened sensitivity to the mysteriousness and wonder that such encounters with Christ, and the divine more generally, might bring. None of this is meant to deny the need for understanding of the meaning of words at some level, most obviously in otherwise unfamiliar anthems. Nonetheless, even these limited conclusions clearly fly in the face of repeated assertions across the centuries of the absolute necessity for clarity of diction, and resultant demands for a return to some ideal standard of purity, not least in Gregorian chant. I turn next to that search.

Repeated Calls for Purity in Music

Here I want to examine three phases in such calls, during the sixteenth, nineteenth, and twentieth centuries. Those already familiar with such history will be expecting some reference to Palestrina and to Solesmes. I include the twentieth century because of the now much more widely disseminated popularity of Gregorian chant among the general public. Its simplicity makes a wide appeal, and this is no doubt one factor in the revival of the works of Hildegard of Bingen, whose career I shall examine in rather more detail.

As already noted, Palestrina's *Missa Papae Marcelli* is often quoted as the ideal intended by the Counter-Reformation Council of Trent. Certainly, the words are clearly audible and there is a complete absence of any secular or non-intrinsic religious material. But not only is the traditional account of this mass setting's origins insecure, it is as well to recall that most of Palestrina's other masses failed to conform to the relevant criteria.[44] In the twentieth century Hans Pfitzner revisited the issue in his opera of the same name, *Palestrina* (1917).[45] Although the opera presents the discovery of the music as the result of an angelic visitation, for Pfitzner the true point of Palestrina's project lay not in clarity of diction but in a proper continuity of tradition, and loyalty to one's own inner creative voice.[46] Palestrina, he suggests, produced such a composition because it was most fully consonant with the musical principles on which his great predecessors had based their work.[47] He wanted to avoid a false turn, just as Pfitzner in his own day had little sympathy with the new directions in which compositional techniques were then turning.[48] Whether accurate as an explanation or not, we are never likely to know. What we can say is that, despite the legend of Palestrina's decisive contribution, much more was eventually owed to composers like Giovanni Gabrieli and the development of a new monodic style, with a basso continuo as harmonic support. Polyphonic masses, however, also continued to be composed.

So far as our present context is concerned, the Cecilian movement of the nineteenth century played a key role in returning the Church to those earlier ideals. Beginning in the collegiate

---

[44] His twelve other masses are quite different. It is true that during his brief reign of three weeks in 1555 Pope Marcellus did complain of the existing state of compositional writing. But the earliest reference to Palestrina specifically composing his mass in response comes from half a century later (from 1607). For further details, O. Toller, *Pfitzner's Palestrina* (London: Toccata, 1997), 215–23.

[45] The key scene is Act I, scene 6. The music sounds as though it might have come from Palestrina's hand, although in fact there are only four direct quotations.

[46] Although not devoid of interest in religious belief, Pfitzner clearly uses Palestrina to explore his own dilemmas. For his religious position, Toller, *Pfitzner's Palestrina*, 66, 85; for the motives he ascribes to Palestrina, 84–5, 88–9, 284.

[47] Nine appear to him in Act I, scene 5. The earliest dates from the thirteenth century. Only two are named, Josquin des Prés and Heinrich Isaac (also known as Harry the German).

[48] As in the Second Viennese School, with composers like Schoenberg.

monastery at Regensburg, through publications and the formation of societies of musicians, it sought to advocate a return to the principles of the late sixteenth century.[49] The use of orchestra and soloists was rejected in choral settings, while Gregorian chant was held up as the ideal under which all were encouraged to participate. That inevitably meant the rejection of most of the church music of the eighteenth and nineteenth centuries. The masses of Haydn and Mozart naturally met with condemnation, but even a composer as devout as Bruckner struggled to conform. Only his Mass in E minor fully met the relevant standards.[50]

It was, however, the work of the great abbey of Solesmes that was to have the most marked impact in restoring the purity of Gregorian chant. Set firmly in the context of French Romanticism, Prosper Guéranger as the founder of Solesmes can be seen in many ways as paralleling the Romantic principles of individuals otherwise as varied as Chateaubriand, Hugo, and Viollet-le-Duc.[51] The difference is that he wanted to go beyond preservation of the past to its recreation. In his desire to restore the purity of Gregorian chant, his ideals were ably advanced by two key figures within the monastery, Joseph Pothier and André Mocquereau. Their methods, however, were quite different. Pothier was someone who sought to enter into that past to the maximum possible degree, even to the extent of trying to recreate the type of books and writing used.[52] By contrast, Mocquereau was the modern scholar content to use photography, comparative analysis, and so on. For Pothier God was found in the inflections of the voice itself as it followed the lines on the page, whereas for Mocquereau it was much more about the resultant sound.[53] By the time of *Motu proprio* (1903) when Pius X

[49] The two key figures were Carl Proske (d. 1861) and Franz Xaver Witt (d. 1888).

[50] As a tribute to the movement he even borrowed a theme from Palestrina (in the *Sanctus*).

[51] Not that Romanticism has been confined to the nineteenth century. Exploring German responses to medieval music in the nineteenth and twentieth centuries, Annette Kreutziger-Herr observes that much modern German interest in Hildegard of Bingen was not unlike what had happened in the nineteenth century: *Ein Traum vom Mittelalter* (Cologne: Bohlau Verlag, 2003), 225–37.

[52] K. Bergeron, *Decadent Enchantments: The Revival of Gregorian Chant at Solesmes* (Berkeley: University of California Press, 1998), 25–62. Style was more important than ease of reading (28).

[53] Ibid. 117.

restored Gregorian chant to its status as the official music of the Roman Catholic Church, it looked as though Mocquereau had won. Pothier, however, had one remaining card up his sleeve. By insisting on a living tradition of interpretation that could never be finally bound by scholarly results, depending on one's point of view authority was now allowed to triumph over scholarship, or the living Church over the dead weight of the past.[54] It is a debate that has continued into our own day.

That debate has also been affected by a quite different and unexpected form of revival. Beginning in 1993 with the widespread dissemination of chant recordings from the Benedictine monastery of Santo Domingo de Silos in northern Spain, Gregorian chant is now found in numerous hitherto unexpected contexts. Not only does it sell in its millions for listening to in the home, it is also the resort of almost every television production that wishes to suggest a religious ambience, even where such chant would scarcely ever, if at all, have found a place.[55] As 'wallpaper' music, listeners are seldom able to distinguish sad from joyful chants or even secular music from religious. In truth, the differences were not as great as they would be now in more contemporary music. Secular melodies were borrowed even then for religious purposes. Perhaps what the phenomenon indicates is the importance of context, the way in which this music has never really functioned on its own but always as part of a liturgy that provided numerous other clues to its meaning.

On the good side of what has happened is the serious attention now given to the reconstruction of what specific liturgies might once have looked like, as well the rediscovery of specific composers. One particular instance that cannot be overlooked is Hildegard of Bingen. Given the time at which she lived, she fits perfectly the desire for relatively simple chants. However, the range of ways in which she is currently presented well illustrates the tensions inherent in any such attempt to recover the past and experience it and her music as once performed. Born the tenth child in a wealthy family, at the age of eight she had been sent to live with another

[54] Ibid. 144–55, esp. 151.

[55] As, for example, in Anglican churches, of whatever period. Such chant has become the visual equivalent of candles, which seem always to be lit for whatever encounter takes place in church, whether liturgical or otherwise.

wealthy person, Jutta, who was a female hermit. Shaped by her for the monastic life, nothing much seems to have happened to Hildegard until at the age of forty-two she started to experience visions, and founded her own convent at Rupertsberg. Though never canonized, she was eventually to die at the age of eighty-one as one of the most revered individuals of the twelfth century. What had transformed her were those visions and the way in which, although without any formal education, she was inspired by them to be totally fearless in proclaiming where she thought her own society had gone wrong. No one was exempt from her critique, neither bishops, nor monks, nor the most famous theologian of the age, St Bernard of Clairvaux, and indeed not even the emperor himself, Frederick Barbarossa.

Before turning to her music, a brief look at those visions may be used to illustrate the difficulty of entering another, quite different world. Her inspiration was divine Wisdom. 'I saw a figure,' she writes, 'whose face and feet shone with such brightness that it beat upon my eyes. She had on a garment as if made from white silk and over it a green coloured tunic which appeared decorated all over with pearls and she wore in her ears earrings, and on her breasts necklaces, and on her arms bracelets, all, it seemed, from purest gold and ornamented with precious stones.'[56] A very worldly picture one might think, but for Hildegard jewels belonged properly only to heaven and not to this world.[57] So in her case it is all part and parcel of her critique of the contemporary Church. Her most famous set of visions ends with the declaration that Charity will confuse the strong and the proud 'through the small and the weak'.[58] And so against all the conventions of the age she even preached in public at Mainz. When excommunicated for burying someone against the Church's express command, she continued her fight until the Church was eventually forced to yield, not her. That feminine

---

[56] Translated from her *Liber divinorum operum* (3. 4. 1) in S. Flanagan, *Hildegard of Bingen: A Visionary Life* (London: Routledge, 1989), 147–8.

[57] Jewels, she suggests, had their origins in heaven and continue to have healing properties: J. Bobko ed., *Vision: The Life and Music of Hildegard von Bingen* (New York: Penguin, 1995), 18. In one of her finest images virgin martyrs are described as a pearl necklace that throttles the Devil: Flanagan, *Hildegard*, 130–1.

[58] Hildegard of Bingen, *Scivias*, Classics of Western Spirituality, (New York: Paulist Press, 1990), 536 (3. 13. 16).

image of Wisdom is of course a tempting one, to draw Hildegard into contemporary disputes. So it is unsurprising to discover some contemporary scholars portraying her as a feminist before her time, as it were. One describes her as *Sister of Wisdom*, while another even allows her to anticipate some of the sexual attitudes of our own day.[59] While one can sympathize with such writers' aims, something important is, I believe, lost: the willingness to see difference and hold it up as a mirror to our own society.

There are similar issues over treatment of her music. Her considerable talent can scarcely be in doubt. Not only is she the author of the oldest surviving musical drama, *The Play of Virtues*, there are also her seventy or so antiphons for the daily offices that make up the collection she entitled *Symphony of the Harmony of Celestial Revelations*.[60] The former is simpler musically, perhaps because the entire community was intended to take part.[61] To the latter's rich poetic imagery is joined extensive use of neumatic rather than melismatic forms, and an anchoring pitch that can nonetheless be combined with a melodic range of sometimes two octaves or more, with the inevitable accompanying demands on singers.[62] Such techniques, it has been suggested, in no way subordinate words to music but rather encourage *ruminatio*, sustained reflection on particular words.[63]

Yet once more there is the question of how all of this should best be appropriated for our own day. If Emma Kirkby sings her works much as Hildegard herself might have intended, Emily Van Evera in collaboration with Richard Souther has produced a much more

---

[59] For the former, Barbara Newman in the title of her book *Sister of Wisdom: St Hildegard's Theology of the Feminine* (Berkeley: University of California Press, 2nd edn., 1997); for the latter, Joan Ohanneson in her novel, *Scarlet Music* (New York: Crossroad, 1997).

[60] *Ordo virtutum* and *Symphonia armonie celestium revelationum*. A fine performance of the former is available on DVD: *Hildegard von Bingen: In Portrait* (BBC/Opus Arte, 2003).

[61] However, a fine melisma is given to the play's very last word: *porrigat*. God is seen 'stretching out' to unite our two worlds.

[62] For the two technical terms distinguished, see my earlier fn. 10.

[63] For an excellent discussion of Hildegard's aims: M. Fassler, 'Composer and Dramatist' in B. Newman ed., *Voice of the Living Light: Hildegard of Bingen and her World* (Berkeley: University of California Press, 1998), 149–75.

modern sound that even draws on pop.[64] As the latter disc has had much better sales, that may seem already to provide some sort of answer. But of course all depends on precisely what question it is that we are putting to Hildegard's works. If we want to enable her to speak to a quite different world from her own, then 'a sister of wisdom' beating her drum or strumming her guitar may well be the answer. But modernizing makes little sense if we are trying to understand her in her own context. The latter, I suspect, will be in the long run the more rewarding, if more difficult, exercise. Perhaps one method might be used as a prelude to the other.

Intriguingly, in responding to the ban of excommunication that prohibited her from receiving the sacraments or even from singing, it was to the latter prohibition that Hildegard took particular exception. It is in singing God's praises, she argued, that we most adequately acknowledge that we belong to an alternative world. Through these means God had demonstrated that it was never his intention that the Fall should be total and complete.[65] In one of her hymns she declares that one can only ascend to heaven if one is prepared here on earth to prostrate oneself before God and God alone.[66] But it is a prostration that on her view then enables one to fly aloft. As she expresses it in one of her visions, what singing grants her is the capacity to be like a little feather floating before the very throne of God.[67] Body and soul then unite in a harmony that is as profound as Christ's own identity in the incarnation: 'the words symbolise the body, and the jubilant music indicates the spirit; and the celestial harmony shows the divinity, and the words the humanity of the Son of God'.[68] So in one of those very rare instances where the religious significance of chant is commented on directly, we have its heart decisively identified. It can link two worlds but, as Hildegard's own life demonstrates, not at all in a way that precludes a deep and profound concern for justice and a bettering of the human condition.

---

[64] For the former, *A Feather on the Breath of God* (Hyperion, 1994). For the latter, *Vision: The Music of Hildegard von Bingen* (Angel Records, 1994).

[65] Flanagan, *Hildegard*, 179–82.

[66] In her *Hymn for Disibod* (an Irish bishop who had evangelized that part of Germany).

[67] Hence the choice of title for the Kirkby disc.

[68] From her concluding vision in *Scivias*, 533 (3. 13. 12).

Reformation and Counter-Reformation Interacting

Once upon a time historians of the sixteenth century would have treated the Reformation as an absolute watershed in the history of the Church, with sharp contrasts drawn between Reformation and Counter-Reformation churches, as also between the medieval and later Church. Now the need for a more subtle approach is widely recognized, and not just among professional historians.[69] These more sympathetic attitudes have, however, yet to percolate properly through to how the history of church music from the sixteenth century onwards is perceived. Among Protestants still widely prevalent is the parody that assumes an unrestrained indulgence of composers by Rome, while among Catholics Bach and Handel are often seen as strange, isolated exceptions in a sea of psalm and hymn singing.

As the deliberations of the Council of Trent and other papal pronouncements indicate, the truth is that Rome was as insistent as any Protestant preacher on the audibility of words. Nor was this a concern unique to Palestrina and his contemporaries and the nineteenth-century campaigns emanating from Regensburg and Solesmes. Early in the seventeenth century Monteverdi coined the name *seconda prattica* for the new style that was then coming into vogue, and which some of his own works illustrate.[70] With clarity of diction and dramatic emotional expression given priority over musical elaboration for its own sake, polyphony was now viewed with some suspicion, and an instrumental *basso continuo* used to support a monodic vocal sound.[71] Far from being dull, its very simplicity sometimes generated strong emotional contrasts that chimed well with the new Counter-Reformation forms of piety.[72]

[69] For illustrations of the change: J. Bossy, *Christianity in the West* 1400–1700 (Oxford: Oxford University Press, 1984); D. MacCulloch, *Europe's House Divided* 1490–1700 (London: Allen Lane, 2003).

[70] The term was coined by Monteverdi in 1607 in defence of the new style that he himself was using in his madrigals, as distinct form those who continued to imitate Josquin.

[71] Monteverdi's most famous religious work, the *Vespers* of 1610, is in a mixture of styles. For example, its five psalms continue the old practice of *cantus firmus*, while the motet *Nigra sum* is pure *seconda prattica*. For a detailed analysis: D. Arnold, *Monteverdi* (London: Dent, 1963), 131–54.

[72] Reflecting its source in the Song of Songs, *Nigra sum* has a warm, radiant feel (the key is G major) in which the music itself adds greatly to the sensuously insistent *surge* (arise).

In evaluating such changes, one must therefore resist jumping to the conclusion that words had simply triumphed over musical considerations. Composers might themselves prefer such a style because clarity of diction could contribute to giving the music greater dramatic intensity. Concern that music functioned as an enactment of the story of salvation was thus present here no less than in more elaborate forms of composition. None of this is to defend the total rejection of the religious works of Haydn, Schubert, and so many others that characterized the Cecilian movement. That was quite wrong in my view. But from that admission it by no means follows that this more austere style does not also have its power to inform and shape religious experience. As with the campaigns of Pugin and his followers for a unique style of religious architecture (Gothic), church musicians have sometimes too quickly opted for opposition. Thereby they have ignored the possibility that competing styles might complement one another in accentuating either different aspects of the divine or else the same aspect but through differing underlying principles and methodologies.

Nor was the missionary potential of music ignored. Oratorios take their name from the new religious order founded at Rome by St Philip Neri (d. 1595). Concerned to use drama and music to evangelize the Roman masses, he stepped outside the context of formal liturgy to use prayer halls (oratories) for such presentations.[73] It was the influence of Carissimi in the following century that ensured transmission of such musical presentations to France, where his former pupil Charpentier (d. 1704) responded to the Jesuits' desire for a similar strategy in Paris.[74] Opera emerged about the same time as the oratorio, and in their earliest versions it is not always easy to tell the two genres apart, musically.[75] Allegedly themes were quite different, but in practice there could be much overlap. So it is perhaps not altogether surprising that operas with

[73] The façade of the *oratorium* next to *Chiesa nuova* (the Oratorians' church in Rome) is almost as grandiose as the front of the church itself.

[74] Carissimi worked at the Jesuit *Collegio Germanico* in Rome. The Jesuits appointed Charpentier music master of their principal Paris church of St Louis. Although his oratorios are now little known, a recent biographer describes them as 'the most genuinely original branch of Charpentier's entire output': C. Cessac, *Marc-Antoine Charpentier* (Portland: Amadeus Press, 1995), 167–96, 265–302, esp. 265.

[75] For that earlier history, *God and Grace of Body*, 376–8.

religious themes were also written, some commissioned by the Jesuits, others actually written by members of that order.[76] More difficult to evaluate is the choice of secular rather than liturgical space for these performances. Was the motive fear of polluting sacred space, or the suspicion that audiences would not attend unless there was a theatre or hall that allowed them greater freedom of response? Both scenarios seem to betoken a rather narrow conception of worship, as though divine adoration could not involve the exploration and offering of the totality of ourselves. What can be said is that, although the oratorio was eventually to migrate through Handel to the Protestant side of the Church, it also continued vibrant within Catholicism, as in the works of Berlioz, Elgar, and Liszt.[77] Equally, the nearest equivalent Protestant innovation, the Passion, was eventually to achieve a similar prominence within Catholicism.[78] Works by Schütz were soon followed by Catholic examples such as Scarlatti's _St John Passion_. While tied more closely to a liturgical context, especially for worship on Good Friday, it too eventually migrated to more neutral contexts, sometimes deliberately so, as in a moving and strikingly original twentieth-century piece like Penderecki's _Passion according to Luke_ (1966).

Nor should we think that such concern with the role of music was confined to a small and very publicly active elite. Its use in mission already hints otherwise. How far such concerns percolated is demonstrated by one fascinating, recent study, of music in seventeenth-century nunneries.[79] Even while Trent's policy of more strict enclosure was being enforced, Sienese nuns were

[76] For two examples of the latter, the Dorian CD _The Jesuit Operas_ (1999). The shorter (Zipoli's of 1755) was intended for the mission field in Bolivia. Kapsberger's (1622) is homophonic with figured bass. It demonstrates a generous spirit in involving different races and nations, and even goes so far as to use the traditional ceremonies for the apotheosis of a Roman emperor as a model for celebrating a more contemporary canonization.

[77] And many more of course. For a helpful survey, K. Pahlen, _The World of the Oratorio_ (Aldershot: Scolar Press, 1990).

[78] Although Catholic compositions do exist that are contemporary with earlier Lutheran works (such as those of Schütz) and so one might talk of a parallel development, in effect its success with Lutherans ensured an eventual similar prominence among Catholics.

[79] C. Reardon, _Holy Concord within Sacred Walls: Nuns and Music in Siena 1575–1700_ (Oxford: Oxford University Press, 2002).

organizing themselves into polyphonic choirs that were used to enhance experience at key moments in their lives.[80] But it was not just a matter of enhancing liturgy. Open to a wider public were operas that included elements of chromatism and word painting and even comic musical dramas that possibly were deliberately subversive of authority in their intention.[81] Nor was any of this done without reflection. As such commentary as survives indicates, instrumental music was sometimes seen as a means towards spontaneous religious ecstasy, while the more routine pattern of eucharistic motets added emotional intensity to the encounter with Christ in communion.[82] Far more credit should be given to such initiatives than is usually the case. What needs to be remembered is that for most of Christian history nunneries were the only place in which women's experience of music was given a valued place.[83] While on the whole the ancient world was well disposed to female singers, by the fourth century women were being prohibited from singing in church. So only the cloister was left to reflect this particular experience of the divine in women's lives.

Just as the Catholic parody needs correcting, so too does the Protestant. In a sense I myself could be seen to be contributing to it, inasmuch as this chapter began with medieval music and not the great choral tradition of the Anglican Church, of which I am a member. Yet the clarity of the Prayer Book settings of the Calvinist John Merbecke (d. 1585) are as fine a riposte to the complexities of Dunstable as anyone might wish.[84] Again, William Byrd (d. 1623), though of quite different sympathies, did manage to combine for his Anglican royal employers richly polyphonic music with careful attention to the words. Marvellous as this tradition is, however, it has remained the experience of only a small minority, particularly

[80] For polyphony and instruments, ibid. 32–3; for a Te Deum to celebrate a new well, 30–1; for music celebrating clothing and profession, 54–5.
[81] For opera, ibid. 123–53, esp. 138, cf. 161; for spiritual comedy, 75–97. In theory the message of the latter was obedience, but this included parody (women dressing up as men etc.): 81–2, 97.
[82] Ibid. 107 (with a lute), 170–1.
[83] For a helpful bibliography, L. Green, *Music, Gender, Education* (Cambridge: Cambridge University Press, 1997), 31, fn.11.
[84] A good example of the problem with Dunstable is his *Veni Sancte Spiritus*, where two different sets of words are sung against each other. English musical style, however, was in any case becoming simpler in the period immediately prior to the Reformation.

cathedrals, collegiate churches and royal chapels.[85] While the Oxford Movement succeeded in spreading such practices, irrespective of churchmanship, to most of the parishes in the land, in retrospect this can now be seen as a happy hiccup in what has turned out to be a more consistent history of neglect.[86]

Even so, two important qualifications must be put. The first can be briefly stated. However deep such suspicions of choral music once were and no matter how seldom performances now actually occur in Protestant churches, in more recent times such music has fortunately come to escape those earlier censures. Lack of resources or inability to reach the young is more likely to be the pretext, along with preference for participation over performance, not theological objections. So the minority who choose may listen in the home without feeling the stern condemnations that would once have been forthcoming; and that applies within Calvinist circles no less than elsewhere.

The second qualification is that, just as early post-Tridentine history is more complex than the parody suggests, so too are attitudes among the Reformers and their immediate successors. In my earlier discussion in Chapter 3, only passing mention was made of the very different attitudes that prevailed, initially at least, within Lutheranism. It is in fact quite wrong to place the three major Reformers on a spectrum that has Zwingli opposed to all music in church, Calvin accepting only the singing of psalms, and Luther also including hymns, some of course his own composition.[87] Luther was much more generous than this. He accepted a major continuing role for choral music.[88] It was only with the rise of

[85] For a history of that tradition, E. Routley, *A Short History of English Church Music* (London: Mowbrays, 1977); for some reflections on its present state, L. Dakers, *Beauty Beyond Words* (Norwich: Canterbury Press, 2000).

[86] This is not to deny the quality of twentieth-century music in 'church composers' such as Wood Bairstow, Ireland, Howells, and Leighton, or more widely with Britten or Vaughan Williams, only to observe that it is the experience of a few.

[87] Zwingli's position resulted in some odd interpretations of Scripture. Colossians 3.16 is taken to mean not actual singing but singing in the heart: for references, P. Westermeyer, *Te Deum: The Church and Music* (Minneapolis: Fortress, 1998), 151.

[88] In his *Worship Wars in Early Lutheranism* (New York: Oxford University Press, 2004), Joseph Herl argues that too much attention has hitherto been paid to theologians' prescriptive comments rather than to evidence from actual practice

Pietism in the seventeenth century and with the Enlightenment movement of the eighteenth that such a tradition was seriously undermined.[89] In the view of Pietism there had to be a more direct and immediate appeal to personal piety in affective song, while for the Enlightenment the rational word was enthroned firmly above the complexities of music.

In his writings Luther alludes frequently to the positive role of music not simply as an adjunct to worship but almost in itself on a level with word in the potential contribution it might make. Thus saying and singing (*sagen und singen*) are closely united in his mind, in much the same way as the composer Michael Praetorius (d. 1621) later combines sermon and song (*concio und cantio*).[90] This is not to say that there were not some early followers who took a different view, but Praetorius' major work in defence of music, *Syntagma Musicum*, demonstrates how plausible a case a Lutheran composer might make.[91] The leading German musician of the seventeenth century was to turn out to be Heinrich Schütz (d. 1672). He had studied under the Gabrielis in Venice and later possibly met Monteverdi. In his compositions he helped to transmit the new style to the court at Dresden and thus more widely. So the way in which music might transcend theological divisions was already evident; as indeed was so in Luther's own case with his praise for the music of Josquin.

However, beyond Pietism and Rationalism and into the nineteenth century, and Lutheran music had been in retreat for some time. If at the Hohenzollern court at Berlin Mendelssohn had to contend with lack of interest in anything apart from settings of the psalms, distrust of Brahms went even further.[92] Despite its inclusion

such as liturgies, ecclesiastical visitations, and so on. These indicate a much more positive attitude not only in Luther but much more widely.

[89] For statistics on the strong bias towards the choral in *Agendas* (orders of service) between 1523 and 1600, Herl, *Worship Wars*, 55. For polyphony defended in explicit opposition to Calvinism, 110.

[90] Praetorius makes the link in the opening dedicatory epistle of his *Syntagma Musicum*. For the link in Luther, M. L. Hendrickson, *Musica Christi: A Lutheran Aesthetic* (New York: Peter Lang, 2005), 10–22, esp. 17.

[91] He worked in a wide variety of different styles: seen, for example, in his Latin motets or in the introductory plea to his *Geistliche Chor* that the earlier counterpoint should not be abandoned entirely in favour of *basso continuo*. For some examples of theological opposition, Herl, *Worship Wars*, 117–22.

[92] Caused in part by the royal household's Calvinist sympathies.

of nothing but the words of Scripture, the first performance of his *German Requiem* was allowed only on condition that it was balanced by an aria from Handel's *Messiah*.[93] Implicit references to Christ's death and resurrection were not enough. Mendelssohn's *Elijah* was in fact first performed in England, in Birmingham, in 1846. The work of a Jewish convert to Christianity, it well illustrates how music can help to comment on the biblical text. Some of the most moving passages are where a distinctively Christian interpretation is given to the prophet's story either implicitly as in the music for the confrontation on Mount Carmel or more explicitly in its Christian ending.[94] Handel went much further in his last oratorio *Jephtha*. Gone is the biblical version that has the judge's daughter die, and in its place comes a deeply reflective struggle towards a self-offering that is not in the end demanded.[95]

As an aside here, perhaps I should add that the point of such examples is not to denigrate Judaism. It is merely to remind the reader that the experience of the divine through choral music is not just about generalities of emotion, it is also concerned with specifics, potentially at least with all the details of the drama of salvation. So assessment is possible at this level as well. Thus, depending on the issue, the choice is not necessarily simply between religions but within and across them. In fact there is as little consistency on musical issues within modern Judaism as there is within Christianity. Cantor and congregation are given widely varying degrees of prominence. There is even some continuing opposition to the use of instruments.[96] To the believing outsider some choral elements emerge with a beauty that is universal in its language, while others

[93] 'I know that my Redeemer liveth': Hendrickson, *Musica Christi*, 168. Implicit allusions such as 'Blessed are those who die in the Lord' were apparently felt not to be enough.

[94] For the use of musical quotation in the Carmel scene, Hendrickson, *Musica Christi*, 159–61. For a critique of the ending, Pahlen, *The World of the Oratorio*, 239.

[95] Contrast Judges 11 not just with the angelic intervention at the oratorio's very end but also with the powerful vision of heaven for Jephtha and Iphis (his daughter) that precedes this.

[96] For a detailed survey of practice in five quite different synagogues in the Boston area, J. A. Summit, *The Lord's Song in a Strange Land: Music and Identity in Contemporary Jewish Worship* (New York: Oxford University Press, 2000). For Al Jolson's dilemmas in abandoning the role of cantor, see Neil Diamond's powerful depiction in the film *The Jazz Singer* (1980).

are problematic even for some Jews.[97] Yet there remains a wide-spread consensus that these issues matter, precisely because singing is so intimately related to religious experience: so much so that to pray (*daven*) is widely taken to carry with it automatic associations with singing, chanting, moving, and swaying.[98]

Similarly within Christianity it is impossible to apply any simple doctrinal tests. There have of course been numerous composers of great faith but what they communicate is by no means necessarily identical with the perspective of their own particular denomination or lack of it. To hear Hubert Parry 'I was glad' in church and Giuseppe Verdi's *Requiem* probably in the concert hall and know that both alike were on the fringes of faith is not at all to answer the question of the possible relevance of their music to religious experience, nor where it should be heard.[99] What matters is how far either entered imaginatively into Christian experience, in Parry's case into the joy of entering into the divine presence, in Verdi's into a sense of one's own unworthiness before a just but merciful judge.[100] It is only the extent of the resources required that makes it appropriate that one is performed in church and the other not. Not that this is always what decides matters. It is sad that Bach's cantatas seem to have migrated permanently to the concert hall, especially since it is only really the rigidity of forms of church service in England that prevent their occasional return. Fortunately, the Lutheran tradition is itself more flexible in both Germany and the United States. Nor should the fact of performance in the concert hall speak of an absence of the possibility of religious experience as a consequence, any more than the hearing of a performance on a CD player in the home.

Enough has perhaps now been said to indicate a more complicated history than is commonly assumed for the last five hundred years in both Protestantism and Roman Catholicism. Communication and

---

[97] An example of the former is the great mystical hymn, *Lekhah dodi*, of the latter use of the Israeli national anthem in the Sabbath service: Summit, *The Lord's Song*, 33–104, 134–5.

[98] Summit, *The Lord's Song*, 26, 33, 88, 94.

[99] Parry, a regular subscriber to the Rationalist Press Association, was perhaps closer to atheism.

[100] Taking, that is, their two best-known religious works. Parry's anthem was written for the coronation of Edward VII (1902), Verdi's *Requiem* (1874) in honour of his friend, the novelist Alessandro Manzoni.

accessibility was a concern in both branches of the Church alike, and the move towards the concert hall was as much a consequence of mission and of the Church's own decisions as it was of secularism.

The Function of Choral Music in Today's Church

Focusing explicitly on what has remained in church, I want now finally in this chapter to consider two interconnected issues. First, there is the question of what is being realized through the music. Glorifying God as one of the principal aims of music has already been mentioned quite a number of times already during the course of this chapter; so needs no repetition here. But a number of additional functions have come to the fore, as the nature of the music has itself changed. Then, secondly, there is the whole issue of the relation between words and music. Music can of course achieve enactment on its own. One witness to this is the long-standing tradition of organ solos in the context of the Lutheran liturgy; another, the development of so-called organ masses, especially by Frescobaldi and Couperin, where organ music replaces choral singing for the Ordinary.[101] Nonetheless, overwhelmingly in church this is achieved through cooperation between words and music, and so the precise nature of that cooperation demands our attention.

As indicated in the first section of this chapter, I do want to resist the fallacy that because experience is not discussed, it is therefore not taking place. Even so, it is clear that from the sixteenth century onwards there is now far more direct focus on the experience of the worshippers themselves. That was part of a more general cultural change that was characteristic of the Renaissance. Its impact can be seen in Shakespeare. Sometimes his allusions to music assume a transcendent dimension; at other times the primary aim does appear to be some effect on the emotions of the listener.[102] This is not to say that the ability of music to convey a sense of a transcendent

---

[101] Part of a once more widely disseminated phenomenon known as verset. The practice was condemned by Pius X's important decree *motu proprio* of 1903.

[102] Much is made of the contrast between the *Tempest* ('Where should this music be? . . .') and *Twelfth Night* ('If music be the food of love . . .') in H. Goodall, *Big Bangs: The Story of Five Centuries That Changed Musical History* (London: Vintage, 2001), 55–6.

presence is thereby demoted. But it now tends to come allied with more specific feelings, such as joy or penitence. Again, it is not that these were absent in earlier centuries, but that in more distant times they usually came through constant association of certain chants with particular seasons rather than because the music in itself intrinsically bore just such a dimension. While it might be objected that such a focus on interior feelings is inevitably at odds with a possible external reference of the music in God, the two do not, I think, operate as alternatives. Emotion can in fact draw listeners nearer to a sense of presence where need is felt (as in sorrow or penitence) or where more positive emotions (such as elation or joy) point beyond themselves to gratitude as an appropriate response. For singers such experience can provide a legitimate alternative to more mechanical forms of interiority, such as the realization of how sound is being generated from within.[103]

My examples thus far still place the divine presence, as it were, over against the music. That is to say, the music is seen as generating certain emotions that then point beyond themselves to God. But another possibility is for God to be actually in the music. That might occur in a number of different ways. The first lies in the nature of composition itself. Where harmonies suggest larger harmonies, the sceptic might complain of a harking back to the now discredited harmony of the spheres, but harmony and communion are after all not unrelated ideas. Such music can encourage not only a stronger sense of communal identity but also communion with one's environment as a whole, and thus with the source of all that is. A more modern dimension would be the extent to which the music under consideration is built on the development of tensions and anticipations together with their subsequent resolution, for that could suggest a possible parallel with the process of salvation itself.[104] Another is the way in which a more immediate impact is achieved in linkage through accompanying words. Pain and its 'answer', for

---

[103] K. Harmon, 'Liturgical Music as Prayer' in R. A. Leaver and J. A. Zimmerman eds., *Liturgy and Music* (Collegeville: Liturgical Press, 1998), 265–80, esp. 272.

[104] A repeated theme in the writings of Jeremy Begbie. For the emotional effect of repeated suspension or *appogiatura* producing tears, J. Sloboda, 'Music and Worship: A Psychologist's Perspective' in J. Astley, T. Hone and M. Savage eds., *Creative Chords: Studies in Music, Theology and Christian Formation* (Leominster: Gracewing, 2000), 110–25, esp. 123.

instance, might be effectively explored not by means of the two-stage process indicated above (with a generated emotion then pointing beyond itself) but by being already there in the particular biblical passage chosen for setting to music. Words and music might then of themselves suggest a particular response rather than require further exploration beyond the actual words and music.

That is one reason why it is essential that musical settings not be allowed to float in isolation, as it were, wholly apart from other non-musical traditions of interpretation on which they so often ultimately depend. Congregations do at times need help in perceiving how particular pieces of music were once integrated into certain specific ways of reading Scripture. A single example will suffice. The issue no doubt repeats itself throughout the land but my experience as a Canon of Durham Cathedral may be used by way of illustration. A few years ago the choral music for the Advent Carol Service contained no fewer than seven references to roses, but none in the passages read from Scripture. The explanation lay in the fact that modern biblical translations now commonly substitute a crocus for a rose in the most directly relevant passage, Isaiah 35.1: 'The wilderness and the solitary place shall be glad for them; and the desert shall rejoice, and blossom as the rose' (AV).[105] So, for instance, Herbert Howells's 'The Rose which I am singing, whereof Isaiah said' now made no sense. In the past the desert flowering to which Isaiah refers was taken as an oblique reference to Mary giving birth to Jesus. She was the rose without thorns that produced the child who would be crowned with thorns in due course for our sake. The result had been choirs regularly singing *Rorare coeli* in her honour, celebrating the fact that her womb would be fruitful as no other, one that could make all others blossom. As Christopher Steel exhorts: 'Furrows be glad . . . Love the rose is on the way,' an obvious allusion to Isaiah 45.8. Again, Joubert informs us that 'In this rose contained was/ Heaven and earth in little space.' In other words, the rose that is Mary's womb contains he who is both God and man. Personally, I cannot see why 'rose' cannot continue to be the translation used on such occasions. Instead of the listener struggling to make sense of the music, the scripture reading will then aid in shaping understanding of the significance of the

---

[105] The issue recurs elsewhere: e.g. Song of Songs 2.1 with its traditional 'rose of Sharon'.

incarnation. Thereby the ideal is achieved of music and words working together in harmony to generate a total experience, rather than appealing to entirely different aspects of the hearers' intellect and senses.

In looking at those kinds of reactions, it is important not to suppose that the aim is only ever to augment or resolve an existing emotion; so, for example, to add to the joy of what is already a festive occasion or to pick up on someone's sorrow and point to its mollifying in the love and compassion of God. Equally relevant is the rousing of such emotions in the first place. If part of Christian discipleship is to try, however inadequately, to match and model one's life on Christ's own, then it is important that at certain seasons and times the believer should enter fully into the type of experience Christ was having at that point in his life, irrespective of the individual's particular mood of the moment. That is why it is quite right to think of music as also having a homiletic or hermeneutic purpose.[106] A short organ solo after a sermon can allow time for reflection on what has just been said. But an anthem no less than the sermon could of itself lead worshippers towards the right response to what Christ has done on their behalf. Stories after all abound of how individuals have been converted by pieces of music rather than by sermons. Recent research suggests that this may even be true of John Wesley's own conversion experience. Possibly integral to it was the music he heard in the days leading up to the experience.[107] The juxtaposition of otherwise unrelated texts in anthems can also play an important hermeneutical role in encouraging reflection, just as sometimes happened at an earlier period with some Gregorian chants, as, for instance, in tropes and sequences.[108]

Yet there is no doubt that the current trend in all the churches is towards the rejection of purely choral pieces. At one level this can

---

[106] Well argued in R. A. Leaver, 'Liturgical Music as Homily and Hermeneutic' in Leaver and Zimmerman, *Liturgy and Music*, 340–59.

[107] Leaver argues from Wesley's own diaries that anthems by Croft, Purcell, and Greene played an integral part in his 1738 conversion experience: ibid. 344–9.

[108] As possible examples from anthems, consider the medley of texts in John Ireland's *Greater Love Hath No Man* or S. S. Wesley's famous *Blessed be the God and Father*. In the later case only trebles and a single bass (the Dean's butler) were apparently available when it was first performed on Easter Day, 1834, at Hereford Cathedral: B. Matthews, *Samuel Sebastian Wesley* (Bournemouth: Mummery, 1976), 5.

be put down to the decline in appreciation of classical music generally. But there are also important ideological reasons that have been repeatedly voiced, not least and somewhat surprisingly in more recent pronouncements from Rome. Whereas earlier decrees had merely insisted upon audibility, to this requirement is now added the need for full congregational participation in the liturgy. With that has come the suggestion that, if settings of the Ordinary are to be employed, these should be of a type in which all can take part. The key chapter in Vatican II's *Sacrosanctum Concilium* identified the proper aim as what was characterized as 'a noble simplicity'.[109] Subsequently, Pope Paul VI even conceded that, in order to achieve this more fundamental goal of full participation, as a likely consequence 'an inestimable treasure', 'that wondrous and incomparable reality' of Gregorian chant, might well have to be jettisoned.[110]

That fortuitous mention of a 'goal' reminds us of what seems to have been forgotten, that deep participation in certain activities is possible without direct involvement: through imaginative identification. It is this kind of ability that has been lost in the modern church. Despite never touching the ball, the football crowd is fully engaged with the actions of their team. Yet congregations are seldom encouraged towards similar appropriate responses towards the choirs they hear. The defenders of church music have sometimes only themselves to blame. Where music is compared with grace and conceived in essentially purely passive or receptive terms, the battle has already been lost.[111] That is quite the wrong model for how to get the most out of particular pieces of music which surely require active engagement and concentration. Our bodies no less than our minds must actively interact with the music in any proper listening: that is, intently. With the decline in musical

---

[109] For a full discussion, M. T. Winter, *Why Sing? Towards a Theology of Catholic Church Music* (Washington: Pastoral Press, 1984), 45–58, esp. 51, 53, 56. The stress on congregational participation had been anticipated by Pius XII in his *Mediator Dei* of 1947: Winter, *Why Sing?* 142.

[110] In an address of 1969: Winter, *Why Sing?* 169–70.

[111] A model adopted by James MacMillan in comparing receptivity in music to the Virgin Mary's response at the Annunciation in 'God, Theology and Music' in S. Darlington and A. Kreider eds., *Composing Music for Worship* (Norwich: Canterbury Press, 2003), 35–50. esp. 48–50; also in Rowan Williams, *Open to Judgement* (London: Darton, Longman & Todd, 1994), 248.

education in schools, it becomes all the more surprising how seldom choirmasters make any real effort to help congregations (through teaching sessions for example) to understand the music that is expected to claim their attention.[112] Moreover, it cannot but be a matter of deep regret that such discussion of music in churches as there is tends to concentrate exclusively on the quality of the performance and not on what might or might not have been said through that performance. There is surely no reason why musicians should not be subjected to exactly the same sort of critique as preachers and liturgists. That way, irrespective of how unwelcome the new forms of critique might be, the value of what musicians are attempting to achieve would be considerably enhanced. Instead of a merely adjunct role, the seriousness and indispensability of their contribution to the whole would at last have been properly acknowledged.

Not that matters would be much helped if this critique were to follow too closely the most common patterns of criticism in the past. Augustine's worries about the seductive powers of music continue to be echoed in our own day.[113] Even in the Roman Catholic Church and as late as the eighteenth century, concern was still being expressed over the potential for purely instrumental music to lead listeners astray. Aquinas was among those quoted as a relevant authority.[114] But music can hardly be pronounced inherently more dangerous than the tricks of any clever orator. Nor can this even be identified as music's characteristic failing, at least so far as church music is concerned. More pertinent are unsuitable combinations of words and music. A beautiful chant, for instance, might be used to lull us into an easy acceptance of troubling words. This is to argue against pleas for return to the practice of singing expressions of hatred such as the concluding verses of Psalm 137 or Psalm 58 in its entirety. While it is of course true that we need under God to work through similar emotions on our own part, this is scarcely

[112] A need acknowledged by T. Hone, 'When in Our Music God is Glorified' in Astley *et al.*, *Creative Chords*, 143–71, esp. 148–50.

[113] e.g. by J. Gelineau, 'The Path of Music' in D. Power, M. Collins, and M. Burnim eds., *Music and the Experience of God*, Concilium (Edinburgh: T & T Clark, 1989), 135–47, esp. 142. Augustine's more positive references ought not to be forgotten, e.g. *Confessions* 9. 6. 14.

[114] For Benedict XIV's lengthy encyclical (*Annus qui* of 1749) in which Bellarmine and Cajetan are used to argue against Aquinas, Winter, *Why Sing?*, 132–3.

helped by chants that fail to draw attention to the sheer vindictiveness of the sentiments or even encourage us to ignore the words altogether.[115] Equally, it must be said that, however beautiful the music, Rossini's *Stabat Mater* leaves Mary too content at the foot of the cross. Because that particular poem is concerned exclusively with the crucifixion, Rossini's version is altogether too operatic and melodic to quite capture the right mood.[116]

However, in such criticism it remains important not to jump to any particular conclusion too quickly. It would be very easy, for example in the modern context, to side with either James MacMillan or John Tavener and endorse the contrast MacMillan himself makes between their music: the strong sense of the pain of crucifixion in his own work and of the joy of the resurrection in Tavener's.[117] It is not as though the choice must be between an exclusive diet of one or of the other. Because of the changing liturgical year, varying anthems, now of one type, now of the other, might be more appropriate.[118] The more interesting question is whether in the two composers' settings particular dimensions have been lost, or not, and so whether they might not after all be used to complement one another. Such one-sidedness is a frequent complaint against eighteenth-century masses. Stravinsky, for instance, described Mozart's church compositions as the 'sweets of sin', and much the same critique might be applied to Haydn. There is nothing of the cost of the crucifixion.[119] But in response it may be said that what Haydn offers, especially through his two oratorios *The Creation* and *The Seasons*, is a challenge that desperately needs to be heard against all who think an exclusive focus on

[115] For the kind of argument I am rejecting, D. Power, 'Editorial Conclusions' in Power *et al.*, *Music and Experience*, 148–51, esp. 150.

[116] In other words, it is the focus of the words that makes the music wrong, not the music as such. So the masses of Haydn and Mozart may be equally operatic and melodic, but the music is in a context (the eucharist) where there is no such exclusive focus on the crucifixion.

[117] As in MacMillan, 'Creation and the Composer' in Astley *et al.*, *Creative Chords*, 3–19, esp. 16–17, or his 'God, Theology and Music' in Darlington and Kreider, *Composing Music for Worship*, 40–1.

[118] Expressed like this because so far MacMillan's religious repertoire has proved less suitable for church performance (largely because of difficulty and resources required, not quality).

[119] I. Stravinsky and R. Craft, *Expositions and Developments* (London: Faber Music, 1962), 77.

biblical revelation is exactly what is required. Thereby effectively ignored is the full wonder of divine creation. In his *Creation* this is exactly what Haydn offers. There is an impressive contrast between the order and unadulterated joy that can be found in creation (as in the parade of the animals in Part II) and the sheer chaos that exists without God, indicated in the opening of Part I by its swirling ambiguous harmonies and suddenly climbing arpeggios.

Again, it is at least worth considering whether Haydn's insistence on always giving a positive tone in the *Agnus Dei* to the concluding *dona pacem* is not after all exactly right, despite the preponderance of composers pulling in a rather different direction.[120] The reason is that, although linked with two other petitions that, as in the *Gloria*, ask for mercy, the prayer is this time being sung after Christ's sacrifice has been re-presented to the Father in the eucharistic prayer. So at this point the service is most open to the exchange of a real and lasting peace between God and humanity. A celebration of peace rather than a renewed plea for its realization is thus entirely apposite. Again, to take a quite different issue, it is important always to bear in mind the century from which a piece is being drawn. So used is the modern listener to the dramatic contrasts of the nineteenth and twentieth centuries that it takes much more effort to hear the gentler contrasts of, say, the sixteenth century.

Earlier in tracing the history of post-Reformation choral music, I noted in passing the way in which such music had begun to migrate to the concert hall. It is a process that has of course accelerated in more modern times.[121] In some ways the Church has only itself to blame. Resources are of course part of the issue, as also the wish of non-believers to hear such music in contexts that do not require commitment of them.[122] But a lack of hospitality on the part of the Church is also part of the explanation. While the late Middle Ages was enlarging the range of words and commentary that might be used in church, subsequent centuries often displayed suspicion of

---

[120] All six of his masses give it a joyful *Allegro*.

[121] As recently as Pope John Paul II, all performances of 'secular' music were banned from Rome's churches.

[122] The last major report from the Church of England was keen to stress potential rather than strained resources, noting in particular the contrast with many churches in the United States: for example Crystal Cathedral in California where over 700 are involved in active music making: *In Tune With Heaven* (London: Hodder & Stoughton, 1992), 111–12.

anything that was not biblical.[123] Yet there can be little doubt that sometimes it is precisely the interaction between biblically inspired words and non-biblical that generates the most profound reaction in challenge and reflection. Obvious twentieth-century examples would include Britten's *War Requiem* and Tippett's *A Child of our Time*. In the former case the words of the Requiem Mass are interspersed with poems of Wilfrid Owen, and to brilliant effect. So, for example, the Latin Vulgate's words of promise to Abraham and his seed are immediately followed by what is perhaps Owen's best-known poem 'The Parable of the Old Man and the Young' that speaks of the slaughter of his son and 'half the seed of Europe'.[124] In the latter Tippett had originally planned something similar, with words specially composed by T. S. Eliot.[125] Although rather disparaging about the words he himself eventually produced, Tippett did achieve a work that transcends any particular age through his decision to offer rather more than his original intention, a lament for the Jews being killed in the Europe of the time. Instead, he deliberately confronts the evil that lurks in us all. In his own words his aim was 'to plough the dark ground of our disorders that we may sow new seeds'.[126]

What the long history of Christian suspicions of certain forms of music reveals is a regrettable tendency to impose certain predetermined norms rather than a willingness to engage with the great variety that is the human spirit. I have already had occasion to call into question whether words need always on each occasion to be heard. Equally, it is not true that the same piece of music will affect us all in precisely the same way. So much will depend on age, education, musical knowledge, personal circumstances, and so forth. There needs, therefore, to be far more openness to the complete range of possibilities than there is at present, where each group in the Church seems to think that it, and it alone, has the right answer. Instead, there should be a willingness to draw not only on music from

---

[123] Or in the case of Rome widened but only to include the early Church Fathers: cf. Alexander VII's decree *Piae sollicitudinis* (1657).

[124] For an analysis at a little more length, see my 'Images of Redemption' in S. T. Davis, D. Kendal, and G. O'Collins eds., *The Redemption* (Oxford: Oxford University Press, 2004), 295–319, esp. 303–4.

[125] For the story, M. Tippett, *Music of the Angels* (London: Eulenburg, 1980), 117–26.

[126] Ibid. 188–97, esp. 190.

different historical epochs but also on a corresponding variety of different styles.[127] Intriguingly, it often takes a public or national occasion like the funeral of the Princess of Wales to spur the Church into that inclusiveness that should be its natural raison d'être.

The Church's own failures in this respect demand, I suggest, more sympathy from the Christian for what now takes place in the concert hall. Surprising as it may seem, commentators without religious belief are seldom dismissive of the spiritual element in works once written for churches.[128] Indeed, they are quite likely to describe in some detail how the piece in question attempts to open listeners to the transcendent, even if it is a path that they themselves have chosen not to follow. So the music remains in its new setting as at the very least a witness to the possibility of experience of the divine, of God himself entering into the drama of the musical action. And possibility of course sometimes becomes reality.

So I end this chapter by refusing absolute dividing lines either between church and concert hall or home, or between music and words. That refusal may seem to undermine any unique quality for the liturgy as such. It does not. It is precisely by building on our experience of God in other contexts that the liturgy will be at its most effective. How exactly that observation applies to its performance in church is the final issue to which I turn in my concluding chapter.

---

[127] For the former, J. Harper, 'Renewing the Past in the Present' in Darlington and Kreider, *Composing Music for Worship*, 155–72, esp. 171–2; for a variety of styles, H. Goodall, 'Music and Mystery' in ibid. 15–34, esp. 24–8.
[128] Seen, for instance, in W. Mellers, *Celestial Music?* (Woodbridge: Boydell, 2002), pp. xi–xiv, 307–10; M. Steinberg, *Choral Masterworks* (Oxford: Oxford University Press, 2005), 5–8.

7
Performance, Costume, Staging

In this chapter I examine the Church's liturgy, but in a manner readers may well not expect. Something has already been said in Part I on how words function, and in particular on the key role played by metaphor. So here I want largely to ignore questions of what is said, and instead apply attention to the wider context against which such words are set. For many that may seem a purely peripheral concern. But that is to ignore the impact for better or for worse of what we do with our bodies in worship. Equally, there is the issue of the kind of things on which our eyes alight, even as the attempt is made to focus on the words of liturgy or preacher. So in what follows I proceed by four stages. First, I examine the relevance of the ritual of bodily actions to performance of the liturgy, then liturgical clothing as one small example of the complexity of the issues involved. A section on architecture and the relevance of such staging and the wider backdrop more generally then prefaces a concluding section on liturgical change and the preservation of mystery. In short, my aim is to set the liturgy as a whole in the context of dramatic performance.

Performance, Ritual, and Bodily Expression

Ritual, it needs to be said at the outset, is not the same thing as ritualism.[1] The latter term is usually reserved for those approaches within the Church that see elaborate ceremony as essential to worship. By contrast, using 'ritual' to speak of how the body is used in worship applies no necessary endorsement of one particular form of worship over another. Indeed, ritual as such is something

[1] Numerous nineteenth-century pamphlets and books on ritualism indicate the difference. For a discussion of the phenomenon, N. Yates, *Anglican Ritualism in Victorian Britain* (Oxford: Clarendon, 1999).

from which no human being can escape entirely, not even the most secular-minded. American identity, for example, is largely a function of various self-generated rituals that are reinforced in various kinds of ways, from the daily ceremony before the flag in schools to the structural layout of the American capital.[2] Nor did the Reformation succeed in banning ritual. It merely acquired new forms. Recall, for instance, in Presbyterian churches the beadle's solemn carrying of a large Bible up to the pulpit immediately before the entry of the minister. Although nothing could be further from the intention, there seem obvious parallels with the procession of the Host in Benediction. It is just that a quite different form of divine presence is being honoured. Indeed, so integral is ritual to human identity that it is arguable that the removal of so much from the sacred sphere at the Reformation merely moved its impact elsewhere into state and civic ceremonial. The increased importance attached to the rituals of the British monarchy in these and succeeding centuries seems to demonstrate as much.[3] So too what happened in many a local context. Take, for example, the city of Durham, in which I am writing these remarks. The longest continuously surviving rituals belong to the legal profession and to the Mayor's formal bodyguard.[4]

Serious academic analysis of ritual only really began in the nineteenth century with the gradual emergence of sociology as an independent discipline. In Emile Durkheim's writings ritual and belief are contrasted, with the former seen as integral to social cohesion.[5] Since then ritual has been variously defined and analysed. Edmund Leach made the term so all-encompassing that its

[2] For the latter, J. F. Meyer, *Myths in Stone: Religious Dimensions of Washington D. C.* (Berkeley: University of California Press, 2001); discussed in my *God and Enchantment of Place: Reclaiming Human Experience* (Oxford: Oxford University Press, 2004), 186–7.
[3] For the increased prominence of royal funerals between 1570 and 1625, J. Woodward, *The Theatre of Death* (Woodbridge: Boydell, 1997); for the impact on Shakespeare's portrayal of monarchy, L. Woodbridge and E. Berry, *True Rites and Maimed Rites: Ritual and Anti-Ritual in Shakespeare and his Age* (Chicago: University of Illinois Press, 1992), 147–295.
[4] The latter still march with their halberdiers, while the annual Assize Sermon has the character of fancy dress parade, with each variety of the legal profession wearing its own strange uniform.
[5] E. Durkheim, *The Elementary Forms of Religious Life* (New York: Free Press, 1964), esp. 51.

usefulness as a category has to be questioned.[6] While the social element is never absent, and in some writers is even more strongly underlined than in Durkheim, in more recent years, particularly among those whose prime interest is religion, there has been a tendency to weaken that contrast with belief.[7] Instead, ritual is seen as belief mediated through action, sometimes consciously so, sometimes not. Indeed, in the opinion of some it is ritual that more naturally entails commitment rather than 'belief'.[8] Christian theologians are likely to be most familiar with work on transformative rituals, not least because such analyses fit quite well with the intentions behind baptism.[9] It is sad, however, that confirmatory rituals are not given comparable attention, and the related term 'taboo' used in a purely negative way. The practice of Orthodox Jews in reciting blessings throughout the day, for example, is best seen as a confirmatory ritual that expresses a particular understanding of the world. More controversially, their food rituals or those of Hindus are not well served by analyses that presuppose only irrational attitudes towards particular animals or groups. Certainly, these sometimes produce unfortunate indirect consequences, as in Hindu neglect of animals in circumstances where mercy killings might be the better option. But on the whole the attitudes concerned do help preserve a sense of the sacred in all of life. Particularly unfortunate has been the usurpation of the term 'taboo' for an entirely derogatory, negative usage. The word is actually a corruption of an original Polynesian term *tapu*, used to indicate areas where *mana* or divine power is made manifest.[10] Applying that

[6] He wanted the term applied to all 'culturally defined sets of behaviour': E. R. Leach s.v. 'Ritual' in D. L. Sills ed., *International Encyclopaedia of the Social Sciences* (New York: Free Press, 1968), 524.

[7] For Bourdieu every social group 'entrusts to bodily automatisms' those principles that are basic to its organization: P. Bourdieu, *Outline of a Theory of Practice* (Cambridge: Cambridge University Press, 1977), 218 n. 44.

[8] Rappaport draws here a contrast with myth: R. A. Rappaport, *Ecology, Meaning and Religion* (Richmond, Calif.: North Atlantic Books, 1979), 193. Since then there has appeared his major study that argues religious ritual is central to the continuing evolution of humanity: *Ritual and Religion in the Making of Humanity* (Cambridge: Cambridge University Press, 1999).

[9] Most obviously in A. van Gennep, *The Rites of Passage* (Chicago: University of Chicago Press, 1960).

[10] S. Hooper, *Pacific Encounters: Art and Divinity in Polynesia, 1760–1860* (London: British Museum Press, 2006), 37–8.

sense to Orthodox Jews and Hindus we might think of its application both negatively (e.g. pork forbidden) and positively (e.g. cows
sacred) as providing a strong sense of God directing all of life
through his care.

In recent years Michel Foucault has made much of social rituals
as powerful instruments of oppression.[11] His account strikes me as
too heavily reliant on a rather old-fashioned contrast between mind
and body, as though ritual was essentially unthinking because
belonging to the body, and so more easily subject to manipulation.
That is no doubt why philosophers have for so long ignored the
topic. But this is changing. Some at least now recognize that human
beings sometimes think through their bodies as much as through
their minds. It can be a way not only of expressing deep commitments, but also of exploring their range. A recent collection of
essays includes one that examines how this works within Judaism.
Another argues that conventional feminist philosophy of religion
falls short, precisely because it is still too strongly in the grips of the
mind-downwards model.[12] Instead of thinking of body and symbol
as two separate realities, the theories of Mauss, Bourdieu, and
others need to be harnessed in detecting a *habitus* or particular
attitude already fully embodied.[13]

More surprisingly, interest in bodies among liturgists is almost as
recent. Admittedly, books about religious ritual have a long lineage,
but their focus in the past was essentially historical. Indeed, historical
research has been the principal concern of liturgists through most
of the period that it has existed as a serious academic discipline.[14]
That is no doubt why in liturgical reform the recommendations
of specialists have usually taken a similar turn. These were directed

[11] Without analysing the term, he continually speaks of 'rituals of execution'
(11), 'penal ritual' (18), 'ritual of public torture' (28), 'liturgy of punishment' (34),
'penal liturgy' (47) and so on: *Discipline and Punish: The Birth of the Prison* (New
York: Vintage, 1979).
[12] S. Kepnes, 'Ritual Gives Rise to Thought: Liturgical Reasoning in Modern
Jewish Philosophy' in K. Schillbrack ed., *Thinking Through Rituals* (London:
Routledge, 2004), 224–37; A. Hollywood, 'Practice, Belief and Feminist Philosophy of Religion', ibid. 52–70.
[13] Unfortunately, the most explicit Christian analysis continues the mind-
downward model: C. Taliafero, 'Ritual and Christian Philosophy' in Schillbrack,
Thinking Through Rituals, 238–50.
[14] But conditioned by the Romantic postulation of a patristic 'golden age': F. C.
Senn, *Christian Liturgy: Catholic and Evangelical* (Minneapolis: Fortress, 1997), 610.

towards the removal of what were seen as medieval encrustations on a purer, uniform patristic pattern. Herein lies the explanation for the very high profile acquired in so many modern liturgies for eucharistic prayers modelled on the early third-century Hippolytus.[15] While Dom Gregory Dix laid greater stress on uniformity of eucharistic action, others detected a common developing pattern that also applied to the words.[16]

In more recent years, however, that consensus has come increasingly under strain.[17] This may explain in part new trends towards more focus on what is actually done and the symbolism involved. Nonetheless, there are still some grounds for worry in respect of the new approach. I want to examiner here three in particular. First, I consider whether liturgy as a discipline is still not too tied to past precedent. What has a meaning and perhaps even a very powerful meaning in one age does not necessarily transmit easily to another. Wider sociological and cultural factors may be more significant. Secondly, I want to explore the open-ended character of symbolic actions, how their impact is much harder to tie down definitively in one direction than is commonly supposed. The result is a plea for recognition of a wider range of options on such activities as offertory processions, postures for prayer, and rituals of fasting. If on both those first two types of question I am rebelling against past narrowness, on the third issue I want to move in the opposite direction, and challenge the modern tendency to seek foci for the presence of Christ almost anywhere else than in the elements. What that traditional focus at least guaranteed was a strong sense of the material: that it is Christ's humanity that matters, not just some vague ethereal presence. All three issues of course ultimately revolve round the question of how a sense of drama about what is taking place can best be maintained.

First, then, the issue of past precedent, and the way in which many 'new' initiatives still often remain largely backward-looking.[18]

[15] Note current questioning of how much of it may be original, e.g. P. Bradshaw, *Early Christian Worship* (London: SPCK, 1996), 48–9.

[16] For Dix's fourfold action, G. Dix, *The Shape of the Liturgy* (London: Dacre, 1945): offertory, thanksgiving, fraction, communion.

[17] For the reasons, P. Bradshaw, *The Search for the Origins of Christian Worship* (London: SPCK, 1990). He talks of 'plundering . . . to fit' a predetermined picture (cf. 101).

[18] That exclusive preoccupation was already being criticized as early as 1947 by Pius XII in his encyclical *Mediator Dei*.

Not that there is anything wrong in seeking inspiration in the Scriptures or in the practices of the early Church, but sometimes insufficient account is taken of the difference of context between then and now. Symbolic actions acquired their meaning against specific backdrops. So repeating practices, however ancient, offers no absolute guarantee of continuity in meanings. Indeed, so much explanation may be required in the modern context that much, if not most, of their original impact may well be lost. As the work of sociologists and anthropologists suggests, ritual is at its most powerful where it reflects implicit commitments of the heart that do not always need to be brought to consciousness in order to be endorsed. In other words, too much thought and explanation should not be required. The issue is best illustrated by examples.

Take the use of incense. Its origins lie in a practical purpose. Jews shared with pagans its use in disguising the smell of animal sacrifice.[19] The sweet-smelling savour was like the nectar of the gods.[20] Eventually conjoined with that role came a more general one, of symbolizing the rising of prayer to the divine.[21] Incense was also used in imperial Rome as a way of protecting the emperor and higher officials from unpleasant smells, as they traversed the streets. This in turn transmogrified into a way of indicating their special, honoured status. Few, if any, of these functions are now in public consciousness. Indeed, most appear to assume that some sort of purification is involved.[22] While that might have legitimacy in the censing of people and altar in preparation for communion, the idea becomes incongruous in relation to the censing of the Gospel book. Even those reluctant to identify too closely text and divinity now find themselves forced into a particular conception of the Bible by

[19] For the Jewish background, K. Nielson, *Incense in Ancient Israel* (Leiden: Brill, 1986).
[20] Presumably the numerous biblical references to 'a sweet savour' (extending even into the NT, e.g. 2 Cor. 2.15; Eph. 5.2) refer as much to the incense as to the meat being offered.
[21] Ps. 141.2; Mal. 2.11.
[22] For a general history of use and attitudes, G. C. F. Atchley, *A History of the Use of Incense in Divine Worship* (London: Alcuin Club, 1909). The analogy between physical and moral purification might be said to make the transition natural.

the rather pedestrian phrases adopted by the Church as an appropriate response to the reading of Scripture.[23] In respect of the Gospel, few are likely to be aware of the original intended analogy with the presence of the emperor. Nor does censing easily suggest a more general honouring of the text. So my suspicion is that for most people present it functions as no more than an ancient honoured custom, if that. Yet incense could be used to conjure up a more dynamic sense of Christ present in the text as Lord, were more thought given to how words and actions might operate in unison. For example, the deacon or reader might pray, 'Lord Jesus, now speak through your word,' as the book is censed. On the other hand, it may just be that this particular form of symbolism has had its day. Either way, what is clear is the need for more reflection on how symbolism and ritual work.

A quite different anxiety is the failure in so much liturgy to allow sufficient interplay between the various symbols, given their often multivalent character. Symbols can, like metaphors, be rich in two main ways; first in pointing in themselves to competing ideas and notions; secondly, by complementing or holding in tension what other symbols seem to imply. Some modern liturgists do demonstrate a willingness to take such interpenetration seriously and consequently suggest exploiting the multivalent character of symbols, most obviously perhaps in an instance such as water.[24] The way in which the Bible acknowledges such competing meanings is no doubt the source of their inspiration.[25] Elsewhere, however, all too soon a heavy dose of rationalism begins to appear, with the tendency to assume that particular meanings can only be conveyed in one way. A pertinent example concerns the question of how to evoke the notion of eucharist as meal. There are repeated calls for a return to the use of an ordinary loaf. The irony in such calls is that a loaf in the modern context would be no less artificial than a wafer.

---

[23] Modern Roman Catholic and Anglican liturgies recommend 'This is the word of the Lord' for other readings and 'This is the gospel of the Lord' for the Gospel reading; strictly speaking, mandated in both cases with Rome, whereas only in the latter case within the Church of England.

[24] e.g. G. Lathrop, *Holy Things: A Liturgical Theology* (Minneapolis: Fortress, 1998), 94–5; R. Giles, *Re-Pitching the Tent* (Norwich: Canterbury Press, 2004 edn.), 167–70.

[25] Discussed in *God and Grace of Body: Sacrament in Ordinary* (Oxford: Oxford University Press, 2007), 156–65.

Readers would, I am sure, look askance at their host if offered just plain bread when invited round for a meal, even if this was accompanied by a bottle of wine. As I observed in *God and Grace of Body*, because of recurring shortages in the ancient world, bread was viewed as a real gift and a serious feeding.[26] In the developed world this is no longer the case. Indeed, the nearer token is brought to reality, the more God (and his Church) is likely to be experienced as a stingy host. The purely nominal character of the wafer thus has its advantages. Symbolic and actual physical feeding are not confused, while the insignificance of the wafer adds paradox to the potency of the Lord and Saviour communicated through it. Indeed, the more basic character of the wafer better balances the wine by itself suggesting care of our most basic needs, while the wine speaks of an overflowing generosity, much as milk and honey might once have been interpreted as complements to one another among the people of ancient Israel.[27]

To take a different example, there are repeated objections to offertory processions and to any form of words that might suggest that human beings could contribute in any way to Christ's own self-offering. Sometimes such complaints even come from otherwise quite Catholic theologians.[28] Yet it is hard to believe that there is a serious risk of such acts undermining the priority of grace when the whole structure of the liturgy is geared to celebration of what God has done for us. If worries do remain, interpreting words such as 'Of your own do we offer you' could act as some form of control. It is identification with Christ's sacrifice that is important, not the absurd belief that anything we do could possibly be placed on the same level as Christ's own act. Even so, the Church of England still continues to veto offertory language.[29] What such prohibitions

---

[26] Again, 136–46, esp. 137–8. Likewise for more details on milk and honey, 143–4.

[27] Milk would have been the basic product equivalent to bread for so long as Israel was primarily a pastoral rather than agrarian community.

[28] For Michael Ramsey it spoke of 'a shallow and romantic sort of Pelagianism': *Durham Essays and Addresses* (London: SPCK, 1956), 18. His objection was that 'we cannot, and we dare not, offer aught of our own apart from the one sacrifice of the Lamb of God'.

[29] In the discussions that led to *Common Worship* (2000) the use of the Roman prayers over the gifts was accepted but conditional on the substitution of 'set before you' in place of 'offer' (London: Church House Publishing), 291.

ignore is the fact that actions and words are in any case richer than any attempted legislation. Priests do not have to disobey and use different words; the raising of the paten and chalice in itself would convey exactly the same meaning. That raises the more general issue of the fact that the way words are read (or performed) can easily ensure quite different meanings from what legislators originally intended. Cranmer would certainly never have endorsed a strong doctrine of the communion of saints, far less prayers for the dead, but both are easily drawn out from the language he adopted. Appropriately sounded, 'the whole company of heaven' in the *Sanctus* can evoke all the saints present with us round the altar, despite that being no part of Cranmer's intention.[30] Again, putting all the emphasis on *with* in 'that with them we may be partakers of thy heavenly kingdom' can speak of concern and prayer for the departed.[31] My point here is not to encourage disobedience of rules. Rather, it is to draw attention to how much richer ritual language and action are than liturgists and legislators commonly assume. The multivalency of words and deeds ensures an openness to alternative possibilities that no one could ever hope to police adequately.

Again, consider attitudes to postures for prayer. Attempts have been made to encourage standing as the norm, especially during the consecration prayer. It is suggested that this creates a greater sense of corporate identity, as well as being more loyal to the normal biblical position for prayer: the worshipper standing with hands uplifted. How much reality actually corresponds with intention I do not know. It is after all possible to retreat into a private dream world from any sort of position, whether standing, sitting, or kneeling. Equally, of course, worshippers can be fully and strongly aware of others around them as they kneel. Where this does not happen, other parts of the service will help bring that reality home, for example through those prayers that are said corporately. So hostility to early communion services seems to me quite unfounded.[32] In a

---

[30] 'Company', as in the original Latin, actually refers to all the divisions in the heavenly host, not to human beings. Nonetheless, the more natural meaning in modern English is easily exploited.

[31] At the end of the prayer for the Church militant in the 1662 Prayer Book.

[32] R. Giles, *Creating Uncommon Worship* (Norwich: Canterbury Press, 2004), 20–1, 162–4.

similar way any potential for idolatry in genuflection is balanced by priest and people alike actually handling the consecrated elements.

The value of such complementarity or creative tension between competing forms of practice is nicely brought out in the amusing history of a popular hymn, John Greenleaf Whittier's 'Dear Lord and Father of mankind'. The author was an American Quaker and poet who rejected all forms of institutional religion.[33] The hymn is in fact part of a larger poem, with the strange but intriguing title *The Brewing of Soma*. Soma is a hallucinogenic drug mentioned over a hundred and twenty times in the Vedic hymns, the earliest version of Hinduism. To this day it continues to play a role in the ritual of the Brahmans or Hindu priests. For Whittier this is religion at its worst, not genuine experience but artificially created through drug and ritual. The poem then continues by asserting that much the same happens in the Christian churches of his own day that use music and ceremony to subvert the senses. What is needed is a simple and undefiled form of experience, not what is actually found in so many modern churches:

> In sensual transports wild as vain,
> We view in many a Christian fane
> The heathen Soma still.

It is against this wider backdrop that the verses now sung as a hymn in most Christian churches should be placed. Their repeated reference to silence, for example, is intended to uphold a Quaker ideal over against the ritualism that characterized Roman Catholic churches of his day and also some Anglican. Indeed, there was once a reference to just such a critique in the second line of the present hymn. Whittier actually wrote, not 'Forgive our foolish ways', but 'Forgive our feverish ways', in other words intensity of ritual and symbol. Yet his words were eventually to find a place in both Anglican and Roman Catholic hymnals. It is not surely difficult to understand why. While those particular branches of the Christian Church would want to reject any claim that Whittier's original position represents the whole truth, such a contention is compatible with admitting that he has a point. Christian faith and practice need

---

[33] For more about him and the poem, J. B. Pickard, *John Greenleaf Whittier* (New York: Barnes & Noble, 1961). For the poem in full, J. G. Whittier, *Complete Poetical Works* (Cambridge, Mass.: Harrap, 1911).

moments of quietness no less than exuberant celebrations full of ritual enactment.

The same point can be made by considering attitudes to rituals of penitence in the Bible. It is very easy to set Jesus in direct, unqualified opposition to the old order. Whereas on the question of fasting the prophet Joel had enjoined the Israelites to 'blow the trumpet' and make a corporate and very public act of penance, Matthew quotes Jesus as emphatically declaring 'do not sound the trumpet before you'.[34] Fasting seems to have been transformed from a public and corporate act to an entirely private and personal one. However, that was not the policy the Church chose subsequently to pursue. Instead, public regulations of increasing rigour surrounded Lent in particular, with corresponding attempts to circumvent the legislation. One of the strangest was what happened in the fifteenth century. Originally the rule in the monasteries had been that no food could be taken before Vespers. Despite its name ('the evening service'), Vespers was moved to before noon, so that the main meal could now be had shortly thereafter.

In the face of such malpractice the temptation is to condemn such public ritual as mere empty form. Joel, however, indicates that there is another side of the coin. Personal penitence was for him not enough. It had to be public and corporate because what worried him was a people over-confident of God's protection. What he wants to force upon his fellow Israelites is perception of divine judgement upon the nation as a whole, and so God's call for new forms of corporate living. So he insists upon a liturgical act of public penitence that is to take place within the Temple itself. 'Call a solemn assembly,' he declares. Earlier generations of biblical scholars used to think of the prophets as in general opposed to temple worship, but Joel clearly intends here that temple worship should of itself be the means of bringing about reform. Likewise when Jeremiah declares of God that he never wanted sacrifice in the desert (7.21), it is highly unlikely that he intended to contradict the books of Exodus and Leviticus. Rather, he employs rhetorical exaggeration in order to underline his critique of ritual where it is deprived of its underlying meaning. His strategy is thus not unlike that of George Herbert, whose approach to ritual I discussed in an earlier chapter. To give Joel a modern application, we might

[34] Joel 2.15; Matt. 6.2.

observe that the Church as a corporate body also needs to be reminded periodically of its sins. Religious institutions too can go wrong, and indeed badly wrong, not only in maltreatment of their members but also in their public representations of themselves to the wider society. So often the Church comes across as an organization that condemns moral failure in others but fails to acknowledge its own deficiencies, not least in the Bible itself, fallible like the community that succeeds it.

Ritual can thus certainly err, but so too can absence of ritual. Without times of corporate penance built into our lives, it becomes very easy to fall foul of an alternative form of arrogance, precisely the type that worried Joel: God viewed as always on the Church's side and so there really being no need for any deep sense of inadequacy or failure in fulfilling God's purposes for the world. It is surely hugely significant that Jesus does not actually recommend giving up fasting, but rather great care in how any such rituals are approached. The formula for the imposition of ashes on Ash Wednesday, 'Dust thou art and to dust thou wilt return,' captures well what is required: the relativizing of all human pretensions. But it is done through body and voice speaking as one.

The last of the three issues I want to mention here is the true focus of the service. Pre-eminent of course is the need to offer God the worship that is his due, irrespective of whether this brings with it religious experience or not. Nonetheless, that conceded, where experience is sought, it is important that this should be the right type of experience. Too often in contemporary discussions it seems entirely subject-led. Perhaps because the presence of Christ is understood in terms of an unproblematic, generalized divine presence, the primary focus for discussion of experience moves to the gathered community and relations between and in them.[35] As I argued in this volume's predecessor, such a perspective contrasts markedly with how Aquinas, Luther, and Calvin would all alike have viewed the situation.[36] What mattered to them was identification with Christ's humanity, the fact of him being an integrated totality of both body and soul, somehow present in the here and

---

[35] Lathrop, *Holy Things*, 10; Giles, *Re-Pitching*, 145. The latter is so far from thinking Christ central that he advocates the bishop's throne as an appropriate replacement for the high altar as focus: *Uncommon Worship*, 60.

[36] *God and Grace of Body*, 407–15.

now to aid us. That way our humanity could also acquire the possibility of being perfected.

It is to that perspective that I would want the Church to return. Although as yet far distant from any such complete realization, human identity can gradually be transformed through an encounter mediated for our bodies primarily by ritual, and for our souls mainly by means of interaction with the words that we hear. It also helps to put into a proper frame those 'Catholic' actions that are sometimes viewed by Protestants with most suspicion. Take the question of genuflection. Its importance lies not in some hidden assertion about how exactly Christ is present, as though transubstantiation or some similar notion is automatically implied. Rather, it is much more a question of cultivating the right kind of attitude to the fact of Christ's presence. Although only invented in medieval times, the gesture allows worshippers to express through their bodies a commitment to place encounter with Christ above all else that is taking place.[37] Not just worldly powers but also bishop, priest, and congregation are all secondary to the Lord who is the source and meaning of the liturgy as a whole. Words such as 'Lord, I am not worthy...' then reinforce that commitment, and help resist any artificial distinction between action and word, body and soul.

It is precisely because of this focus that I find some of the terminology currently associated with liturgical action misconceived. 'President' as a term for the presiding minister is as old as the second century.[38] Nonetheless, it badly misleads in suggesting that the individual concerned is the most important personal agent present, but the true president is surely Christ himself, with the chief minister only one of a number of individuals charged with the task of making the presence of Christ manifest. Readers, intercessor, preacher, acolytes all contribute to the greater whole. That was allegedly the reason for getting rid of the term 'celebrant': that all present should be seen as celebrants in what is taking place. But the advantage of celebrant over president was that at least it demoted priests. They were responsible for actions (we celebrate things or events rather than directly the people concerned, as for example

[37] A hostile but still useful account historically is to be found in the relevant chapter of V. Staley, *Ceremonial of the English Church* (Oxford: Mowbray, 3rd edn., 1904).

[38] From Justin Martyr, *First Apology* 65.

someone's birthday or a wedding anniversary). So the lordship of Christ remained unaffected.

In actual fact in contemporary liturgical discussion hierarchy with a strong focus on the clergy seems as strong as ever, with assumptions about everything needing to proceed from the top down still depressingly common. Presidents, it is said, derive their authority from an absent bishop.[39] They in turn should make it clear that all that takes place in the service is now done under their direction. It is, therefore, essential that the celebrant should open and close the intercessions, the deacon be blessed by the celebrant before reading the Gospel, and so on.[40] Such ideas crystallize around the notion of the priest acting *in persona Christi*. With offertory processions so frequently attacked, it is puzzling why such an account of priestly ministry is not faced more often with a corresponding critique. An even larger role for human initiative is claimed, and for no good reason.

The whole question of the nature of ordained ministry is too large an issue to open out here. All I can therefore do is indicate what troubles me about such terminology. Most Church of England dioceses now follow the Roman Catholic practice of summoning their clergy on Maundy Thursday for an annual communion service (with blessing of oils) at which the bishop presides.[41] The implications of the symbolism, whether intended or not, are obvious for all to see. The bishop is implicitly claiming that he is now in the place of Christ, who first celebrated the rite that day. The Second Vatican Council sought to pull Rome back from the notion canvassed at Vatican I that only the Pope properly represents Christ.[42] Yet at that Council the assembled bishops still claimed a comparable status for themselves, whereas what the

---

[39] *In persona Christi*, however, is sometimes used as a way of denying *in persona episcopi*: e.g. P. Bernier, *Ministry in the Church* (Mystic, Conn.: Twenty-Third Publications, 1992), 228, 277.

[40] Giles combines abolition of robed choirs in the name of equality with every act needing to receive explicit endorsement from the president: *Uncommon Worship*, 69–71, 75, 110, 154.

[41] Though now abandoned by some Roman Catholic bishops because of the pressures it puts priests under on what is already a rather crowded day.

[42] What is often forgotten is that for much of Christian history bishops were seen as simply priests with more executive power: A. Nichols, *Holy Order* (Dublin: Veritas, 1990), 48–50 (where Jerome and Chrysostom are given as examples).

practice of the New Testament Church surely suggests is attempts, however halting and inadequate, to govern through plurality of representation, not through a single person. Move to the local level, and it is quite absurd to talk of the bishop as the normal or customary celebrant, when he is virtually always absent.[43] Even so the language of *in persona Christi* locks in, to give the priest a comparable status to the bishop locally. But it is surely Christ who is properly both priest and victim. The functioning minister is simply the agent who helps to make manifest an already existing reality, the timeless offering of Christ to his Father in which worshippers can now be incorporated. So symbols that imply continued delegation actually destroy what should be the true focus of the community's worship, not something the priest is doing but something done through him, a common sharing in Christ's sacrifice. Nor is there just a sharing in sacrifice. It is also a carrying forward of the believer into Christ's present reality as risen and glorified humanity. Authority thus comes ultimately from Christ himself and mediately from the Church as a whole and particular dioceses and congregations rather than specifically from one person. The irony is that those who claim to be most concerned to get rid of hierarchy often reintroduce it with the force of a hammer blow when the nature of human priesthood is under consideration. Extravagant claims for human priesthood can only give an unfortunate focus to the rite, with the human priest effectively substituting for a now absent Christ or else, worse, with Christ's body turned into a mere thing to be manipulated by others.

Such details of ritual are not only of vital importance in securing the right kind of attitude, they can also help explain why drama is after all the best, more inclusive category against which discussion of Christian liturgy should be set. Words can of course achieve much, but without the commitment of our bodies, only half of our identities will be, as it were, addressed, and it is the totality with which the present risen Christ is concerned to interact. Not that this is by any means the sole reason for treating liturgy as a form of drama. Both of the next two sections are concerned to strengthen

---

[43] Even as late as the fifteenth century priests (abbots, missionaries) were still being allowed to ordain: J. Galot, *Theology of the Priesthood* (San Francisco: Ignatius, 1985), 186.

that case. Liturgical costume suggests a form of acting, while the architectural setting can in my view be regarded as a form of staging. Although for many what the clergy wear in church is viewed as a quite trivial, indeed insignificant, matter, this too, as I shall seek to demonstrate, can make a significant contribution to the drama, even where clergy seem unaware of their acting role.

Liturgical Costume

Although my principal concern here is with what is worn in church, a much wider range of reference has proved necessary. That wider look is important. The sociology of clothes is now quite a well-researched topic, and has much to teach the Church. It would be folly to suppose that the major symbolic role elsewhere of clothing is not also active within liturgy, despite the almost flippant way in which the issue is so often discussed within church circles.

Admittedly, it is all too easy to make fun of the arbitrariness of what the clergy do wear in church. Take, for example, Anglican choir dress, that is what they wear at non-eucharistic services. Largely the result of late medieval developments, it had originally more to do with practical considerations than with providing elements of symbolism.[44] Thus the familiar black cassock began as a northern outdoor garment which the clergy had brought indoors as a way of warding off the cold in the days before churches had adequate heating. Indeed, it was only because of that migration indoors that the white surplice that is worn on top in quite a number of denominations finally emerged: a fact that becomes quickly apparent from its Latin name, *superpellicium*, in other words, something put on top of a fur-skin coat. Originally, at all services the oldest of clerical garments was worn, the long white garment now known as the alb, which remains the most popular form of wear at Communion. The trouble, however, with putting an alb on top of a fur cassock was that it was all a bit tight, and so the looser surplice evolved, made still looser in the eighteenth century so that wearers could easily get it over the head without needing to

---

[44] H. Norris, *Church Vestments: Their Origin and Development* (Mineola, N K: Dover, 2002 edn.), 165–7, esp. 166.

take their wigs off.[45] Even academic hoods once had a more practical purpose: they could be raised over the head to keep out the cold. When that function disappeared, the black scarf emerged as an alternative use for the surplus material.

The arbitrariness in all of this can scarcely be challenged. Even so, this is not necessarily the last word. While the detailed arrangements might well be changed, the symbolism in the white of surplice and alb should not be forgotten. The churches of the Reformation on the whole went for black and so for an alternative rationale in austerity and penitence. That imagery almost prevailed also within the Church of England, but fortunately never quite so. The changes that began in the second half of the nineteenth century were, therefore, much easier than they might otherwise have been. The result was that surplice and alb had once more become the norm by the late twentieth century. With that development also came the possibility of renewing connections with what white is taken to mean in the Scriptures. Consider the magnificent description of the worship of heaven in the Book of Revelation (ch. 4). It is no accident that the elders seated before the Father's throne are robed in white. It speaks not only of the purity that is necessary to enter the divine presence but also of a joy that will arise once there, reflected in the rainbow that surrounds the divine throne and which offers a reminder of God's faithfulness.

Yet even so there is not total escape from ambiguity. The elders are wearing what we might now call an alb, but in those days was the ordinary secular garb of the better off, those who did not need to sully their hands with manual labour.[46] It thus also spoke of a dubious entitlement to difference, the Empire's upper-crust way of reminding inferiors of the absence of any need for ordinary toil. What is more surprising is the degree to which the Bible in general is infected with such ambiguities. Even Christ's own robes, as the New Testament records them, are not immune. Wool was cheaper than linen, but not always regarded as pure: sheep can after all be rather dirty animals. So significantly Ezekiel bans all wool from

---

[45] P. Dearmer, *The Parson's Handbook* (London: Humphrey Milford, 1928 edn.), 128 n. 2.

[46] Norris, *Church Vestments*, 11–20, esp. 15. The alb developed out of the linen undergarment worn by the better off underneath their *himation* or *pallium* (togas were so cumbersome that they never really caught on in the eastern Empire).

those who serve the new Jerusalem (44.17). Joseph is honoured by Pharaoh with fine linen and the virtuous woman in Proverbs sells and wears such linen.[47] Whether because of its greater purity or not, Jesus is also presumed to wear the more expensive linen. At the Transfiguration his garments are made to glisten so intensely 'as no fuller on earth could bleach them' (Mark 9.3).[48] The description would have been powerfully evocative at the time, given the imperfect processes of dying that characterized the ancient world. Even so, in the image it is earthly extravagance that is made to reflect heavenly values.[49]

Those in the know may object that at least the chasuble or eucharistic over-garment has respectable working-class origins. Meaning in Latin literally 'the little house' (*casula*), it was the poncho that was worn in the late empire (particularly in the east) by ordinary people as a way of keeping warm and warding off the rain.[50] So it contrasts nicely with the origins of the alb. But in between is the stole, originally a towel like the now seldom used maniple. Both were once employed in the late empire for various roles at the imperial races. The maniple's nearest modern equivalent is the lavabo or washing towel given to the celebrant just before the consecration prayer. So, were readers to think of the servers at this point engaging in a little off-course betting, they would not be too far wrong about the mixture of secular and sacred, rich and poor that characterizes the Church's symbolic gear. So it comes as no surprise that the poor man's poncho eventually became the Church's richest garment. Practicalities, symbolism, and ostentatious display of wealth have fought it out, sometimes with good results and sometimes to the detriment of the Church's mission.[51]

[47] Gen. 41.42; Prov. 31.21–2.
[48] Thus paralleling the Son of Man of Dan. 9.7, angels (e.g. Luke 24.4; Acts 10.30) and the elect in heaven (e.g. Rev. 1.13; 3.5).
[49] Given the association of leprosy with white (discussed below), on the other side could be set the fact that the colour may also have hinted at Jesus' close identification with these outcasts.
[50] Although the 1604 canons of the Church of England cannot possibly have had chasubles in mind, it is amusing to note how hair is treated as though it were a sort of thatched roof for the lower garb. Those who are bald are urged to use a skull cap as an alternative covering for what is called their 'infirmity'.
[51] Practicalities explain the changing shape. The Gothic form made easier the elevation of the host, the Baroque the weight of stiffened embroidery on the back: B. Dean, *Embroidery in Religion and Ceremonial* (London: Batsford, 1981), 47–51.

Nor is the situation any better once focus moves away from actual practice to how the story of the Christian faith is represented in art. The sixteenth-century painter Caravaggio got into difficulty when he included the shabby clothes and dirty feet of poverty in his religious paintings.[52] Our natural impulse is to side with Caravaggio. Yet to attribute wholly bad motives to resistance to such portrayals would be as misguided as to attribute wholly good. Beautiful colourful robes worn by the principal figures of the Christian faith were primarily intended as a way of honouring symbolically such persons, however poor in actual life they may have been. But because symbols of honour have of necessity to be drawn from worldly contexts, they almost invariably carried with them some degree of ambiguity. Was the Church after all really on the side of the wealthy? Matters were not otherwise, when Christian art first adopted the halo. Gold honours with its reflective glow, but it is a worldly standard that is also used in the process.[53] Much the same can be said about the later adoption of symbolic colours for the Virgin Mary's dress and cloak. In many a medieval and renaissance painting she is portrayed dressed in a red gown and blue cloak. Eventually the blue was taken to symbolize the blue of heaven (her future destiny), while the red indicated the suffering that characterized so much of her life.[54] But probably far more pertinent to begin with was the cost of the dyes concerned, purple from murex shells, deep blue from lapis lazuli, and red from the kermes insect.[55] Divine value thus apes human values, in selecting the most costly for what is seen as also spiritually the most precious.

I draw attention to such developments, not to mock (though they are sometimes amusing) but because such a mix seems to me

---

[52] Dirty feet are most obvious in his *Madonna of Loreto*, shabby clothes in his *Supper at Emmaus*.

[53] Introduced not always without protests, e.g. Jerome, *Epistles* 22. 32. The halo was borrowed from pagan culture. Where gold was already used as a background, jewels were sometimes employed by way of differentiation. See further, esp. D. Janes, *God and Gold in Late Antiquity* (Cambridge: Cambridge University Press, 1998), 143–5.

[54] The complexity of the issues and how much depended on context is emphasized in M. Hall, *Colour and Meaning: Practice and Theory in Renaissance Painting* (Cambridge: Cambridge University Press, 1992), e.g. 16.

[55] The deep blue produced by lapis lazuli was expensive because, although small amounts were found near Rome, the two main sources of supply were far distant in Afghanistan and near Lake Baikal.

integral to what it is to be an incarnational religion. The mix of the good and the base here is in fact no different from what I have suggested elsewhere is encountered both in the Bible and in the history of the Church.[56] It is not that anywhere is immune from human sin, the temptation to speak of corrupt human designs and aspirations as though they came from God. The solution is not to retreat to some sanitized realm, but to engage with the mix. That way such resources can function as a reminder both of human folly and sin and also, no less importantly, of the power of God to draw us through them into more profound dimensions of reality.

To observe the latter potential, it is worth noting the regulations for clerical dress in Exodus 28. All priests are required to wear white tunics. In addition the High Priest is enjoined to wear a blue robe on top (called an ephod). Affixed to this on the front is a jewelled, multicoloured breastplate, while on his head he wears a turban inscribed with the most sacred name of God, the tetragrammaton.[57] Apart from his more familiar role on the annual Day of Atonement, each day just outside the main temple building the High Priest appeared facing west, while all the other priests faced east towards the Temple. As he raised his hands in blessing, and uttered the sacred name of God (Yahweh), all the clergy then prostrated themselves, rather like Muslims do in a modern mosque. Only then was an already prepared lamb sacrificed, and the trumpet or shofar blown and cymbals sounded, as the choir of Levites burst into song with one of the psalms.

I recount all of this because it is very easy to jump from the prohibition of images in the second commandment to the assumption that all forms of art were therefore precluded from Jewish worship. Far from it! The ear and the eye were assaulted, and there seems little doubt that the appearance of the High Priest must have had something of the character of a divine theophany. Indeed, he seems to have worn a blue over-garment, precisely because he was seen in this role as marking the meeting of heaven and earth, just as in later Christianity one reason for the Virgin Mary being dressed in blue was to suggest that her body was likewise just such a meeting place between heaven and earth, through the incarnation.

---

[56] A recurring theme in both *Tradition and Imagination* (1999) and *Discipleship and Imagination* (2000).

[57] The four consonants YHWH.

But added to that was the splendour of the breastplate. We are told that it was made of gold, blue, purple, and scarlet stuff, and had four rows of various types of precious stones.[58] Mention of these might make us think that it was just a matter of copying the secular world, with an ostentatious display of wealth. Almost certainly, there was an element of this. But a deeper, quite different motivation is also detectable. The aim is to reflect the divine 'glory'. Despite its frequent application to God in the Bible, *kabod* (the relevant Hebrew word) is a rather difficult word to translate. It does not mean simply majesty but also splendour and brilliance, terms that we might think more naturally applied to physical things. It is what has 'weight' or impact upon us, and for the ancient world generally this was taken to mean not particular colours as such but rather their intensity or brightness.[59] Such facts help explain why ancient languages in general have relatively few colour words and call by the same name what in the modern world is more likely to be identified by a number of different colour names. In the case of Hebrew, light and dark is the most common contrast, with white and red then used to identify two different forms of sheen rather than the actual colours inherent in them. One interesting consequence is that dark (or whatever is drained of luminosity) and not black then becomes the normal negative term. So, although in English until relatively recently it was common to hear such expressions as 'black as sin' or 'having a black mark against one character', in Hebrew neither would be a natural form of expression. Instead, pale white was quite likely to be viewed just as negatively as black is treated in these English usages. The skin disease that the Bible calls 'leprosy' drew brightness out of the skin and left the individual with a dry, pallid complexion. So 'white and leprous' became the Hebrew world's corresponding metaphor.[60]

---

[58] Used as the basis for Innocent III's legislation on liturgical colours in 1195: J. F. White, *Documents of Christian Worship* (Edinburgh: T & T Clark, 1992), 32–4. Even as late as fourteenth-century England, however, distinctions between festive and ferial were still made largely on the basis of quality rather than colour: W. S. Hope and E. G. C. Atchley, *English Liturgical Colours* (London: SPCK, 1918), 12.

[59] For a more literal use of *kabod* as something 'weighty', cf. Gen. 13.2; 31.1 (both of wealth).

[60] For the colour of leprosy, 2 Kgs. 5.27: 'a leper as white as snow'.

That interest in natural brilliance suggests a society fascinated by colour and display in liturgy, however hostile it may have been to the use of representational art in the worship of God. Certainly it is totally untrue that there went with this a rejection of drama, performance, and music. Consider one further example. In much the same way as the sanctus bell used to be rung in Catholic churches during the consecration prayer, so the High Priest's robe had bells on it, to warn worshippers of the advent of the most solemn aspects of the service. So far from anything being deemed essentially idolatrous in the sound or in the brilliance of the priestly vestments, they were assumed to provide a means of alerting worshippers to the glory of God and his immanence now in the Temple's worship. The lustre and splendour of the High Priest's costume helped mediate a sense of the brightness of the divine glory now being made sensibly present in what was being done there in the Temple in his name. It is thus no accident that the word 'glory' occurs no fewer than fifty times in the psalms.

The vagaries of history have produced what the clergy now wear—practicalities of warmth, adaptation for wigs, and so forth. Even so, the whiteness of light, the brilliance of gold, the blue of heaven are there to remind worshippers that the Christian religion is fundamentally one of joy, a summons out of darkness to share in God's own marvellous, splendid glory. What clergy wear is thus not just about legitimating a representative role on behalf of the congregation, it is also equally about expressing the point of that role: that incarnation brings with it the hope of glory, however much suffering may need to be endured in the interim. That is why, in my view at least, black and more negative colours should never be allowed to dominate. Instead of resisting colour and drama, the Church should be confident in offering such worship.

This defence does not of course entail that such expressive possibilities need necessarily be tied to those particular costumes. Others might serve equally well, or better. The point is that the Church should be consciously aware of what it is trying to communicate through them, not suppose that the issue of costume is of only minor or negligible relevance. Dressing up indicates that something of importance is taking place. The advantage liturgical costume now enjoys is that, irrespective of the complexities of past history, over the course of time it has for the most part succeeded in freeing itself from the vagaries of any specific cultural association.[61] Inevitably, there are some exceptions. That is why, for instance, the Roman Catholic Church of our day has chosen to simplify the garb of the pope and his cardinals. The monarchical associations of the papal tiara and the other trappings that went with it rightly had to go, as also the elaborate trains with page boys that once character-ized the attire of cardinals.[62] Clergy sometimes naively suppose that they can circumvent such problems by wearing ordinary clothes. The problem is that there is no such thing. Whatever is worn communicates. Jeans, for example, were once spoken of as the new universal language of informality.[63] But that is precisely what they now singularly fail to be. Not only does the prominent display of designer labels complicate matters, there is also the issue of how jeans are worn, the nature and size of the belt that accompanies them or not, their tightness or bagginess and so on. Young black ghetto use, for example (baggy and hung low), is set in deliberate opposi-tion to the style adopted by cowboys and white middle-class youth.

Sociologists and historians now write extensively on the subject of clothes. In particular attention is drawn to the wide variety of meanings that they can communicate. So long as Christianity continued to look back to the defining story of Adam and Eve, the natural association of clothing in a Christian society, it might have been thought, was quite likely to have been the need for modesty, a sharing in the first pair's shame.[64] Yet matters were never quite that simple. Nudity was in fact much more widely accepted over Christianity's long history than was the case, for instance, in nineteenth-century Europe.[65] Nude bathing and sleeping naked were apparently the norm through most of this

[61] Perhaps that provides some justification for Percy Dearmer's decision largely to ignore history in his influential *Parson's Handbook*.

[62] The triple tiara was given up by Paul VI. Originally a simple white Phrygian cap, it had acquired a single crown in the eleventh century, and two more at the beginning of the fourteenth.

[63] A thesis still being defended as late as the early 1990s in F. Davis, *Fashion, Culture and Identity* (Chicago: University of Chicago Press, 1992), e.g. 68, 70; though he does note some threats on the horizon (e.g. 72).

[64] Stressed in E. Rouse, *Understanding Fashion* (Oxford: BSP Books, 1989), 8.

[65] F. Piponnier and P. Mane, *Dress in the Middle Ages* (New Haven: Yale University Press, 1997), 99–103.

period. So shame at nakedness is not always the message. Equally, however, where positive value is assigned to clothing, this can be for reasons other that the primeval pair's sin. Some paintings appear to suggest that the pre-fallen state was really altogether too close to the animal for comfort. Adam and Eve are given an almost shaggy appearance that hints that the benefits of civilization are still to come.[66]

That lack of uniformity in attitudes perhaps makes it less surprising that late medieval Europe rebelled, and began seriously to engage with fashions that did not shrink even from fairly explicit expressions of sexuality. Even so, it was apparently not till the Renaissance that the word 'fashion' lost its more basic meaning of 'making' (and so of an act in which God could also engage) and moved closer to the modern sense of restless change.[67] Inevitably, there was a negative side as there is today in such change, in conspicuous consumption. Sumptuary laws were periodically passed throughout the Middle Ages and beyond that sought to limit such extravagances of display.[68] But the variety of colour in creation provided the medieval world with an alternative rationale for pursuing beauty elsewhere. So, as in ancient classical temples, churches were almost always a riot of colour. Elsewhere I have described the shock the eighteenth century experienced at the discovery that classical sculpture had once been painted.[69] Even today most people seem unaware of how much bright paint and decoration there once was on the pillars and walls of both classical temples and medieval churches.[70] Sometimes the clothes of the congregation were just as gaudy. Although lack of resources militated against such ostentation on the part of the majority, the natural desire of human beings to form sub-groups within the more general

[66] A late example from Rembrandt (1638) is considered in A. Hollander, *Seeing Through Clothes* (Berkeley: University of California Press, 1975), 185–6.

[67] A. R. Jones and P. Stallybrass, *Renaissance Clothing and the Materials of Memory* (Cambridge: Cambridge University Press, 2000), 1–5, 269.

[68] For sumptuary laws, Piponnier and Mane, *Dress*, 83–6.

[69] *God and Grace of Body*, 25.

[70] English churches occasionally preserve small flashes of medieval colour, for example at St Albans Abbey. But for the real thing one must turn elsewhere, for instance to Albi or Issoire in France. The latter (St Austremoine) is illustrated in H. Pleij, *Colors Demonic and Divine* (New York: Columbia University Press, 2004), no. 20.

amorphous society did mean that such desires percolated further down the social scale than might otherwise have been expected. The result was dress sometimes functioning as a distinctive badge of identity.[71]

Some such badges were imposed. Yellow, for instance, became the mark of a Jew, striped clothing that of a suspect profession. The latter as a sign of suspicion is at least as old as the book of Leviticus. Used to identify prostitutes, jugglers, and eventually convicts, the different colours were taken to suggest the unnatural and difficult to interpret.[72] Even Marian blue acquired some negative undertones that continue into our own day, as in expressions such as 'feeling blue' and 'blue movies'.[73] Of course it is always possible to rebel against such meanings. Although the veil is later than Muhammad himself, some Muslim women of today choose to interpret it not as an indicator of the suppression of female freedoms but as a way of achieving liberation from male values (not least the male gaze). While such arguments are not wholly successful, there is certainly a case that can be made.[74] So in considering the development of a distinctive clerical garb in the black cassock and in parallel developments for nuns, it is worth pondering how far these are, like the veil, prisoners of their past.

As with the cassock, nuns' habits and veils originally closely followed secular conventions. Nuns not only declared their marriage to Christ in ceremonies that paralleled marriage, they also wore the normal garb of married women of the time.[75] As the centuries advanced, secular wear changed, and so the nuns' clothes became more distinctive, and in the opinion of some more

---

[71] The twin pulls of identity and difference are a key element in G. Simmel's analysis in his article on 'Fashion' in G. Wills and D. Midgley eds., *On Individuality and Social Forms* (Chicago: University of Chicago Press, 1973), esp. 295, 301.

[72] Lev. 19.19. For a history, M. Pastoureau, *The Devil's Cloth* (New York: Columbia University Press, 2001). For church legislation,13; for the resultant suspicion of zebras, 24.

[73] For a fascinating but far from comprehensive history, M. Pastoureau, *Blue: The History of a Color* (Princeton: Princeton University Press, 2001).

[74] Among the best is F. E. Guindi, *Veil: Modesty, Privacy and Resistance* (Oxford: Berg, 1999). For lack of early acceptance, 152; for the harem as a corruption of the sacred *haram*, 77–96; for male covering, 117–28.

[75] E. Kuhns, *The Habit: A History of the Clothing of Catholic Nuns* (New York: Doubleday, 2003). For the clothing ceremony aping marriage, 22–5; for their habit aping classical married dress, 53–7.

quaint.[76] So long as enclosure was the norm, no major issues arose. But the more nuns became involved in ordinary jobs such as teaching and nursing (from the sixteenth century onwards), the more practical issues raised themselves about the usefulness or otherwise of wearing such dress.[77] The arguments of the second half of the twentieth century on this matter need, therefore, to be set in that much wider context. Practicalities and the desire to return to less conspicuous forms of attire were not just signs of increasing secularism (though this no doubt played its part). They were also indicative of worries about the extent of departure from earlier ideals: identification with ordinary life whilst maintaining a distinctive but supportive approach.

However, there remains an irony here. It was precisely at the time when so many nuns were seeking to break free of symbolic clothing that new groups in society discovered the potency of such signs. So, for instance, a skinhead or punk is not someone who has acquired a certain, definite philosophy and then chosen to demonstrate it by adopting a particular form of dress.[78] The dress actually 'incarnates' or 'sacramentally' embodies the identity in question. That makes me wonder whether the issue for nuns was not wrongly formulated. In the modern context their former wear all too easily suggested repressed women dominated by a male hierarchy. But what they really needed were new positive symbols rather than their total abandonment.

By contrast, the black cassock of an overwhelmingly male clergy may seem relatively innocuous. But the fact that St Francis deliberately opted for grey for his new order illustrates how even a colour once chosen to indicate penitence and humility could acquire quite different associations.[79] For Francis it spoke of status and privilege. It was several centuries later before the Reformation was faced with similar decisions about dress. In turning once more to black, what of course was being rejected was what was seen as

---

[76] Although uniformity developed less slowly than is often supposed: C. Warr, 'Religious Dress in Italy in the Late Middle Ages' in A. de la Haye and E. Wilson eds., *Defining Dress* (Manchester: Manchester University Press, 1999), 79–92.

[77] The great change came with Angela Merici (d. 1540), and the founding of the Ursulines.

[78] The terminology is mine, but the idea developed in M. Barnard, *Fashion as Communication* (London: Routledge, 1996), e.g. 30, 41–3, 129–32.

[79] Pleij, *Colors Demonic and Divine*, 32.

the extravagant and corrupt colours in churches of the pre-Reformation period. Even the Catholic Erasmus thought that stripping statues of colour might make the populace turn to the saints themselves rather than the sculpted figures that it was claimed embodied them.[80] In the case of both Luther and Calvin, black came in almost by default. Luther retained the black cassock from his time as an Augustinian canon, while with Calvin the black gown indicated his training as a lawyer.[81] Even so, precisely because of the high social status of the clergy in the sixteenth and seventeenth centuries, the wearing of black soon spread to the laity as a means of marking respectability.[82] It was in this capacity that black became the mark of the moneyed middle classes in the nineteenth century. So, for much of its history, so far from hinting at a revolutionary religion, the wearing of black has demonstrated deep conformity and respectability, though this may be changing.[83]

To say this much is in some ways to state the obvious, that the Church cannot help but be affected by the surrounding culture and its values. But it is amazing how often that same Church pretends that matters are quite otherwise. There is a real need among Christians for more social awareness of the wider social setting that conditions and changes whatever the Church might be trying to say through its symbols and ritual actions. Even as basic a garment as the cassock is not as innocent as it seems, despite its antiquity.

Similarly, taking off clothes may no longer imply the meanings it once did. In the past washing feet on Maundy Thursday clearly proclaimed the care of a serving Church, and that remained true for so long as those whose feet were being washed were the poor or prisoners. To this day the papacy continues the practice of washing the feet of prisoners in local Roman prisons. Even the pretentious and absolutist French monarchy had an eight-hundred-year-old tradition (known as *La Cène*) of the king washing the feet of thirteen poor children and then serving them with a meal. Now, however, dramatic though the action is, it cannot be said

---

[80] Erasmus, *The Praise of Folly* (Princeton: Princeton University Press, 1970), 67.

[81] J. Harvey, *Men in Black* (London: Reaktion, 1995), 85–6.

[82] Helped by an already existing tradition of black to indicate respectability, e.g. in Burgundy, in Venice, and in Spain: Harvey, *Men in Black*, 55, 66, 72.

[83] For the new associations of black with fetishism, P. Calefato, *The Clothed Body* (Oxford: Berg, 2004), 109–15.

to preserve the powerful symbolism and moving quality that it once did. The recipient is quite likely to be well-to-do, to have washed his or her feet carefully beforehand, and of course to have changed into a clean pair of socks. The result is that the ceremony is more likely to evoke in the eyes of the casual observer the Victorian drawing room than anything to do with humility.

There is also a need to be on guard against the rampant individualism of modern society and its impact, even where we may not always be conscious of it. The great advantage costume can potentially give to the liturgical setting is the transcending of individuality, that what is mediated is clearly seen as more important than the human mediator. This is not, therefore, the place where gender or racial representation should be to the fore. I recall once attending a eucharist at an American cathedral where the white, middle-aged celebrant was accompanied on one side by a woman and on the other by an African American. Although the desire for equality that such action expressed was commendable, it actually diverted attention away from the proper focus of the liturgy into more mundane concerns. My point is not that the mundane is irrelevant. It most certainly is, but such applications should not be bought at the expense of where such applications find their ultimate rationale in the lordship of Christ. So it seems to me quite wrong when the attempt is made to focus on individual priests rather than on what they are trying under God to mediate.

Perhaps the issue can be made clearer, by considering a little further the question of sexuality in such a context. In the modern world the nature of the sexual gaze is undoubtedly changing. Women now exercise the right to use their eyes in the way that men always have. Even the male gaze has changed. Partly this is because of increasing male insecurity about gender roles. Partly, it is a consequence of the way in which gay liberation has encouraged heterosexual males also to be more self-conscious about the potential of the body to communicate.[84] That consciousness means that even suits no longer enjoy the innocence that they were once presumed to have.[85] Some may regret this. At the very least what

[84] For one version of the latter argument, A. Sharkey, 'New Media, New Men: The Lost Paradigm of Male Normality' in G. Malossi ed., *Material Man: Masculinity, Sexuality, Style* (New York: Abrams, n.d.), 170–9.

[85] That presumption is challenged in A. Hollander, *Sex and Suits* (Brinkworth: Claridge Press, 1994).

is entailed is that in the 'secular' world Christians must cease regarding sexual messages as necessarily suspect (they are in any case inescapable).[86] More pertinent here is the need to transcend that gaze in the context of the liturgy such that whatever the gender, the celebrant is made firmly subordinate to the larger drama in which all are being encouraged to participate. Here liturgical costume can undoubtedly play an important role, in minimizing (though not eliminating) sexual identity. To my mind, however, what is most needed is the cultivation of a requisite *habitus* or attitude appropriate to the occasion.[87] In the costume drama that is the liturgy, sexuality and personality need to be subsumed beneath the greater goal of allowing Christ to be sensibly experienced as present and so as the true focus of all that takes place.

I turn now to the wider setting or 'staging' of the liturgy. It too suggests that liturgy operates as a kind of drama, especially where congregations are alive to the architectural setting within which the story of Christ is re-enacted.

The Staging: Architecture and Integration

Here I want to consider the architecture and art of the Church not only in its role as background staging but also in its capacity to contribute to the overall impact of the liturgy as a whole. As some of these issues have already been considered in *God and Enchantment of Place*, here I shall focus more narrowly, at least to begin with, by considering in detail one particular example.[88]

Liturgists often write as though worshippers should be wholly focused on the words. No doubt some are, but more, I suspect, think equally through their bodies (as I have tried to indicate) and also through their imaginations. So in modern liturgy with clarity so often bought at the expense of range and richness of imagery, it is scarcely surprising that attention sometimes wanders into reflection or prayer that is quite far removed from the actual words on the

---

[86] As I argued in *God and Grace of Body* (35–56) the sexual gaze need not automatically imply the desire for consummation.

[87] For an example of Bourdieu's term applied to fashion, J. Entwistle, *The Fashioned Body* (Oxford: Polity, 2000), 36–9.

[88] *God and Enchantment of Place*, 245–371.

page.[89] It is important that, when attention returns, the words should be adequate to the task. But such wanderings should not be despised, as though they somehow lessen the possibility of encounter. Eyes wandering round the church building during a poor sermon, for instance, need also to be fed. That is one reason why the setting in the building is important, the staging, as it were; another is that, as worshippers arrive, they have some sense of where their faith is taking them.

In *God and Enchantment of Place* I offered a sustained critique of utilitarian views of church buildings.[90] Their role is not simply to serve the community or its purposes of worship. They also have a natural expressive function that contains the potential to stimulate various types of experience of God, depending on the type of architecture concerned. There I spoke in general terms, without offering a detailed analysis of any specific building. That would in any case have complicated the task since church buildings are so often a hotchpotch of competing architectural and artistic influences. Even so, such medleys can sometimes make a highly effective contribution to the type of transformation expected of the liturgy as a whole. Since the choice of any building as an example is inevitably arbitrary, I may as well consider the cathedral at Durham, where I served as a Canon for seventeen years. This is not intended as an indicator of local pride. While the building's Romanesque architecture is among the finest in Europe, depredations at the Reformation and under Cromwell were severe, and much of what arrived subsequently is of second-rate artistic quality. Nonetheless, it illustrates surprisingly well how an apparently disparate ensemble can be moulded into an overall coherent theme. As in such circumstances key contributions often come from the Victorian period, its artists and architects clearly deserve to be accorded greater credit than is still usually the case. Sadly, these days few worshippers, far less visitors, use their eyes and imaginations to engage with the implicit programme, but they could.

We may begin our tour with arrival at the north door. As in most parish churches the visitor is first confronted with a baptismal font,

---

[89] I continue to regret the replacement of the rich image of Christ coming under our roof (as in the story of the centurion's servant, Matt. 8.8) with the bland, 'I am not worthy to receive you'.

[90] *God and Enchantment of Place*, 17–22, 245–349.

in Durham's case so elaborate (with its fine seventeenth-century wooden canopy) that they may not appreciate immediately what it is.[91] That is unfortunate, since in their long history not only have many fonts been decorated with relevant carvings, even their shape has been adapted to convey symbolic meanings of various kinds, among them most obviously the hope of new life.[92] While then Cosin's font cannot be pronounced altogether a success, more immediately legible is the great west window that lies behind it. A nineteenth-century version of a form of window once common-place, it is generally known as a Jesse window from the fact that the tree in question traces Jesus' ancestors through Jesse the father of King David, and down to Mary and the nativity.[93] On either side Old Testament prophets observe the tree. Both window and font thus speak of beginnings. The font reminds of how life as a Christian begins, in God's mysterious action through others in bringing individuals to faith. The window emphasizes that the Christian story as a whole did not begin with the nativity but rather with all that led up to it, the whole sweep of the Old Testament dispensation, including prophets, kings, and so forth. Worshippers thus enter the church, not as isolated individuals but as part of a community, already heavily indebted to others.

But it is a community on a voyage. As the great nave opens up before visitors' eyes, they may possibly think of an inverted ship, especially if they look up to the ceiling. *Navis* is the Latin for a ship and was adopted as a term to conjure up the notion of the church as a sort of Noah's ark.[94] But to the less-well-informed public of today, it is that inverted ship that is more likely to come to mind, clearly more obvious in some church buildings than in others. If so, it suggests a community sailing upside-down. If Durham's ceiling is not as conspicuous in this respect as some, in bringing such imagery to mind, it can nonetheless share in people's perception more

[91] Even the dove on top of the tall wooden structure is a strange mix. The wings and scale are more suggestive of an eagle, presumably necessitated by the visual demand that the bird should at least be visible.

[92] The great range of possibilities is explored (with illustrations) in R. Kuehn, *A Place for Baptism* (Chicago: Liturgy Training Publications, 1992).

[93] A Clayton and Bell window of 1867 that followed closely the pattern of an earlier fourteenth-century window.

[94] This is the most common explanation, but the origin of the term is uncertain. It may even possibly be derived from the Greek for a temple, *naos*.

generally of the curved or pitched ceiling of so many churches: that there is an element of entering a world of topsy-turvy values, where, as further exploration will demonstrate, power is found in weakness and self-assurance in self-giving concern for others.

At the same time it is a ship that is going somewhere. The whole direction of vision is towards the east, to the dawn of a new day. That eastern orientation is characteristic of churches generally, but in Durham it is reinforced by its massive Romanesque pillars, whose carvings were almost certainly deliberately intended to pull the eye eastwards. Although there are competing explanations for such orientation, one commonly canvassed view is that Christ's second coming would be from the east.[95] So, appropriately, in the great east window (again Victorian) is to be found the adoration of God as described in the Book of Revelation. Christ in majesty is surrounded by twelve apostles in the inner circle and twenty-four elders in the outer. Twelve and twenty-four were in the symbolism of the time signs of completion and perfection. Even if that piece of symbolism is now lost on most contemporaries, the circular form of the window still makes the same point. The Christian's ultimate destiny is union with Christ in heaven, in a destiny that will bring believers through God's grace to a perfection (like the circle's) that they currently lack.[96]

That might suggest only some distant, utterly unimaginable prospect, of little relevance to the here and now, but once more the building intervenes, and insists on things happening in the here and now. First, and most basic of all, is the assertion that we are not alone in our quest. Even if visitors notice little else in the cathedral, they cannot but be overwhelmed by the sheer solidity of the Romanesque pillars that speak of God's majesty and power. They are like great oaks solidly set in the ground and destined to endure long after all else in the vicinity has perished in the dust. So likewise with God's grace. Walking down the nave, its windows are not likely to attract immediate attention, partly because of distance and partly because of the intervening pillars. So the next most likely

---

[95] Based on passages such as Ezek. 43.2–5. Another is in terms of Christ as Sun of righteousness. But the most likely explanation is as a continuation of pagan practice, in facing the rising sun as symbol of new life.

[96] For the symbolism of rose windows, P. Cowen, *The Rose Window: Splendour and Symbol* (London: Thames and Hudson, 2005 edn.), esp. 195–239.

visual engagement will be with two windows in either transept balancing the nave altar in between. Both speak of how such grace is mediated.[97] The right arm has four key pictures of scenes from the life of Christ, most obviously a crucifixion, but no less than three of what happened thereafter: resurrection, ascension, and glorification. God promises a change as dramatic for the believer as what happened in the story of his Son. To allay any doubts about such divine action continuing into the present, the window on the left arm acts as a reminder that the story of God's action in human history did not end with the incarnation. There are to be found the so-called four Doctors of the Church along with two other saints. The theme may not sound promising, but included in their number are Pope Gregory the Great, responsible for sending Augustine to convert England, Cuthbert the great saint of Durham, and Mary to whom the building is dedicated (along with Christ and Cuthbert). Beneath Mary is a petition in Latin asking her to pray for us. We are not alone. Not only has God continued to act throughout the history of the Church, those others who have gone before us, the great multitude of the saints, now pray for us.

But it is not just the windows that speak but also the architecture itself in those cross arms or transepts. The pattern was adopted for larger churches to remind worshippers that transformation comes not through the pursuit of power but through identification with a cross, the cross of Christ, and all that says of humility and self-giving. But it is not just a message of self-effacement, it is also one of transforming power. That is indicated by both pulpit and altar. The iconography of the pulpit can be explained quite briefly.[98] In common with countless churches worldwide, the brass pulpit is based on an eagle. An eagle beginning to soar from beneath reminds viewers that the proclamation of the Scriptures can give new strength to mount aloft. As Isaiah puts it: 'They who wait for the Lord shall renew their strength, they shall mount up with wings like eagles, they shall run and not be weary, they shall walk and not be faint' (Isa. 40.31)

But that renewal will not come from the preaching of the word alone. No less relevant is the altar. In Durham's case the nave altar's

---

[97] Both are again by Clayton and Bell.

[98] The eagle is more commonly associated with lecterns. Both pulpit and lectern are part of George Gilbert Scott's reordering and date from the 1870s.

lack of any obvious symbolism is compensated by the lectern's use of explicit eucharistic imagery. Before the Reformation a silver pelican hung before the high altar with a gold pyx beneath containing the reserved sacrament, while to the left was a gilded lectern with the same image. Bishop Foxe of Durham was so fond of this image that when he founded Corpus Christi College in Oxford he had a pelican installed in its front quadrangle, today perhaps the best-known example of that particular symbol. Nevertheless, the Durham of today is not without its pelican. The imagery returned in a permanent lectern that balances the pulpit on the other side of the entrance to the quire. Pelicans swallow food whole and then regurgitate it for their young. It was from this practice that there developed the legend that, when too weak to regurgitate, the mother would allow the chicks to bite away at its gullet and feed on her own blood. That is what the chicks are doing here. Modern translations lose the allusion, but the way in which art and text once nicely interacted can be seen in older versions of Psalm 102 (v. 6). There talk of a pelican in the wilderness was taken to allude to the way in which Christ, spiritually fortified by his struggle in the wilderness, could now feed us through his offering on the Cross and current presence in the eucharist.

How far such imagery may strike the modern viewer as merely quaint is an open question. Certainly, anyone who investigates the symbolic resources of the Middle Ages is in for something of a shock. Even if attention is confined to architecture, most of what is said on the subject lacks the clarity that is to be found in Abbot Suger.[99] The suggestions in Durandus' *Rationale divinorum officiorum*, the most widely read treatise on the matter, often seem forced and artificial. The four walls, for example, are supposed to be the evangelists, towers preachers and the piers bishops.[100] This is not to say that such symbolism could not be taught. But the further question would remain, whether, even when learnt, it could actively engage a congregation. It is this fact that is so often overlooked in nostalgic defences of a pre-Vatican II world. Such writers

---

[99] Discussed in my *God and Enchantment of Place*, 272–7.

[100] I. 15, 21, 27. For an edition and commentary, J. M. Neale and B. Webb eds., *The Symbolism of Churches and Church Ornaments* (London: Gibbings, 1906).

are often quite astute in identifying problems in present patterns.[101] Nonetheless, it does not follow that the earlier forms were without difficulty, or that the Church did not need to act in order to halt a decline in engagement with its symbolism. The Church's liturgy often seemed remote from the problems of everyday life, and the real focus of devotion lay not so much in the mass itself as in what might be called sacramentals, the saying of the rosary, pilgrimages and so on. That is why it strikes me as a mistake for Anglicans to accord any comparable unqualified approval to the past.[102] Catherine Pickstock provides a powerful and carefully nuanced interpretation of the medieval mass.[103] But the very richness she imposes on it is not only not how it was experienced by the great mass of the laity, it is also doubtful whether her analysis would have met with many resonances among the clergy themselves. For me at least it sounds too cerebral.[104]

But I also have a deeper worry, and that is the lack of embodiment in the analysis. It is largely the words that are given this exalted status, not an experience of the eucharist as a whole. Hitherto, in respect of my discussion thus far I myself might be charged with a similar fault, in that I have only mentioned the impact of the building on arrival or when attention begins to stray from the words. But of course that is not how churches have been used in the past. Especially in the medieval period, there was a great sense of movement in the building, with different liturgical acts reserved for specific parts. Not only did processions to shrines include such an element, so also where baptisms and marriages were performed, as well as sometimes certain stages of the liturgy. Most obviously the Gospel procession is a case in point. The symbolism reminded the congregation of the need for the Church to proclaim its message to the world. But there were plenty of other occasions too, with Easter sepulchres and so on. Some

[101] e.g. D. Torevell, *Losing the Sacred: Ritualism, Modernity and Liturgical Reform* (Edinburgh: T & T Clark, 2000).

[102] In Pickstock, there is one brief admission of substantial faults, C. Pickstock, *After Writing: On the Liturgical Consummation of Philosophy* (Oxford: Blackwell, 1998), 172. It is a pity that more attention was not devoted to them, as some of her critiques of the value of what was lost are entirely apposite: 121–66, e.g. 140–5 (on non-blood kinship); 149–52 (on the rise of a more juridical approach).

[103] *After Writing*, 167–273.

[104] As in her analysis of the opening trinitarian formula or ambiguities inherent in *Gloria in excelsis*: 181, 203.

contemporary liturgists have sought to recover that sense of movement, and that is all to the good.[105]

Even so, one wonders whether such ideas could not be carried
further. So, for example, currently it is only ever at their initial
dedication that stained glass windows or other works of art are the
focus of services in church. Yet in aiding the totality of the drama
there is every reason to suppose that they could contribute much
more significantly. In generating and enlivening a sense that the
building is an integral part of the power of the drama that occurs
within it, they could add to the roundedness of the resultant
experience. Sermons on themes illustrated in the windows could,
for example, be delivered beneath them, and so on. Special services
in cathedrals now quite commonly use the whole of the building
with movement at least of the choir and clergy through each aspect.
But that pattern could also be repeated in the parishes, with the
congregation also moving, depending on the nature of the theme.

Reticence about introducing such practices has, I think, less to
do with traditional English reserve, and much more with failure
even to appreciate such potential in the words themselves. With so
many alternative translations now available, it is absurd that reverence for the biblical text still seems to preclude readers from making
a real effort at performing it. But even divine texts can only
communicate with human aid. That means helping God to speak
through the text, not assuming that this can be carried off without
any effort on the human side. The reading, therefore, needs to be
performed in a way that allows it to be understood on its own
without antecedent knowledge. As I mentioned in an earlier chapter, this is why not only is some kind of introduction usually
necessary but also occasionally alterations to the text as well.
Where the latter is not easily intelligible on its own, those with a
little education can often make quite a big difference, for example
by supplying identifying references or changes of speaker. Moves
between God, the prophet, and the people speaking are quite
commonly not distinguished in the biblical text, but need to be
orally, if the words are readily to be understood by the congregation.
Even the English style might sometimes be improved. Translators'

[105] The best-known English example is the work of David Stancliffe in the
reordering of Portsmouth Cathedral. David Kennedy has also done some excellent
work as Precentor of Durham Cathedral.

concern for accuracy means that the same English word is often used repeatedly where in English we would expect more variety. Again, especially in the Hebrew scriptures, readings that might naturally come to some sort of climax are sometimes spoiled in translation by uncertainty about meaning, too many obscure references, and so on. That is emphatically not to suggest manipulation of the meaning. Even where the content is problematical, it should still be allowed its own right to speak first. Challenge belongs with the sermon rather than at this point. But it is to suggest that it is not the text as such that is sacrosanct but the ability of God to communicate through it.

Change such unthinking deference towards the text, and people might be more willing to see the particular architectural and artistic staging also there to make their own distinctive contribution to the drama. Another stimulus to change could be alternative types of dramatic performance within the church itself, since these could well help congregations to draw parallels with the liturgy itself. Admittedly, special dramatic performances and dance are quite often not done well, but they could be. That is why I find Benedict XVI's curt dismissal of dance so disappointing, as indeed his rejection of all kinds of music except traditional church forms.[106] While dance to be done well does need the guidance of experts, the mistake is to assume that huge resources are required.[107] The minimalist approach to props in modern theatre which I discussed in Chapter 5 demonstrates otherwise. Music too need not take conventional forms, in order to have much to offer.[108]

Effective liturgy needs to escape Christianity's two long-standing but ultimately unsustainable oppositions: between the divine word and all other forms of communication and between biblical word and all other words. The Bible speaks of a people on a pilgrimage of faith like ourselves, and so contains similar foibles and faults to our own, as well of course as the means to salvation. So reverence and critique need to go hand in hand. The Bible also comes to us from

---

[106] J. Ratzinger, *The Spirit of the Liturgy* (San Francisco: Ignatius, 2000), 198–9 (dance); 147–8, 155 (music).

[107] e.g. L. M. Goens, *Praising God Through the Lively Arts* (Nashville: Abingdon, 1999), e.g. 22.

[108] For a defence of spectacle and electronic music as a means of generating a sense of transcendence, T. Sample, *The Spectacle of Worship in a Wired World* (Nashville: Abingdon, 1998), esp. 105–22.

what is now a quite different and in some ways alien cultural world. So transitions need to be made. Selections of readings from the history of the Church and from the long tradition of Christian poetry are not always well made, but the principle at least is a good one.[109] What is often forgotten is that, as with the Scriptures, some attempt at context and introductory explanation is usually essential. Poetry can of course be quite often difficult to comprehend on first hearing, and so demands some preliminary elucidation. But repeated reading of certain poems could only enrich a congregation's reflection and experience, giving them new and enriching metaphors. It is sad but true to observe that Anglican ordinands of the present generation are far more likely to know about the latest version of non-Anglican German or American theology than they are about the great poetic tradition that once constituted Anglicanism and in a sense still does (if only just). The enriching of existing metaphors through such poetry might also encourage contemporary hymn-writers to be more adventurous in their own work.

Willing openness here, as in the performance of biblical readings, could well lead to more openness not only to the art in the building but also to the role of music, so often treated as a mere optional adjunct. Whereas medieval versions of the western canon tended to focus rather narrowly in the consecration prayer on the crucifixion, and in this the Reformation followed suit, now at last the whole span of Christ's life, death, and resurrection is brought into play.[110] But long before this change, the Creed had already embodied such a holistic perspective. Nowadays complaints are often made about the dryness of credal language. One way of rectifying this might be to return to the earlier dialogue pattern from which the Apostles' Creed appears to have emerged.[111] But another is to encourage the

[109] Better attempts include *A Christian's Prayer Book: Psalms, Poems and Prayers for the Church's Year* (London: Geoffrey Chapman, 1974) and *The Cloud of Witnesses* (London: Collins, 1982), with its additional readings for saints' days.

[110] The Ambrosian tradition of the church in Milan was an exception in preserving a much wider range of eucharistic Prefaces: A. Griffiths ed., *We Give You Thanks and Praise: The Ambrosian Eucharistic Prefaces* (Norwich: Canterbury Press, 1999).

[111] Usually associated with baptism, and reintroduced into that context in a number of liturgies. For details, J. N. D. Kelly, *Early Christian Creeds* (London: Longman, 1972 edn.), 40–9; F. Young, *The Making of the Creeds* (London: SCM Press, 1991), 6.

use of musical and visual memories. Those fortunate to hear regularly musical settings might deepen commitment by recalling how
key moments in Christ's life are set; those with visual memories
might recall some of their favourite paintings and meditate on
them. It is not formulae that are being absorbed but how such
formulae apply to the living Saviour being made sensibly present in
their midst. Local churches could even provide occasional sessions
where music and art were combined to enable subsequent recall in
a way that secured real engagement with the Creed and its description of saving history. Bows and crossings during the Creed would
then cease to be purely nominal, but rather symptomatic of profound
interaction with what is being said or sung: body and mind as one.

We live in a period of liturgical renewal, with more changes to the
nature of liturgical performance in the past half-century than some
churches had witnessed over several centuries. Even so, I want to
question whether the change has gone far enough. There is so much
unrealized potential. Christ is of course present in the eucharist even
in a dark and gloomy church where the service is read by the
minister in a flat, deadpan voice. But it is one thing to acknowledge
that fact; quite another to put unnecessary obstacles in the way of
the believer's capacity to experience the living reality of Christ.

Change and Changelessness: the Divine Mystery

It is natural in human beings to seek some element of stability in
their lives. The result is that it is seldom the case that individuals are
consistently in favour of change. Nowhere is that paradox more
marked than in the extraordinary phenomenon of theologians who
are otherwise at the liberal end of the Church being often the most
intensely conservative in their forms of worship. It would be
invidious to mention names here, but during the course of my
own life I have certainly known quite a few who would fall into
such a category. However, it does seem to me a temptation that
must be firmly resisted. Liturgy of course has a constant element in
the great divine drama that is being retold. But how that is best
communicated will inevitably differ radically, depending on the
nature of the society in which the Church is set. What I want,
therefore, to note in this final section is how pressure for yet more
change is not something new but an issue that has always been with

the Church. However, I shall end with that constant element, the divine mystery that is thereby disclosed.

As I constantly sought to stress in *Tradition and Imagination* (1999) and *Discipleship and Imagination* (2000), neither revelation itself nor its interpretation can be divorced from its wider cultural context. In the case of liturgy, this helps explain why its performance has often taken quite different forms over the course of the centuries, even where doctrine has appeared to remain constant. As noted earlier, in the early Church it now looks as though the charismatic open form to liturgical performance may have survived much longer than liturgists in the past supposed. However, that may have been less to do with loyalty to scriptural precedents than influence from values in the wider society. In Chapter 4 we saw how rhetorical composition and associated concerns with performance achieved an exalted status in the wider culture at that time that they were only briefly to recover once more at the Renaissance. It is these factors that may well have been determining in the earlier open shape of the liturgy.[112] In other words, the opportunity and free-dom for a fine rhetorical performance was deemed more important than set details.

Although concern for theological orthodoxy in the face of various heresies eventually greatly reduced such variety, even then rigid uniformity only emerged very slowly, partly under the impact of state interference and partly through the controls made possible through the invention of printing. Byzantine emperors used the liturgy as a way of proclaiming and reaffirming their control over the city of Constantinople. In this respect the papacy as a secular power behaved no differently.[113] So, although Charlemagne's desire was not focused on a particular city, his request to the papacy for a fixed liturgy can be read as similarly motivated, in the wish for imperial control rather than simply the desire to do a job well.[114] However, it was only with the invention of printing that really tight

---

[112] For the influence of rhetoric on liturgy, S. J. White, *Christian Worship and Technological Change* (Nashville: Abingdon, 1994), 40–5, 138 fn. 14.

[113] Discussed in M. D. Stringer, *A Sociological History of Christian Worship* (Cambridge: Cambridge University Press, 2005), 58–88. For the way in which the relationship between the various churches in the two cities was conceived, 62–75.

[114] Resulting in the so-called *Hadrianum*, allegedly an account of how the rite was celebrated in the Rome of the time, but perhaps modified locally.

controls became possible. Before that time, although the spread of the Benedictine houses in particular across Europe pulled in the direction of uniformity, local pride and the actions of individual scribes moderated any such effect. The complexities of medieval manuscript traditions indicate as much.

Nor will it do to suggest that the late medieval tradition then continued relatively constant until the reforms of Vatican II. While the elevation of the host did indeed remain a permanent and prominent feature, the playfulness of baroque performance was quite different from the solemnity envisaged by Trent, and cannot properly be understood except in the wider context of related movements in art and architecture.[115] It is against the background of redundant balconies introduced into churches to suggest a theatre that apparently flippant extras such as an abundance of lace and even silk slippers and gloves can be more easily under-stood.[116] More seriously, false ceilings helped to create a sense of heaven and earth merging as one, with the often histrionic gestures of the accompanying statuary inviting not mockery but a new sense of worshipper and saint alike engaged in a common drama.[117]

Even apparently very dissimilar forms of change may be seen to stem from common wider roots. So, for example, the new focus in the Protestant churches in the eighteenth and nineteenth centuries on a more personalized form of experience had a related impact on Roman Catholicism, though expressed quite differently. While within Protestantism this especially took the form of emotionally charged hymns, within Roman Catholicism there was an almost constant stream of new devotional practices, especially in new cults of the Virgin Mary and in increased popularity for the practice of Benediction. Again, in the case of the changes effected within the nineteenth-century Church of England, it is impossible to divorce the Oxford Movement from the literary and artistic movement

---

[115] See further *God and Enchantment of Place*, 289–97 and *God and Grace of Body*, 41–6.

[116] They all encouraged a feeling for performance and joy, and indeed even fun, in that performance.

[117] Flat ceilings were decorated with *trompe l'oeil* paintings of heaven that suggested the vault of heaven itself joining in the performance of the mass.

known as Romanticism.[118] So, in spite of its familiar doctrine of
reserve, the desire for a more experiential faith lies at its roots.[119]
This is evident in Newman's own origins as an evangelical. But
conjoined in Romanticism with its new emphasis on experience
was nostalgia for the past in the face of growing industrialization
and other change. It was that potent mix that ensured that a movement initially uninterested in liturgical change eventually came to
champion so many controversial practices that divided the Church
of England in the later nineteenth century. The fact that during this
period Anglicanism replaced Lutheranism as the branch of the
Church nearest to Roman Catholicism is thus not simply a function
of intellectual argument, it also reflects the fact that changes in its
liturgy were profoundly affected by a wider cultural context.[120]

None of this is to imply determinism. Such influences can be
resisted, and sometimes should be. But a heavy penalty may be paid
in the inability of the Church to communicate, since we are all
creatures of our own time and circumstance. At present there seems
little agreement about the religious character or otherwise of contemporary culture. Personally I am optimistic, and agree with Grace
Davie's analysis of a society that is 'believing without belonging'.[121]
More negative estimates have of course also been advanced.[122] But a
recent influential work argues strongly that religious aspirations are
in fact widespread among the population at large, and that this
is found reflected in pop culture.[123] In outline, the author (Tom

[118] Newman's enthusiasm for the novels of Sir Walter Scott offers one small
illustration.

[119] Although Isaac Williams's famous tract 80 on 'Reserve in Communicating
Religious Knowledge' spoke against discussions of personal experience, in effect
the movement made implicit appeal to such experience, most obviously perhaps in
the poetry of Keble and Newman.

[120] Nicely illustrated in J. F. White's tabulation of 'Protestant Traditions of
Worship', where a switch over time on the right wing between the two denominations is indicated: *Documents of Christian Worship*, 7.

[121] G. Davie, *Religion in Britain since 1945: Believing without Belonging* (Oxford:
Blackwell, 1994).

[122] e.g. S. Bruce, *God is Dead: Secularisation in the West* (Oxford: Blackwell,
2002).

[123] T. Beaudoin, *Virtual Faith: The Irreverent Spiritual Quest of Generation X* (San
Francisco: Jossey-Bass, 1998). Generation X as a way of referring to those born in
the1960s and 1970s comes from Douglas Copeland's novel of the same name
(London: Abacus, 1992).

Beaudoin) identifies four main underlying assumptions among those whom he has labelled Generation X: institutions are suspect, experience is the key, suffering has a religious dimension, and ambiguity is central to faith. The group R.E.M.'s song 'Losing My Religion' is used to illustrate the first point, Madonna's video *Like a Prayer* the second, Nirvana and grunge clothing's expression of an absence of self-worth the third, with the last found, among other things, in the bending of gender distinctions.[124] An appropriate response from the Church to each is then indicated. A liturgy that includes mystery, ambiguity, and sensuousness is recommended, with an unauthoritarian and affirming approach in its teaching and pastoral care.[125] Interestingly, analyses produced in response by evangelicals, practising and lapsed, are alike hostile.[126] No doubt they are right that Beaudoin is too confident about the extent of the dissemination of such attitudes. Nonetheless, their own analyses in turn seem flawed by too much of an either–or approach. They seem to assume a dichotomy between either vague aspirations with absolutely minimal content, or else explicit Christian belief.[127] But even within the Church the activity of God scarcely always takes this form. Individual Christians remain the same mix of good and evil that characterizes humanity as a whole. Equally, not every experience of the eucharist will generate an emotional 'high'. As with the themes of the pop videos to which Beaudoin refers, much of the impact of the eucharist remains subliminal. It is not the case that in order for a celebration to 'work' its impact must be perceived. Rather, it is in the individual's openness to such an impact that Christ's often hidden work will gradually be made manifest. So the response to pop music and to the eucharist is not necessarily wholly different.

Whether Beaudoin's analysis is correct or not is too wide an issue to raise here. Certainly, preceding pages will have already made it abundantly clear that it is the sort of account with which I myself would be in general sympathy. However, there are formidable

---

[124] Beandoin, *Virtual Faith*, 51–142, esp. 53–4, 74–5, 100–2, 138–9.

[125] e.g. 167–8.

[126] G. Lynch, *After Religion: Generation X and the Search for Meaning* (London: Darton, Longman & Todd, 2002). S. Savage, S. Collins-Mayo, B. Mayo, and G. Clay, *Making Sense of Generation Y* (London: Church House Publishing, 2006). Lynch is by his own admission a lapsed evangelical (*After Religion*, 1).

[127] Complicated in the case of the multi-authored work by the fact that they are supposed to be analysing a different generation. Y refers to those born after 1982.

obstacles in the way of the churches adapting to such attitudes. Official approaches to liturgy often continue to be strongly authoritarian, whether it be liberals or conservatives that hold the upper hand. Our own age is unparalleled in its possibilities for control. Governments often feel themselves ineffective, unless each day brings some fresh new initiative, allegedly to achieve greater efficiency in delivering some presumed valued goal. It is all too easy for contemporary liturgists on both the left and on the right to adopt a similar model of control from above.[128] If Benedict XVI speaks of uniformity as a good, there is no shortage of those on the left wishing to impose their own particular, no less dogmatic recipes.[129] The Church as a community on the move, for example, may be claimed as the norm, with any models drawn from the Temple rejected as Israel's purely human action and therefore, strictly speaking, the dereliction of its own proper role.[130] What the proposed ideal ignores is the theological necessity to take seriously the totality of Israel's history as part of the story of revelation and not just the bits we happen to like.[131] Equally, Benedict in pleading for more emphasis on cosmic symbolism ignores how difficult it might prove to communicate such notions to contemporary congregations.[132] Facing east during the Creed can be made easily intelligible, if it is seen as an act of turning towards the altar as source of Christ's presence made effective in our midst. But if it is towards the sun as symbol of Christ or the place from which he will eventually return, much more work would be needed to engage the imagination.[133] Cosmological and agricultural symbolism do not, I think, come easily to the modern mind.

[128] In the key role exercised by committees, Susan White detects 'the bureaucratization of the liturgy': *Christian Worship and Technological Change*, 50–8.

[129] 'The greatness of the liturgy depends . . . on its unspontaneity (*Unbeliebigkeit*)': Ratzinger, *Spirit of the Liturgy*, 166. American decisions about the content of hymns (discussed in ch. 3) provide an obvious example on the other or liberal side.

[130] 'The building of the Temple . . . was apostasy': Giles, *Re-Pitching*, 25.

[131] For an attempt to argue for a continuous early appropriation of the principles of temple worship, M. Barker, *The Great High Priest* (London: T & T Clark, 2003).

[132] For cosmic elements in Benedict's thinking, Ratzinger, *Spirit of the Liturgy*, 24, 68, 99, 101.

[133] Anglicans might have an advantage with Keble's hymn, 'Sun of my soul, thou Saviour dear'.

Where Benedict is undoubtedly correct is in lamenting the loss of mystery in much modern liturgy. He has been much derided for suggesting that at least for the consecration prayer the focus should once more be eastwards, with the celebrant and people now facing in the same direction.[134] That would, he suggests, provide a more transcendent dimension to the proceedings. It would in any case, he adds, be more compatible with forms of eating in the ancient world where the couches were always left open on one side for the servants to approach. The point is underdeveloped, but we might think of Christ drawing alongside us to unite us in his own self-offering to the Father. This is not to marginalize the bonding of the community. It is to place it in its own proper context. The Spirit is there indwelling believers so that all may become part of the corporate body that is Christ's and so part of his self-offering. No doubt those who suspect at every turn the existence of an all-too-human desire to be the real agent of the offering (either in the worshippers themselves or through mediation of the priest) would object to such change of direction as automatically carrying such a meaning. But to face east is not necessarily to place the priest in control of Christ. Indeed, in some ways it would seem to lessen that sense of control so prevalent in modern liturgy, with the 'president' exercising so obviously dominant a role. It is that human-centred focus that Benedict seeks to correct. Of course, Benedict's real desire may be for the priest in fact to face east for the whole service, and so for the Church to return to an earlier pattern. If that really is his meaning, it would seem to me quite misguided, since so many undoubted benefits have come with westward facing altars, not least a greater sense of the involvement of the entire congregation Even so, just because the proposal comes from a conservative pope, it should not simply be dismissed out of hand. As I have stressed a number of times, metaphors and symbols do sometimes need to be played off against each other, and at present there is too little pulling towards transcendence and otherness. Against such a backdrop the symbolism of genuflection could play an important role, especially where immanence appears to be the more natural description of a people gathered round what looks like an ordinary table.

One of the great liturgists of the past, Odo Casel, placed great stress on mystery as the best key towards a proper approach to the

---

[134] *Spirit of the Liturgy*, 74–84, esp. 77–9.

liturgical drama.[135] It is the totality of the mystery of Christ's life, death, and resurrection that is once more being made present and timelessly so. Eastern Orthodoxy seeks to express such mystery by making each stage of the liturgy re-enact the incarnation. Already present in the theology of someone like Theodore of Mopsuestia, such symbolism gradually became codified in various commentaries on the liturgy, among them the *Mystagogia* of Maximus the Confessor, the *Mystical History* of Germanus, and Nicholas Cabasilas' *Commentary on the Divine Liturgy.*[136] Western liturgy eventually became trapped in a narrower focus on Christ's death. Even so, a timeless and indispensable character was attributed to the medieval mass, which one recent commentator finds not unlike how the Aztecs conceived their own sacrificial system. Both societies saw the world as held in being by just such a performance.[137] Fortunately modern liturgies have widened the focus once more but without resort to the detailed symbolism that characterizes the east. Arguably, such details in any case undercut the historical reality of what happened two thousand years ago. The performance becomes too mythic when even the nativity must be represented by speaking of a star hovering over the elements.[138]

While it is easy to see how the transformative character of the eucharist might be used as an interpretive principle for understanding the nature of reality as whole, it is harder to communicate an actual dependence of the world on the continuation of such a drama. Yet that must surely be the ideal for the Christian, for whom the whole of history revolves round what Christ has done and its continuing significance. The restoration of some sense of mystery and awe to the liturgy would at least aid such perceptions. One liturgist of an earlier generation suggested that this might be expressed by returning to what he saw as the original place of the *Sanctus* at the conclusion of the eucharistic prayer: greeting

[135] O. Casel, *The Mystery of Christian Worship* (London: Darton, Longman & Todd, 1962). For an introduction to his thought, G. Guiver, *Pursuing the Mystery* (London: SPCK, 1996). Casel died in 1948.

[136] From the fifth, seventh, eighth, and fourteenth centuries respectively. Theodore's comments, spread through a *Baptismal Homily*, are usefully summarized in Bradshaw, *Early Christian Worship*, 67–8.

[137] Stringer, *Christian Worship*, 139–40.

[138] Cabasilas, *Commentary on the Divine Liturgy* 1.11 (London: SPCK, 1960), 41.

with the awed recitation of 'Holy, Holy, Holy' the presence of the clue to all reality now once more made manifest in our midst.[139]

I cannot pretend to have the answers. Instead I end by appealing for more dialogue with ordinary human experience. The Church has the greatest possible gift to offer the world in the God who became human for our sake and adopted a bodily identity that continues into his present existence.[140] So it has rightly things to say about and through the body.[141] That was a repeated theme of this volume's predecessor. Here, I have focused on how that fact is mediated in the liturgy through language and its related accompanied drama. As I have repeatedly affirmed both in the first part of this work on language itself and in the second part on drama, language and the dramatic action that goes with it in liturgy should be seen as operating not to quench mystery but rather, if anything, to ignite it. Certainly, metaphor helps to disclose surprising and unexpected interconnections that the Creator has built into the very fabric of things, but, if metaphor is to retain its power, such disclosure should never be seen as complete. Equally drama, when functioning at its best, hints at other worlds rather than forces them on our imaginations. It is into such a world that liturgists should induct us, not one in which the desire for plain teaching has taken over entirely from the inexhaustibility of words and where the decisive spotlight in the drama is turned on an all too readable human agent (usually the priest) rather than the ultimate agent: Christ, who must remain the ultimate mystery. The danger otherwise is that, as the Church simplifies and seeks constantly to explain rather than enjoy Christ's presence in its own right and with no further object in view, it will force people to find mystery in God at work everywhere else rather than in this, its greatest gift, the liturgy itself.[142]

[139] E. C. Ratcliff, 'The Sanctus and the Pattern of the early Anaphora', *Journal of Ecclesiastical History* 1 (1950), 29–36, 125–34. Ratcliff was an Anglican. For the notion of mystery within Anglicanism, H. R. McAdoo and K. Stevenson, *The Mystery of the Eucharist in the Anglican Tradition* (Norwich: Canterbury Press, 1997 edn.).

[140] Bodily in the sense of the totality of what it is to be human, however now expressed. The issue is discussed in *God and Grace of Body*, 410–11, 419–21.

[141] Perhaps even as elementary as teaching the value of correct posture in walking: so P. H. Pfatteicher, *Liturgical Spirituality* (Valley Forge, Pa.: Trinity Press International, 1997), 110–11; cf. 9.

[142] For such a meaning for *mysterium* in patristic and medieval liturgical texts, see B. Gordon-Taylor, *Mystery*, Ph.D. thesis (Durham, 2007).

Conclusion

THIS volume concludes a series of three works, *God and Enchantment of Place* (2004), *God and Grace of Body* (2007), and now *God and Mystery in Words*, all on the same theme of religious experience as mediated through the arts, and culture more generally. They were preceded by two earlier companion volumes *Tradition and Imagination* (1999) and *Discipleship and Imagination* (2000) that explored the theme of biblical revelation and its appropriation over subsequent centuries. Although my original intention was to treat the two projects as quite distinct, rightly or wrongly many commentators have seen all five volumes as interrelated. So it behoves me here to say something of how I myself understand that relationship, not least because this is the most obvious point at which to reflect on the whole.

Although an interest in arts, culture, and the imagination has been maintained throughout, none of the volumes is intended as an exercise in aesthetics. The art, music, architecture, and literature referred to are essentially illustrative of a more fundamental thesis: that both natural and revealed theology are in crisis, and that the only way out is to give proper attention to the cultural embeddedness of both. Religion does not operate in isolation, and so theology and philosophy as it reflects on religion is equally incapable of escaping that wider influence, however much it may pretend otherwise.

Such has been the focus in this volume that the connection with natural theology may have been less clear than in its two predecessors. Even so, as in them I adopted the same strategy of moving from the wider culture to more specific Christian contexts. So experience through metaphor and drama more generally were allowed to introduce their application to Christian worship. In a similar way in *God and Grace of Body* extensive reflection on the great range of symbolic meanings that the human body bears prefaced a specific application to the eucharist, while *God and Enchantment of Place* opened by advocating a return to a wider sense of 'sacrament' that allows Christian sacraments to be seen as particular instances of a more general phenomenon, God acting through the material universe. 'Acting', however, is not always quite the right word.[1] Sometimes it might perhaps be better to speak of human beings tapping into presence, as it were, rather than God having to do anything specific in addition. Even so, it would be quite wrong to deduce from this an inferior sort of contact. In such experience of presence God is still perceived under one particular category rather than another. It is just that it lacks the specificity that philosophers of religion tend to like when they employ the so-called argument from religious experience to justify belief in God.

That immediate move to specificity seems to me a mistake, but all too common not only with this argument but also with arguments for God's existence more generally. Examine the premises, and almost invariably something like the Christian God has been smuggled into arguments that establish, if anything, very much less. Indeed, what the conventional arguments seem best at offering is rather suggestive sketches of what might possibly be the case rather than what is necessarily so. That does not deprive them of a role, but it does make it odd that they continue to be presented as the essence of how God might be known outside the historic revelations of specific religions.[2]

Such intellectual claims seem in any case far removed from what inclines most people away from or towards belief. Such research as exists tends to point towards various sorts of appeal to experience, often far removed from the more conventional types that make it into philosophers' discussions. Here a narrow focus on experience in worship, prayer, and specific religious traditions continues to be the norm.[3] Thereby effectively marginalized is the immense variety of contexts where most people continue to believe that they encounter God. As the national millennium census indicated, the great majority of the British population still inclines toward reli-

---

[1] St Teresa of Avila offers a good example of how the Christian obsession with divine action can mislead. Until reassured by her confessor, she was deeply depressed by the conviction that God must always be supposed to be acting in some way or other whenever his gracious presence is felt: *Life* in *Complete Works of Saint Teresa* (London: Sheed & Ward, 1946), i. 110–11.

[2] Why, for instance, should this continue to be assumed as necessarily the right approach in the study of religion in schools?

[3] For my critique of contemporary approaches, in particular William Alston's: 'Experience Skewed' in K. Vanhoozer and M. Warner eds., *Transcending Boundaries in Philosophy and Theology* (Aldershot: Ashgate, 2007), 159–75, esp. 160–5.

gious belief.[4] Yet it is a belief that no longer corresponds to attendance at church, nor, one suspects, to the sorts of experience that are seen as central within those communities. That phenomenon is repeated across Europe and more widely. No doubt the sociological explanations are complex. But one key element to my mind is the way in which the Church and its theologians have in fact retreated from most of the areas that give rise to the sort of experience upon which such popular belief is so often based. People still find God in the great range of human experience that their ancestors once did. It is just that serious consideration is no longer given to such experience within the Church. Instead, an intellectual system is offered that now hangs free of the once universally shared assumptions on which it was based: the divine reality available everywhere to be encountered.

I would like to see that retreat reversed, which is why I have investigated in these volumes such a great range of mediated experience. Just as this volume touched on clothes and fashion as well as poetry and drama, so in its predecessor I examined pop music (including hard rock and rap) and sensual and sexual bodies as well as more obvious themes such as food and gratitude. My motivation was not merely the desire to be comprehensive. It was to alert the reader to how God continues to impinge on all of life. We may no longer have sports and dramatic festivals like the ancient Greeks' deeply based in religion, but many sports movies continue to explore religious themes, while quite a few of the major dramatic theories of the twentieth century found their raison d'être in notions that have obvious religious parallels.[5] The problem is that most of these continuities remain ignored by the Church and its theologians. There are of course some exceptions, film perhaps being the most obvious.[6] It is little wonder, therefore, that even in major forms of culture such as dance, religious issues are now pursued almost entirely without reference to Christianity.[7] In some instances, such as dance, sophisticated discussion has survived. But elsewhere it often amounts to little more than a vague intuition.

---

[4] 76 per cent indicated belief in God.

[5] For the former, *God and Enchantment of Place* (Oxford: Oxford University Press, 2004), 387–402; for the latter, this volume, ch. 5.

[6] Though even here I discovered no significant writing on religious themes in films about sport.

[7] *God and Grace of Body* (Oxford: Oxford University Press, 2007), ch. 2.

Gardens are in my view one such instance. Gone are the often
subtle discussions of the Christian past but in their place has not
yet come any deep reflection on the garden's spiritual significance.
Yet claims to religious experience are still associated with gardens, and
rightly so in my view. The unfortunate result is phenomena such
as Feng Shui effectively replacing what might instead have been
contributions from Christian theologians.[8]

Nor are matters any better in respect of revealed theology, the
focus of my two earlier companion volumes, *Tradition and Imagination* and *Discipleship and Imagination*. In the modern world all three
major monotheistic religions have had to face major challenges to
their self-understanding. All three have responded by seeking
renewal in their historical roots, in their classical texts. While this
has undoubtedly brought many benefits, it has also had its corresponding downside. With Judaism the most obvious response to
the Holocaust has been in recovery of a sense of the land of Israel as
divine gift, an idea that was marginal to Jewish self-conception for
most of the past two thousand years. In the process much that was
valuable in medieval and later Jewish thinking and practice has been
demoted or else gone altogether.[9] Particularly sad has been the loss
of those elements that as a religion it might have contributed to
human religious sensibilities more generally, for example how
obedience to law, so far from being a burden, might actually
bring delight and liberation. Again, perhaps mainly under the
impact of universal literacy, Islam has largely retreated from the
emphasis once placed on the Prophet's hadith and oral tradition to a
somewhat narrow and exclusive focus on personal reading of the
Qur'an.[10] The result has often (though by no means uniformly)
been the abandonment of that faith's traditional liberal tolerance in
favour of a frightening and dogmatic fundamentalism.

There have also been unfortunate consequences for Christianity.
In my view Christianity is now progressively entering into a world
of self-deception where it must inevitably seem less and less

[8] For Feng Shui and gardens, *God and Enchantment*, 15–16, 371–87. John
Evelyn (d. 1706) might be cited as one such Christian example from the past.

[9] For the positive side in the past, *Tradition and Imagination: Revelation
and Change* (Oxford: Oxford University Press), 136–51; for the more negative
present, *Discipleship and Imagination: Christian Tradition and Truth* (Oxford: Oxford
University Press, 2000), 301.

[10] *Tradition and Imagination*, 151–67.

plausible in the modern world. Take the case of the equality of women and men. Book after book appears that finds such teaching in the New Testament and by implication blames the later Church for two thousand years of misrepresentation. For reasons I gave in *Discipleship and Imagination* I find such claims utterly implausible.[11] But even supposing them true, the way in which such changed perceptions have come about would still prove the underlying contention that runs across those two earlier volumes: that the stimulus or trigger for such change comes not from the text itself but from external changes within the wider culture where God is also to be found operating. It was change in experience of what women were capable of in industrial and post-industrial society that made plausible the demands for a new way of understanding the relationship between the sexes, and the first to see this was not the Church or individual Christians (with few exceptions) but wider society at large.

A new model for understanding revealed religion is therefore required. That is why I proposed the notion of revelation continuing to grow and develop under God within the traditions of the community. The tradition generates trajectories that under stimuli, sometimes from without, sometimes from within, lead to new implications being discovered at a later date, and sometimes even to the correction of what had hitherto been seen as the fundamental direction of the tradition. The New Testament was one such time. It is quite wrong for Christianity to claim that it more accurately represents the fundamental thrust of the Hebrew Scriptures. In many ways Judaism was more nearly right. This is certainly true of the most appropriate meaning of the passages we continue to read at Christmas carol services.[12] It is also true of how Abraham's calling should be understood. As I argued in *Tradition and Imagination*, faithfulness in action is the correct historical reading, even though as a Christian I would want to support Paul's gloss on the relevant chapters of Genesis as now in the light of Christ legitimating talk of justification by faith.[13] Both the rise of biblical criticism and proper respect for those of other faiths necessitates that

[11] *Discipleship and Imagination*, 11–31.
[12] For my attempt to tackle this issue, D. Brown, *The Word to Set You Free* (London: SPCK, 1995), 17–21.
[13] *Tradition and Imagination*, 213–37, esp. 218–19, 232–4.

as Christians we be honest and admit that the arguments that once brought the community to a particular position are no longer adequate in themselves.

That of course raises the issue of what then is. While I did offer a general list of relevant criteria, it does seem to me that there are no simple answers.[14] Rather, each particular instance will be in some sense unique. So the best way of proceeding is to examine each contested case in some detail. If one believes in divine providence at all, the fact that the community of faith in general has changed its mind creates at least a basic presupposition of a move in the right direction. But it offers no absolute guarantee. As I sought to indicate in my discussion of Reformation and Counter-Reformation and other such conflicts, it may take centuries before a proper balance is achieved.[15] Both sides were wrong, and it was only really in the twentieth century that a more balanced view was achieved on both sides of the Church.[16]

Such complexities may make even some naturally sympathetic to my position want to retreat from such a view. But, sadly, criteria drawn wholly from within the scriptures give only a superficial appearance of fewer problems. Apart from the arbitrary imposition of new meanings that I claim has happened in respect of female equality, even where original meanings are preserved such appeals often ignore the wider context of how the arguments that led to change have in fact been played out.[17] Take decline in belief in the existence of hell as a place of eternal punishment.[18] It may sound plausible to suggest that New Testament stress on divine love is sufficient to cancel out the relevant verses, even if these are read literally. But that is to ignore the earlier history of interpretation whereby love was taken not to exclude just such an implication. The new understanding of divine love only began to make any sort of sense, as fresh understandings of moral responsibility as limited liability began gradually to emerge. Go back in history to Anselm,

[14] For criteria, *Discipleship and Imagination*, 389–405.

[15] Ibid. 293–342, esp. 325–7.

[16] To take obvious examples, Roman Catholics underplayed the importance of Scripture, Protestants the centrality of the Eucharist.

[17] By the phrase 'imposition of meaning' I refer to Gal. 3.28, which is now usurped to speak of a more general equality that was no part of its original meaning: *Discipleship and Imagination*, 12–14.

[18] Discussed in ibid. 130–45, 150–62.

for instance, and such an argument would have been found utterly incomprehensible. For him we owe everything to God and so cannot have any rights or expectations.[19] Yet just as in the following century someone like Abelard was able to carry the Church beyond the more social understanding of responsibility implicit in Anselm, so F. D. Maurice in the nineteenth carried that sense of individual responsibility a stage further into the notion of limited obligation and so of a limited charge against us. What love entails is thus set in a context that presupposes the growth of talk of rights, the economics of limited liability, and so on.

That in turn of course raises the question of how God could allow his Church to go wrong for so long. In seeking an answer, I suggested that doctrinal error is seldom without its compensations, and so needs to be seen in a broader light. In the case of hell, the doctrine undoubtedly brought with it a more serious sense of responsibility, strongly directed self-examination, and a lively sense of the Church as a corporate body charged with the task of mutual support. Again, there may not be sexual equality in the Gospels but there is what is in my view a far more fundamental insight, and that is equality of regard, the view that, whatever one's status and abilities, all are equal in the sight of God. So those with severe learning difficulties, for example, are not to be seen as in any sense inferior to any other brother or sister in Christ but deserve a prominent and valued place in the community.[20]

Our understanding of biblical revelation thus turns out to be dependent again and again on developments in the wider culture. So that is why I recommended, as with my three later volumes, a listening process. To some degree that happens in any case, even if the Church pretends otherwise (as over the equality of the sexes). My desire is simply to see the entire process more explicitly acknowledged by my fellow Christians. This is in no way to suggest that revealed religion then becomes redundant. Rather, it is to take seriously the reality of any true engagement, that it will be a careful listening that should sometimes make a positive answering response,

---

[19] Which is why in his atonement theory, only Christ's death counts and not his life nor antecedent suffering. See further my 'Anselm on Atonement' in B. Davies and B. Leftow eds., *The Cambridge Companion to Anselm* (Cambridge: Cambridge University Press, 2004), 279–302.

[20] That might include ordination to celebrating the eucharist, even if such ministry had to be greatly limited in other ways.

but, equally, on other occasions not. Realism about Scripture and the history of the Church requires recognition that some of the worst examples of nasty human behaviour and limited vision come from the biblical writers themselves. A religion like Christianity can scarcely allow itself to be too facile in its judgements, when within its own biblical traditions are to be found launching pads for equally contestable behaviour. Aztec sacrificial victims were at least honoured for a time before death in a way that was never true of the native population of Palestine whose extermination is recommended by the Hebrew scriptures under Israel's *herem* or sacred ban.[21] Nor should the anti-Semitism implicit in at least two of the Gospels be forgotten.

Equally, a generosity of spirit that reflects divine grace may sometimes be better found in those who espouse another religion or none. The danger is that unless we are fully aware of such external influences, the Church will always eventually follow the wider society rather than sometimes, entirely legitimately, stand firmly against current trends. That is why, although most of my examples have come from the history of Christianity, I did not hesitate to range more widely, in order to hear better alternative understandings of God at work. So, all of the world's major religions have been drawn on at some point: for example, Buddhism on beauty of body, Hinduism for the significance of dance, Islam for religious drama and architecture. But I have deliberately not stopped there. It is so easy to despise as primitive otherwise now defunct cultures, when in fact they may have the capacity to throw up interesting and challenging perspectives of their own. It is only relatively recently that Roman religion has begun to escape the contempt that for some inexplicable reason was never extended to the Greeks.[22] As part of that process of recovery I therefore attempted in *God and Grace of Body* a positive estimate of ancient

---

[21] e.g. Deut. 20.16–18. John's use of the term 'Jew' is often treated as anti-Semitic. For Matthew, cf. 27.25.

[22] For a good example of positive attitudes, M. Beard, J. North, and S. Price eds., *Religions of Rome* (Cambridge: Cambridge University Press, 1998), 2 vols. For the continuation of old assumptions, cf. the novelist Robert Harris's best-seller *Pompeii* (London: Hutchinson, 2003). Here Roman religion is always treated as superstition, with sexual imagery never anything more than mere talisman. Contrast Allan Massie's recent admission that failure to give enough attention to Roman religion is a weakness in his own novels: *Classical Association News* 32 (2005), 2.

Roman attitudes to the symbolism of sexuality, just as in *Tradition and Imagination* I did not hesitate to accept parallels between changes in the telling of Greek myths and the developing Jewish and Christian traditions.

What I am above all concerned to ensure is that Christianity be seen as a religion to be practised and not just a doctrinal system that may or may not be internally coherent. That is why I was so adamant that among relevant criteria should always be included a degree of imaginative engagement. What led to change across the centuries in the interpretation of the Book of Job were different, historically conditioned, conceptions of the nature of human suffering.[23] What led to the way of reading the infancy narratives with which we are all now familiar was a new value placed upon the child as such, an idea quite foreign to Matthew and Luke.[24] Even so, more important than either of those externally induced changes was the resultant ability the new readings gave to live more closely in identification with Christ.

None of this is to deny the limitations of what I have so far achieved. So let me end by admitting three in particular. First, there is great need for a more technical analysis of some of the claims that I have made. That would include not just the question of criteria but also greater precision in description and categorization of the types of experience I have identified. Secondly, because I have been dealing with aspects of experience often ignored, I have sought to be uniformly positive about them, so far as possible. Clearly, there are more negative aspects to such experience, and these have to be acknowledged. Indeed, sometimes despite people's belief to the contrary one might well want to speak of a divine absence rather than presence. Even so, my suspicion is that there will be some surprises, for surface negativity does not always imply deep-seated wrong. As I have noted a number of times, even the most positive of experiences can have unfortunate, vicious sides to them, including within the Bible itself.[25] So, the reverse may also be possible, and what appears wholly evil may not be entirely so. Finally, I have developed these ideas largely without any critique

---

[23] *Discipleship and Imagination*, 177–225.
[24] *Tradition and Imagination*, 72–105, esp. 77–9.
[25] To quote my favourite example, the conclusion of Psalm 137, despite its wonderful initial impact.

of other contemporary theological and philosophical writing. Clarifying deficiencies elsewhere might well help to make it clearer why
I so strongly favour the approach I do.

How I shall develop these points further is as yet undecided.
Instead, I want to conclude here by alluding to an image that more
than once has appeared over the course of these five volumes:
Augustine's marvellous image, of God as the water that permeates
every aspect of the sponge that is the world.[26] It is that very
universality that I believe needs to be taken much more seriously
by modern theology, even as it also honours the Bible's own
inherent distinctiveness: a God of mystery who has disclosed something of that divinity to humanity but with a inexhaustible richness
that means that, although that mysteriousness will never be fully
captured by us, there remains always something more to discover,
something more to delight the senses and the intellect.

[26] Augustine, *Confessions* 7. 5.

INDEX

288 *Index*